Psychoanalysis, Culture and Social Action

Dieter Flader explores how current social and cultural concerns are connected to the unconscious, and how this affects our responses to them. Flader focuses on the role of the ego, assessing how our feelings about these issues in adulthood grow from childhood fears and desires, and integrating the existing psychoanalytic theories of Winnicott, Lacan, Kohut, and others with sociological and political theory. The interdisciplinary approach not only analyses current social issues but also generates new perspectives and solutions, and examines examples including climate change, bullying, and vegetarianism.

Dieter Flader is co-director of the Berlin Institute for Applied Human Studies and adjunct professor at the Free University of Berlin, Germany.

Psychoanalysis, Culture and Social Action

Act Signatures of the Unconscious

Dieter Flader
Translated by Bettina Vestring

Routledge
Taylor & Francis Group

LONDON AND NEW YORK

First published in English 2022
by Routledge
2 Park Square, Milton Park, Abingdon, Oxon, OX14 4RN

and by Routledge
605 Third Avenue, New York, NY 10158

Routledge is an imprint of the Taylor & Francis Group, an informa business

© 2022 Taylor & Francis

Translated by Bettina Vestring

The English edition is based on:
Dieter Flader: Vom Mobbing bis zur Klimadebatte.
Wie das Unbewusste soziales Handeln bestimmt
© Psychosozial-Verlag, Gileßen, 2016, www.psychosozial-verlag.de

Library of Congress Cataloging-in-Publication Data
Names: Flader, Dieter, author.
Title: Psychoanalysis, culture and social action : act signatures of the unconscious, or, from mobbing to climate change awareness : how the unconscious shapes social action / Dieter Flader ; translated by Bettina Vestring. Other titles: Vom Mobbing bis zur Klimadebatte. English
Description: New York, NY : Routledge, 2022. | Includes bibliographical references.
Identifiers: LCCN 2021038411 (print) | LCCN 2021038412 (ebook) | ISBN 9780367363635 (hardback) | ISBN 9780367363642 (paperback) | ISBN 9780429345449 (ebook)
Subjects: LCSH: Psychoanalysis and culture. | Social psychology. | Subconsciousness--Social aspects. | Social action--Psychological aspects. | Families--Psychological aspects. | Bullying. | Narcissism.
Classification: LCC BF175.4.C84 F6313 2022 (print) | LCC BF175.4.C84 (ebook) | DDC 150.19/5--dc23
LC record available at https://lccn.loc.gov/2021038411
LC ebook record available at https://lccn.loc.gov/2021038412

ISBN: 978-0-367-36363-5 (hbk)
ISBN: 978-0-367-36364-2 (pbk)
ISBN: 978-0-429-34544-9 (ebk)

DOI: 10.4324/9780429345449

Typeset in Bembo
by MPS Limited, Dehradun

Contents

Preface

When I first started talking to my friends and colleagues about my ideas for this book, their spontaneous reaction was enthusiastic. "The aim of this book is to find out how the unconscious shapes social action? How exciting!" "Yes", I replied, "I find this interesting because so many individual and collective conflicts have their roots in unconscious speech and action."

Naturally, my friends' and colleagues' curiosity and their many follow-up questions spurred me on. I began to think about which unresolved social conflicts I should chose to investigate the effects of the unconscious. It seemed obvious to me that I should start with communication processes: Why and in which situations does an element of the process remain unconscious, and what problems can this cause? Our social environment offers a multitude of examples, including conflicts that occur in relationships, at work, in society, and in politics.

Why does something remain in the unconscious, and what are the consequences? This question initially sounds abstract. It may remind us of a famous saying of Sigmund Freud – a statement that his contemporaries found profoundly offensive (this was the third major blow to the general public after it had already been told that the Earth is not at the centre of the universe and that man is supposedly descended from apes). "We are not masters of our own house", Freud said. In other words, human beings, despite their awareness, self-confidence, knowledge, reason, and intellect, obviously do not speak and act at the conscious level alone.

Since we cannot look inside a person to know what he or she is conscious or unconscious of, there is only one way in which we can possibly capture the unconscious: By looking at speech and action. This is where unconscious processes come to light and where they can be perceived and analysed. Good examples of how the unconscious works are the slips that occur when we do or say things that we do not want to do or say at all.

The consequences of these slips become visible in speech and action, but the causes – for instance, an inner unresolved psychological conflict that precedes the slip – remain obscure. This means that conflicts which arise unconsciously cannot be solved. This, in turn, results in difficulties not only for the individual but also for society and collectives.

The origins of this book

How does the unconscious take effect? This question has been at the heart of my entire professional life.

It was a great discovery for me to find answers in Freud's works. I have pursued this issue in my lectures, publications, and research projects. As a young research assistant and leader of a project funded by the Deutsche Forschungsgemeinschaft (DFG, German Research Foundation), I used linguistic theories to analyse a series of psychoanalytic sessions recorded on tape with colleagues. I was already on the trail then that I also follow in this book.

During the DFG project, it became evident that not only are we shaped by our families but that we and our families are part of society. Wars, political events, trends, and the zeitgeist leave their mark on every family and on every individual, and vice versa: Society consists of people who are active in shaping the culture in which they live by speaking and taking action at work, in their families, in their leisure time, and in and with the media.

In my book *Psychoanalysis in the Focus of Action and Language* (1995), published by the German publishing house Suhrkamp Verlag, I developed methods to analyse this connection between the unconscious and speech and action. This was not the first time that I had been working on combining linguistic and psychoanalytical theories. In 1974, I published the book *Strategies of Advertising. A Linguistic-Psychoanalytical Attempt to Reconstruct Advertising Effects*, in which I demonstrated the effect of advertising on social issues. These are only two examples of my writings which are part of the prehistory of this book, apart from numerous other publications to which I contributed as editor.

My research and writing have always had this double focus: On the one side, the connection between unconscious processes, as evidenced by language and action, and, on the other side, the interaction between individual and society. Obviously, it is a very broad field. But as both major connections are active at all times and in all places, they can be examined for content, forms, and context of interpersonal communication not just theoretically but also empirically. The reason is simple: Every conflict today − and in the past and the future − arises or becomes manifest through speech and action. This is true for all current crises that affect both individuals and society.

I used this same approach in 2018/2019 for a research project on "The So-Called Climate Sceptics. Argumentation Patterns and Psychosocial Backgrounds" which was funded by the Deutsche Bundesstiftung Umwelt (German Federal Environment Foundation) and in which I cooperated with Dr Barbara Strohschein. We conducted interviews with climate sceptics as well as members of the wider public, people from all generations, professions, and social classes. Our research strategy was designed in accordance with my approach of combining a psychoanalytic theory of action with linguistic theories. The aim was to find out which life-historical and political attitudes give rise to opinions on the climate issue. We found out that such opinions reflect feelings, knowledge, values, hopes, and visions of the future, which provide information about what people think and feel about climate change without having to be aware of them. These public opinions, as we made clear in the final report and our recommendations, are highly relevant in the climate debate, and policy makers and academics should be aware of them.

Science should serve enlightenment

In the course of my work as a university professor for communication science, linguistics, and basic research in psychoanalysis, holding a fair number of visiting professorships in Germany and abroad, it became clear to me that profound existential questions cannot be answered by one science alone. Even psychoanalysis based on the tradition of its founding father Freud is not enough.

Freud discovered the unconscious. While he did not have a satisfactory answer to the question of how this unconscious is reflected and as the invisible becomes visible, he did take the crucial first steps. I consider it an ongoing challenge to continue along his path and to also include insights from other humanities and social sciences in my research. Linguistics serves to analyse speech acts; theories from the social sciences help to examine social action; and the narcissism theories from psychoanalysis provide clues to the unconscious sources of speech and action.

But what is the point of all this? I believe that every academic and scientist who is serious about his or her work not only feels the responsibility of providing good teaching lessons and of carrying out and publishing meaningful research projects. For me, there is more to it, despite all the limitations we face as human beings. I have a great desire to try and shed light on what is still in the dark. And perhaps we can best describe the unconscious as something "dark" – a dark that holds treasures, myths, powers, and mechanisms of action worth bringing to light. But how can we find the key to the front door in the dark if we don't have a flash lamp?

It is my intention to try and bring problems that would otherwise remain unsolved into a solution perspective. This is not a matter of finding something for the sake of it. Many people today suffer from a lack of self-esteem, anxieties, and feelings of powerlessness. The stress in their professions is so constant that they often feel unable to cope with the enormous demands made on them. In addition to their own conflicts, there are societal issues that generate anxiety, denial, repression, and aggression. They are triggered by the pandemic, climate change, increasing terrorism, far-right populism, and the difficulties of integrating so many migrants and refugees, all of which are causes of conflicts that are hardly or never resolved. There is not a single person who is not directly or indirectly affected.

In this convolution of conflicts, I believe that science has the crucial task of sifting through the deeper causes of conflicts, articulating, analysing, and explaining them, and proposing solutions. The purpose is to advance enlightenment in the classical sense – not in a moralising way, and not just as an appeal to reason, but through "explanation and understanding", as the Finnish philosopher Georg Henrik von Wright said in his eponymous book.

Science – and this is my goal, which I hope to achieve with this book – can then also be helpful for people who are not scientists. This is possible if they recognise themselves and their problems in the concrete examples I present, for instance as regards mobbing, and understand the root causes of conflicts and how to deal with them.

Acknowledgements

Many suggestions and ideas for this book can be traced back to my seminar "Psychopathology of Social Institutions", which I conducted from 1996 to 2001 at the Graduate School for Social Research at the Polish Academy of Sciences in Warsaw. Some of my work is also based on lectures I gave at a psychoanalytic training institute in Berlin.

When doing research from a deep psychological point of view, supervision is indispensable. The reason is that the author's own unresolved conflicts can interfere unnoticed if the subject of the investigation touches on these conflicts. I owe the supervision of my research results to several experts: Professor Regine Reichwein (psychotherapist) supervised the pointed psychoanalytic interpretations, Monika Hirsch-Sprätz (graduate psychologist and head of the Berlin-Brandenburg Mobbing Counselling Centre) and Ralf Müller-Amenitsch made important comments on my investigation of mobbing, while Stephan Kaiser (psychoanalyst) supervised this same investigation.

I am also very grateful to Dr Irene Roski for her careful comments on the manuscript. Christiane Bassyouni, Lilly Stock and Manfred Stock, Gabriele Mirbach, and Hartmut Lange have also influenced crucial passages of my book. Tita Gaehme and Roland Schäfer contributed valuable text revisions and clever comments. I would like to thank Sven Lüder not only for his technical assistance in the preparation of the book manuscript but also for his always stimulating text comments. Johannes Strohschein and Christina Schmidt very carefully reviewed the manuscript and suggested corrections.

I would like to thank Heide Dürr and Heinz Dürr for the interesting discussions and for the friendly support of their foundation. I am also very grateful to my translator Bettina Vestring, not only for her professional competence, but also her advice and constructive suggestions. Last, but not least, I would like to thank my partner Dr Barbara Strohschein for her clever suggestions during the revision of many chapters as well as for her tireless support over many years, without which I could not have written this book.

Introduction

Why and to what end is it important to examine the unconscious in culture?

Investigating the unconscious in the realm of culture brings us insights into correlations that we cannot gain otherwise. Mental problems become apparent which would otherwise remain unrecognised. Psychoanalysis provides orientation and a guide to serenity. It also gives us the courage to address the dark side of both a person and a cultural phenomenon instead of disregarding it as so many others would do. Using selected examples, I will show how a psychoanalytical cultural critique can reveal correlations about disturbing cultural phenomena which remain mostly hidden to other sciences. Such discovery is more than an end in itself; it allows us to find solutions through insight.

Let us begin with some questions: What actually happens during mobbing? How can the depth dimension of such harassment be made visible so that its effects can be adequately understood? If we look at tomorrow's leaders, are we dealing with managers who are getting overloaded with tasks that nobody knows how to solve? In business, are we seeing the beginnings of a maternalistic corporate culture that may gradually replace the traditional paternalistic one? How can we explain that casting shows are so popular among young people? Physicists as well as sociologists and psychologists often ignore the depth dimension of action in the public discussion of climate change. But what are the consequences for the public's understanding of climate change? How much of the context is inevitably getting lost? What should vegans and vegetarians pay attention to if they want to become politically effective, given the risk that their actions – as much as any action in the political field – may be affected by unsolved mental problems?

The term "subject" can help us understand why neither philosophy, sociology, nor cognitive psychology is able to give us an insight into mental problems. There, it has a completely different meaning than in psychoanalysis. In sociology, for example, a subject is always a bearer of competences – of moral judgment, action, language, and so forth. This is quite different from psychoanalysis where subject always means subjectivity, which can be individual or collective.

DOI: 10.4324/9780429345449-101

What does this refer to? Traditionally, subjectivity is what we call the "inner soul world" of an individual or of a collective. Such a collective can be a generation, a group, a community, and so forth.

Here, I will refer to such a collective and its inner soul life. My fundamental idea is that society must rely on the ego of which Freud said it was "not master in its own house". More than that: The ego is the place of the soul where old wounds of childhood can reopen; where unfulfilled longings can persist and push for fulfilment; where existing contradictions can always assert themselves anew – and much more.

The main point is: All of this happens not only to specific people as individuals but also to everybody within their own culture. In a therapeutic approach, one would take the perspective that the ego, under the influence of the unconscious, produces problematic and unadapted phenomena in individuals. These phenomena are seen as an indication of disorder and mental suffering of the individual, which is diagnosed to help that person.

But the ego, under the influence of the psychic unconscious, can also produce phenomena that are perceived as collectively significant, simply because the unconscious, which makes its presence felt, exists frequently in a society. The result then becomes part of our everyday culture. In that case, it makes little sense to speak of disorder or deviation outside the therapeutic context. What does make a lot of sense is to look for indications of existing mental suffering and problems that are of a collective nature. They always leave behind evidence of their own origins in the respective cultural phenomena. If we are able to see these, we can better understand and shape ourselves as well as our social reality.

Some concepts for the analysis of the collective–unconscious dimension of cultural phenomena

A starting point of my research is that relationships that were traumatically experienced in childhood can, under certain conditions, be re-actualised in the present time, as if under a compulsion to repeat.

But how can we know what the corresponding emotional problem situation in childhood would be like? And when can we consider it typical for a generation?

Freud focused on the effect of the Oedipus complex on cultural phenomena, which – because it was often not well resolved – persisted in people's psychic unconscious and thus had a hidden effect on cultural creations.[1] Freud could only imagine social order as a paternal order. But if social and paternal order are considered identical, the perspective on culture is much reduced, because two other forms of social order are left out: The social order of equals (in social groups) and the maternal order.

If we followed Freud's view of the social order today, the scope of psychoanalytic cultural criticism would be much reduced. We must understand that with social change, the psyche has also changed fundamentally. The Oedipal conflict in its traditional form has largely lost its significance today and has been replaced by other widespread psychological problem constellations. The traditional conflict between instinctual drives and superego prohibitions, which Freud believed central, has shifted towards narcissism.[2]

Moreover, in exposing the Oedipal complex, Freud interweaved various contexts that we should carefully separate. I mean the distinction between which parts of this complex are specific to a culture and which are (probably) universal. The concept of positions when analysing the psychodynamics of a family can help clarify some of these elements. For some time now, clinical-therapeutic case reports have indicated that in the present time, the father has become a "weak father". This result is quite independent of the specific therapeutic school involved in the treatment interview.

How can we get a better grasp on the meaning of this metaphor? The person who is in the position of the father has to fulfil the various functions that are linked to this position. The person is weak when he does not fulfil these functions well or when he fails at them altogether.

Regardless, however, of what is meant by the metaphor of the weak father, I would like to distinguish between two groups of functions. The functions, which are probably universal, that serve to confirm the genealogy, that is the line of ancestors, into which a subject – through the prohibition of incest and the prohibition of killing – falls. These functions are largely intact today. However, there are other functions which are culture-specific and in which – as the metaphor possibly suggests – the subject does not perform well at all. These include, for example, the function of providing orientation and of enforcing those small everyday prohibitions that a father can impose on his child. The execution of these functions has obviously become uncertain in Western culture today.

Why therapy and cultural analysis cannot be equated

I have already pointed out that the distinction between healthy and sick is not relevant to my investigations. Of course, the wealth of experience that psychotherapists or psychoanalysts gather in their therapeutic practice is enormously important. But a psychoanalytic cultural critique, as I understand it, does not gain much if the therapeutic perspective is merely extended to society. The popularity of books such as those by Wolfgang Schmidbauer (1981) or Hans-Joachim Maaz (2012) about the narcissistic society or the narcissistic personality of our time should not blind us to the fact that they simply find in social phenomena what was previously learned from patients in a therapeutic context. In doing so, one relies – as Freud did – on a mere analogy of findings between the therapeutic context and social phenomena. How such an analogy is justified in each case is usually left open.

The psychoanalyst Wolfgang Mertens (2005 [1981]) in his therapeutic descriptions of symptoms unintentionally demonstrates why such an analogy is problematic. His symptom descriptions are based on concepts that are functional for psychoanalytic therapy (such as "illness", "abstraction of patient behaviour from the social context", and "personal responsibility of the patient"). However, these become dysfunctional when the symptom descriptions are related to social reality outside the therapeutic context. Society is not a mere collection of actual or potential patients, even though it may appear so from a therapeutic perspective.

My analytical approach: The systematic perspective

How can a psychoanalytical critique of culture be developed with an approach that meets today's cultural and psychological challenges?

As I said, my analytical approach focuses on the ego, because society can only build on this ego. But the ego is also the place where, under certain circumstances, psychological wounds that have not healed well can reopen. Repressed longings can make themselves felt, or anxieties from childhood can be revived. Outside of therapy, this cannot be evaluated as a symptom, that is as a sign of an existing psychological dysfunction. I therefore do not understand psychoanalytical cultural critique as a psychology of deviance. Rather, it should, in the manner of a psychosociality, draw attention to new phenomena for which so far no adequate terms exist. Then, conflicts that have so far been excluded from action can become accessible and be resolved.

There is certainly more than one approach to the object of psychoanalytical cultural critique, which should be understood as research that uses cultural phenomena to highlight the connection between the unconscious and the social in each case. According to the approach I have chosen, interactive action is at the heart of the analysis. It is itself a part of culture, if by this we mean the habits of thinking, acting, feeling, and communicating. This interactive action creates an inner connection between the four seemingly heterogeneous social fields of my research – mobbing, future leaders, new mass media, and the public debate on climate change.

The "act signatures of the unconscious" are the focal point of my investigations. Interactive action in various social contexts is examined to see how it can be influenced by psychologically unconscious processes and to analyse the consequences. The basic concepts of my analytical approach are also explained in Chapter 1. I will concentrate on knowledge which informs collective action. If it is in the grips of an unsolved emotional problem of childhood that it attempts to address, it will be knowledge of a psycho-pathological nature that henceforth guides interactive action. We can then observe anomalies of action which can be evaluated as irrational, non-conformist, strange, and so forth but which have long since become part of social reality.

An interdisciplinary research perspective is an important prerequisite for these investigations. For if we want to find out how culture, interactive action, and the unconscious are connected, we need knowledge that traditionally comes from different subjects, not just from psychoanalysis, but also from sociology and possibly also from linguistics.

There are two very different models for interdisciplinary research: One results from a desired cooperation between representatives of different academic disciplines, who above all try to find a common language. In the other model, one scholar is proficient in two or three different academic subjects. The advantage of the latter is that the inevitable tension between the subjects will be dealt with within the scholar himself. This is the easiest way to test the limits and the respective scope of a discipline. Implementing this second model is certainly a difficult undertaking, but if it is successful, it is also quite productive. My own research is based on this second approach.

The three different narcissism theories that I use all share a prerequisite which is necessary for my approach to this research: They presuppose a coherent self. I believe this is justified because each of these theories relates to a particular psychological development phase of the child and also gains its explanatory power from this phase. In Kohut's psychology of the self, the reference to the second year of life is of particular interest to my investigations. Mahler's concept of individuation covers important narcissistic aspects of mental development from the second to the fourth year of life. I see both theories as linked to each other in the description of the "seesaw relationship".

We can see the narcissistic dimension of the so-called Oedipal phase, which is the focus of Legendre's study (based on Jacques Lacan), in the fourth and fifth years of life.[3]

Since Freud, there are two methods of investigation which give us access to the psychic unconscious. However, there is a fundamental paradox in their application. During therapy, it is not possible for the psychoanalyst to take up the relationship offer of his patient through transference and countertransference in a controlled manner and, at the same time, investigate the unconscious meaning of jokes, mistakes, and neurotic symptoms. While we cannot solve this paradox, I believe we can avoid it. I will draw on my earlier proposal (Flader, 1995) to replace Freud's associational psychological concept of meaning with an action-theoretical one. In this book, I will expand it to include a time reference, that of the past.

For my investigations I distinguish between two levels of meaning: The level of a currently existing emotional conflict of the participants and the level of the re-actualisation of an emotional problem during childhood. Outside of therapy, such re-actualisation will seldom take place eruptively. Instead, it will manifest as a compulsion to repeat which makes use of the affected person's existing knowledge. A prerequisite for re-actualisation is that this person (unconsciously) perceives a structural analogy between a given action and its contextual characteristics on the one hand and the respective relationship pattern of childhood on the other hand. This produces meaning because the various structural elements of action – such as motif, inner images, situation concepts, and maxims – are shaped by the respective childhood relationship pattern.

Freud's tendency to hypostasise the unconscious made it difficult for him not only to distinguish between different types of unconscious but also to explain in different ways why a particular mental phenomenon should be considered unconscious (i.e. systematically withdrawn from reflection). In Chapter 1, Section 1.2, I propose to differentiate. Among other things, I pursue the following questions:

In what way is it becoming difficult or even impossible to reflect upon the unconsciously persisting close connection to the primary reference person? Why is it so difficult? Is it, as Legendre assumes, the weakening of paternal authority and the uncertainty of the reference (or father as a metaphor) that make such a reflection impossible? Is it that the position of a third, which one would need to be assume, is missing?

It is not the fact that narcissistic mental disorders have been found in these fields, which are known in the therapeutic context as symptom descriptions (cf. Mertens, 2005 [1981]), that shows the objectivity of my interpretations, reconstructions, and analyses. It is the fact that many readers can recognise themselves, in whole or in part, in my investigations of connections between the psychological and the social. In order to check my suggested interpretations, I have submitted individual chapters of this book to psychoanalysts and therapists for supervision.[4]

Concrete examples of act signatures of the unconscious

Chapters 2–4 will explain how act signatures of the unconscious can be captured in different social fields. The aim of these investigations is to show, based on concrete current examples, how to proceed with a psychoanalytic cultural critique. We will also be looking at the reasons we can use these insights to gain an understanding of correlations that no other discipline can yield. As early as 1978, Paul Parin raised the question – rightly in my opinion – why psychoanalysts so rarely take a stand on the hot issues of their time, and why they neglect the cultural-critical tasks of psychoanalysis. Has this currently really changed as much as the many book titles written on the topic suggest?

Chapter 2 deals with *mobbing* in great detail – this is still a taboo subject in many areas of our society. I believe that the destructive effects and the inherent dynamics of this process can only be properly understood if its psychological dimension is taken into account. The intended narcissistic devaluation of the victim is the crucial element.

To my mind, the real taboo of mobbing is the re-actualisation of a mental problem situation of early childhood, which is linked to maternal dominance and its destructive side. For all the constant talk about mobbing, this new and destructive phenomenon of our society is hushed up.

Chapter 3 focuses on a detailed analysis of our failure to take action against *climate change*. With regard to the work done by Claus Leggewie and Harald Welzer (2009), which I will discuss at the end of my concrete investigations, I will concentrate on a striking explanatory deficit and its consequences: The authors never even refer to a psychoanalytical explanation – let alone make it fruitful. The same is true when scientists publicly discuss the disturbing results of their research. Here, too, the question arises: If they fail to consider the depth dimension, will the public's understanding of global warming not lack some important explanatory context? With the help of my interaction-related cultural critique, I will make some suggestions as to what we may find concerning this dimension. Finally, I will present the findings of two eminent British psychoanalysts, Sally Weintrobe (2013) and John Keene (2013), regarding our attitude towards climate change.

After these two detailed studies, Chapter 4 consists of five shorter sections on current social phenomena that I propose to look at.

1. *Leadership* is a reference point of modern corporate culture. I examine the numerous theses and remarks that recognised leadership experts have collected and put forward for discussing their "Global Agenda" (Geneva, 2012). I am particularly interested in the nature – both psychological and cultural – of the new challenges that the experts have identified for the "leadership of tomorrow".

2. Next, I propose to look in detail at the theses and advice given by Peter Kruse (2004) on *successful management*. In his highly differentiated model of contemporary management tasks, I am particularly interested in the metaphorical transfer of the concepts of self-organising systems, which have their origins in the natural sciences, to companies and the management tasks related to them.

   I will also investigate the question of whether the guiding principles of a modern organisational culture in any way indicate the difficulties that can be caused by abandoning the traditional paternalistic style of management.

3. The next part of my research focuses on the *mass media* as a mirror of narcissistic problems. I will interpret the different types of narcissistic satisfaction in football reports, political television discussions, modern casting shows, computer games, and discotheques.

4. After that, I will use an *analysis of three films* by Alfred Hitchcock and Stephen King to focus on the medium as a mirror of its time

5. Regarding the analysis of *vegans and vegetarians*, I am particularly interested in the question of how they can influence politics today. Apart from the concept of "politics through consumer decisions", which has become very popular among the younger generation – how can vegans and vegetarians influence legislators? This is where the concept I developed bears fruit: It points out that all interactive action, including political action, may be influenced by the actors' unsolved mental problems. I conclude this study with some practical advice on what this social group should pay attention to in terms of politics.

So what conclusions can we draw? Are there patterns of thought and behaviour that are rooted in our Western culture? In Chapter 5, I propose to investigate the perspectives offered by different social sciences.

In the sense of the sociality of the psychic, I as an author hope that the research perspective that I have developed will be taken up by others to draw attention to other cultural phenomena of our time, which I have not been able to examine here, and to establish connections in the depth dimension that have often been overlooked until now.

Ultimately, my psychoanalytical approach is about finding a way to recognise and, as far as possible, to understand the psychological conflict structure or problem situation that underlies certain cultural phenomena and that mostly eludes consciousness. Only then will it be possible to make proposals that allow a reflected approach to these phenomena.

Notes

1 In his research, Freud always focused on his father as the promoter of order: In *The Man Moses and the Monotheistic Religion* (1939a [1934–1938]), this part of the Bible is understood as a hidden story of patricide. In *Totem and Taboo* (1912–1913a), a psychoanalytical reconstruction of the formation of society in the early days of mankind is developed, and in *The Discontent in Culture* (1930a), it is stated that the feeling of guilt is widespread because in the memory of mankind, the patricide of the early days is preserved.

2 As far as the analysis of narcissistic problems and their genesis is concerned, I largely follow Heinz Kohut (1973), combined with Margaret Mahler's writings (1972) on the developmental phase of detachment and individuation. I use the term "depth psychology" whenever I orientate myself on Kohut's self-psychology, otherwise I generally speak of psychoanalysis.

3 The well-known approach of Otto F. Kernberg (1978), for example, which refers to so-called severe narcissistic personality disorders – such as psychosis and borderline cases – is not relevant to my approach, since it presupposes a non-coherent self.

4 I am particularly grateful to Gabriele von Bülow, Stephan Kaiser, Gabriele Mirbach, Regine Reichwein, and Irene Roski.

Chapter 1

Basic assumptions and some concepts of the psychoanalytic theory of action

1 The act signature of the unconscious – a new approach of psychoanalytic cultural critique

This book puts the focus on psychoanalysis not as a method of therapy but as a research approach – the research paradigm (Kuhn, 1973) developed by Freud. I am referring to the collection of exemplary research that Freud initiated to develop his theory of the unconscious. I assume that such research has the potential of providing us with explanations without which we cannot adequately grasp important social phenomena of our time. In a systematic perspective, I now propose to examine selected social fields to find out how the unconscious can determine interactive action.[1]

We should distinguish the socio- and psycho-historical perspective from the systematic perspective. From the latter, the urgent questions arise: How do we find a viable approach for an analysis of the relationship between psyche and culture? What can be the basic element of such an investigation? In other words, how do we actually see the interrelation of psyche and culture? Which phenomena should we choose in order to investigate this relationship?

Mendel (1969) has emphasised that as a psychoanalyst, he has only "imagines" – meaning inner images – at his disposal in therapy. We can add that this must also refer to his conclusions about the overall cultural changes of his time. From this historical perspective we can at least gain some orientation about the theoretical foundation of narcissism research that is relevant here as well as the psychological changes that have been documented in therapy. But are these "imagines" really the only existing basic unit of this investigation?

Let us look at scientific tradition in this field of research. It is worth considering because we can learn which elements still make sense and which parts of the tradition seem problematic today. If Freud (1927c, p. 367), for example, diagnosed (Christian) religion as a collective compulsive neurosis that spares the believer from having to form an individual neurosis – is such a diagnosis plausible? Freud's approach simply consisted of drawing an analogy between

DOI: 10.4324/9780429345449-1

symptoms of obsessive-compulsive patients (their tendency towards ceremonies and rituals) and a corresponding neurotic problem of the Christian religion or church. Both ceremonies and rituals seemed comparable to him.

But is that really true with regard to their likely psychological background? According to Freud's model of mental development, both groups – the group of compulsively ill patients and the social group of believers – have quite different mental backgrounds. For his patients, under aspects of drive development, the fixation on the anal phase of development was characteristic, while the group of believers received support by society's cultural institutions for coping with the Oedipal complex. In addition to legal institution, ethics, and state institutions, these also include the social institution of religion (Freud, 1924f, p. 426). In this respect, according to Freud's development model, the two groups are not at all on the same psychological level. Thus, the psychological background of both social groups is also different.

I assume that Freud believed them to be comparable primarily based on an analogy procedure. Freud took the description of symptoms and the genesis of obsessive-compulsive disorder from his therapeutic perspective. It was this perspective that he then extended to religion. In the process, however, the social content of this social institution disappeared. With it disappeared the question that I regard as central to a psychoanalytical critique of culture: What actually is the connection – using religion as an example here – between the social and the psychological?[2] The Freudian approach cannot give us any information about the unconscious dimensions of social institutions, for example those of Christian doctrine.

Should we not consider that from a therapeutic perspective, when it is simply extended, society may appear as an ensemble of patients? Winnicott (1973) provided us with an example. He drew up the following list of mentally ill people who are part of society: The psychopaths, the neurotics, the melancholy, the schizoids, the schizophrenics, and the paranoids (ibid., p. 157).

This list corresponds to a viewpoint from where society actually appears as a collection of potential patients. Such a list may be a useful marketing strategy for the profession of therapeutic psychoanalyst. But there is a danger that this extension of the therapeutic perspective to society, if it is intended to help us gain insights in the sense of a psychoanalytic cultural critique, will fail. Instead, it will result in the loss of its object – and thus also its content.

Since Lasch (1979), several attempts have been made to diagnose Western society as narcissistic in the therapeutic-clinical sense of psychoanalysis and to interpret conspicuous behaviour of individuals as "typically narcissistic". In most cases, the result is at best essayistic. To my mind, the main reason for this is the application of symptom descriptions to social phenomena outside the therapeutic context, which is problematic. Since this procedure is quite common among psychoanalysts working in therapy, I will go into this in more detail.

1.1 The description of symptoms in psychoanalytic therapy

Therapeutic descriptions of symptoms are firmly linked to the therapeutic context. They are part of the defining conditions of psychoanalytic therapy because, from the outset, they are tailored to the demands made by the psychoanalytic-therapeutic discourse – not only on the analyst but also on the patient. The patient will need some time to meet the specific demands of this discourse. For example, the person seeking therapeutic help will frequently not see himself as a psychoanalytic patient in the beginning. He often has to be instructed to do so, because the psychoanalytical concept of illness differs from the medical one, which a patient usually knows. The study on "The Effect of the Basic Rule of Psychoanalysis", which I conducted together with Flader & Grodzicki (1982), illuminates these requirements from a perspective which combines communication-related linguistics with psychoanalysis.

While these symptom descriptions thus have an important functional significance for psychoanalytic therapy, they do not work for analysing non-therapeutic phenomena of collective subjectivity. They obstruct the view rather than sharpen it.

In my view, the following aspects of psychoanalytic-therapeutic descriptions of symptoms are particularly relevant here: (1) The problematic assumption of normality as a yardstick for diagnosis; (2) the concentration on the individual; and (3) holding the patient responsible for the symptom.

The following examples are taken from the highly differentiated and concise "description of the different facets of self-esteem disorders close to everyday life" given by Mertens (2005), an experienced therapeutic psychoanalyst (ibid., p. 128).

I What is assumed to be mental normality becomes the yardstick for a diagnosis

The idea that there is a standard for health, by which individual behaviour is measured and abnormalities can be detected and registered, is important in the therapeutic context. The therapeutic diagnosis establishes a link between a traumatic childhood relationship experience of a patient and the conspicuousness of his or her actions outside therapy. The latter is understood as the expression of certain character traits that are considered typical for a certain mental disorder. Mertens characterises in detail what he calls a "healthy narcissistic personality". This is a person who

> can appear self-confident and self-assured, who loves to be the centre of attention occasionally and is not too shy to talk about himself. As he can convince other people, they like working with him without feeling ignored or exploited. His talents and gifts, especially his unshakable conviction of the meaningfulness of his goals and visions, allow him to realise many

projects. If he is able to create a benevolent environment for himself, his creative urge knows practically no bounds. (ibid., pp. 181–182)

Mertens adopts a concept from folk psychology to diagnose narcissistic behaviour. He makes the following comments on when to use it:

> One [describes] someone as a 'narcissist' when the person concerned tends to be egocentric and overconfident; if he has a pronounced predilection for manipulating other people; if he has not only an extreme self-centredness, but also an overpowering feeling of how important it is that he is right in his views, convictions, and actions. One also finds in him a reluctance to empathize with and listen to others, an exaltation of constant attention and admiration, the spending of unusually long periods of time on observing himself, his appearance, talents, and abilities. (ibid., p. 129)

This psychological description can be functional in a therapeutic context if it leads the patient to understand himself or herself as sick. This can be a starting point for gradually introducing the patient to the specific psychoanalytical concept of his or her illness.

However, this psychology, when applied to the extra-therapeutic context of human action, has a potentially dangerous dimension: It assigns to a group of persons all the negative characteristics which in the political context correspond to the discrimination of minorities.

In contrast, one of the goals of my research is to circumvent the collective defence against the narcissistic or, rather, to contribute to it becoming unnecessary over time. After all, narcissistic problems are not an issue of the mentally ill but part of our social reality – albeit in a form that is often difficult to understand.

Ultimately, this therapeutic assumption – which is based on the idea of mental health, insofar as it is understood as a standard for normality – follows the inner logic of a psychology of deviance. It proceeds in the following steps: First, an assumed normality is taken as the standard; then abnormalities of individual behaviour are registered according to this standard as deviation; finally, the persistence of such abnormalities is determined as a character trait of a person. As I understand it, this deviance psychology marks the exact opposite of the psychoanalytic cultural critique that I propose here.

In everyday life, the word "narcissistic" is often used as if a narcissistic issue was a personal flaw attributable to others but not to oneself. Mertens does not address the fact that the psychological concepts of narcissism and narcissistic behaviour can be used in an extra-therapeutic way to achieve a certain psychological defence against one's own anxieties and feelings of smallness.

But he also says that psychoanalysts have a certain susceptibility in this area:

> However, from a psychoanalytical point of view it is always necessary to recognise one's own prejudices and offenses. Certainly, it is rare for

someone to be admitted to psychoanalytic training who has a serious narcissistic disorder. But wounds to a child's self-esteem, traumatisation which has made one feel insecure in certain areas, or the lasting effects of narcissistically compensatory fantasies are part of the basic equipment of almost every person and thus also of every therapist. These, too, therefore react to the narcissistic airs and graces of certain personalities, and it takes quite a lot of experience not to immediately put a diagnostic label on every personal insecurity in interpersonal encounters. (ibid., pp. 168–169)

If we see the increase in narcissistic problems today in the context of processes of social change – as pointed out by the sociological discussion of individualisation – then these problems are by no means only a part of the human basic equipment, as Mertens believes. Rather, they are phenomena that we are all dealing with in a certain psychological way because we are all children of our time.

2 The focus on the individual

The concentration on the individual in therapy has a side effect: The patient's behaviour outside of therapy is removed from the complicated social contexts in which he or she behaves and interacts with others in everyday life. It may seem as if the psychoanalyst who works in therapy would also be concerned with the behaviour, modes of experience, and action strategies of his patient. Mertens reports in detail on this. After all, the analyst receives a great deal of information regarding the patient's extra-therapeutic behaviour, which he or she also explains during the course of therapy.

But this information is always tailored to the patient as an individual and to the possibilities of helping the patient therapeutically. Especially, the therapeutic descriptions of symptoms do not show the connection between social and psychological aspects in certain phenomena outside of therapy. Mertens explains politics, for example:

> Politics is in any case an outstanding field of activity for narcissistically disturbed people. Being in the limelight, appearing as a guest on countless talk shows, and being used by complementary narcissistic journalists and consumers as a mirror of their own grandiose dreams, means that early violations of self-esteem can be compensated for at least for a while. (ibid., p. 155)

This interpretation of politics explains next to nothing. A complex social phenomenon, such as that of politics, is reduced to the defensive strategy of politicians who suffered narcissistic childhood mortifications. It is assumed that they compensate for these mortifications with a contrasting public performance that is intended to confirm their own greatness. Since journalists (and their readers) are also included in the interpretation, everybody involved in politics is considered to be affected.[3]

Mertens, for example, believes that today's societal problems have primarily been caused by the increasing reduction of the ability to empathise and sympathise. The fundamental shocks to the cultural foundations of our society, which we must accept as real today – for example, the increasing insecurity of parents about imposing limits on a child's actions; the consequences of the fact that the social relevance of the Christian churches is becoming fragile; the increasing helplessness of experts to react appropriately to climate change; the widespread uncertainty as to how leadership in social organisations can still be possible today; and much more – all of these are reduced to the therapist's fundamental skill, which he needs to bring to his or her profession and then differentiate further.

The extra-therapeutic assignment of negative character traits to a person or a group of people in society does not only block out the mental conflict behind it. It also blocks out continuing social differences. It abstracts from successful interpersonal relationships and from concrete actions. No matter how negatively a person is judged, he or she will never be as completely absorbed by those traits as other people are inclined to believe. This is how Mertens describes people in leadership positions:

> Narcissistically disturbed personalities can be socially well adapted and successful. Not infrequently, they even occupy top positions in our society as bosses, managers, politicians, or professors. Yet as they are led by appearances and market values and attracted by success and fame, interpersonal contacts are usually only a tool for them. They use them to motivate employees on their behalf and to instrumentalise them for their ideas. Words such as empathy, tolerance, participation, and corporate culture are part of their normal vocabulary, but they are basically empty words. Strictly speaking, they secretly despise those who stand up for these values in the company. According to their philosophy – although they do not say so loudly to their fellow human beings – basically everyone is fighting everyone else. (ibid., pp. 131–132)

3 The self-responsibility of the patient

In the psychoanalytic-therapeutic context, it makes sense to assume that patients are responsible for themselves. The mental suffering which brought them into therapy is linked to them. In a certain sense, they have produced the symptoms (for example their narcissistic character traits). The only people who can make them disappear – with the help of the therapist – are the patients themselves.

A mentality of entitlement, self-pity, self-righteousness, dogmatism, and a sense of aggrievement are considered typical narcissistic traits. For the purposes of therapeutic work, this process of generalising individual behavioural ab-normalities as character traits can indeed be helpful. Such character traits can provide a relatively tangible clue to help patients overcome their resistance to treatment. However, Mertens makes it very clear how difficult this process is:

> As with the analysis and overcoming of other narcissistic traits, the greatest difficulty in the analysis of such patients is for them to recognise and accept their attitude of self-righteousness as a defensive measure. This shakes the whole structure of their ideals and values. (ibid., p. 154)

Here, the defensive instrument of self-righteousness is actually linked to the structure of ideals and values in a sense of taking action. In my opinion, however, an attitude is not a concept which we can really use to shed light on non-therapeutic social phenomena. Such character traits individualise the phenomena we mentioned. Rather than understanding them as the creation of an interrelation between culture and psyche, they are analysed as behavioural abnormalities of a person.

The conclusion from all of this is that we cannot use the therapeutic de-scriptions of symptoms to adequately investigate contemporary social phe-nomena. The therapeutic descriptions of symptoms, which are part of the essential conditions of psychoanalytic therapy, should not be confused with descriptions and analyses of non-therapeutic social phenomena, even though they are often used to that end in relevant publications.

1.2 The concept of the act signature of the unconscious

By simply extending the therapeutic perspective to society, one recognises there what is therapeutically already well known and now is easily identified again in the non-therapeutic context.[4] This procedure reduces the object of investigation of a psychoanalytic cultural critique which has to do with the fact that psychoanalytic therapy to a large extent limits the ability to act. On this, there is a broad consensus, no matter how one defines this restriction in theory. Analysts working in therapy – Mendel, for example, whom we have already mentioned (1969) – have emphasised that in the course of the treat-ment interview, they essentially see the "imagines", the inner, unconscious images of the patient's self and objects. It is these inner images that are con-nected to the particular pattern of emotional relationship which a patient develops towards his analyst and which the analyst (in countertransference) takes up in a controlled manner.

As a consequence of this limitation, other structural elements of action, such as the maxims of childhood (super-ego), situational concepts, and the child's sexual desires, which directly guide action, are not at all covered by the method of transference and countertransference. There is absolutely no awareness of them in a therapeutic context.

The activity of speaking, insofar as it mainly serves the purposes to regulate narcissistic tendencies, is reduced to a monologue in the examples given by Mertens. His view largely ignores the social character of speech – as a form of social action – as well as the social context in which it takes place. In the examples given by Mertens, "the counterpart is meant to be impressed, kept at a distance, or invited to come closer. He or she are meant to be dominated or suppressed and subdued by a flood of words" (ibid., p. 164). But this kind of speaking is only possible if the person makes use of certain linguistic acts that serve his or her psychological purposes. But this is not something we learn anything about.

Let us look at an example from politics to illustrate the problem of this limitation of action: If unconscious processes in politics are to be uncovered, we need a factual debate about the current demands the public media make on politics. Thomas Meyer (2001) has called these the "colonisation of politics by the media". Here, psychoanalysis could make an important contribution if it addressed the assumptions and models of political science and sociology in the sense of scientific criticism. It could then prove that important psychological connections and processes are neglected as far as modern politics is concerned.

Then again, a psychoanalytical contribution would also have to show concretely how personal feelings of one's own grandiosity, together with the feelings of smallness and inferiority that are warded off thereby, can be embedded in different phases of contemporary politics. For this to happen, however, an interdisciplinary perspective would be needed that can complement the therapeutic perspective because it is aware of the latter's limits.

The extension of the therapeutic perspective to society poses another problem: Similar to the therapeutic practice, in which the psychoanalyst takes the side of the individual patient and wants to help him or her, the application of psychoanalytic concepts to social phenomena can all too quickly turn into a criticism of existing social conditions, which are denounced as repressive.

Thus, Gruen (2002) interprets the "majority of cultures … as instruments … to create and maintain divisions in human consciousness" (ibid., p. 131). Here, too, one can ask whether Gruen did not simply generalise the therapeutic experiences he had with many of his patients, attributing the cause of their difficulties to the development of culture. If we understand culture as a system of social values and norms, of models and rites, then it can be both: It can be restrictive, but it can also be supportive. Freud's position on this issue was rather sceptical.

As long as such criticism was directed against a social sexual morality that was recognised as inhuman (cf. Freud, 1908), it was justified. It could easily identify the mental dimension of individuals that caused their illness – their overly strict super-ego – in the therapeutic experience and relate it plausibly to the corresponding social authorities (the Christian religion, the parental home, etc.). These authorities could be considered responsible for the mental suffering of many, although an existing interrelation between the mental structure of individuals and the cultural norms of society was not excluded. The studies presented in Chapters 2–4 of this book are intended to do justice to both sides of culture. Where the restrictive side is in the foreground, I hope that those involved in a particular cultural phenomenon, once they have recognised the destructive power of the unconscious processes at work, will be able to free themselves from it, either on their own or with outside help.

Let me sum up: When discussing how psychoanalytic cultural critique could proceed today and what insights it should convey, many suggestions share a striking flaw. They apply the same simplification of psychoanalytic interpretation, which is necessary in a therapeutic context, to the investigation of social phenomena. This refers not only to the extension of the therapeutic perspective (and the associated descriptions of symptoms). There is also the reduction of the object of research to expressions of imagines and the widespread lack of awareness of the methodological dilemma of psychoanalysis. One of the exceptions is the work of Johann August Schülein (1999).

The question arises with which method of investigation can we now find a reasonably viable access to collective subjectivity.[5]

About the methodological dilemma of psychoanalysis

There are two fundamentally different methods of investigation in psychoanalysis for uncovering the so-called inner world of the soul, which are largely mutually exclusive (see following table).

I	II
The re-actualisation and interpretation of the fantasy world of childhood through the method of transference and countertransference in a therapeutic context. This is supplemented by interpretations of the patients' reports and their behaviour during the therapy interview.	The uncovering of unconscious processes of dreams, jokes, mistakes, and symptoms in a non-therapeutic context through the method of analysis of the "unconscious meaning".

Re I: The method of transferring patterns of traumatic relationships experienced by the patient in his or her childhood to the therapist and his or her countertransference (the therapist's emotional reactions to those patterns against the background of his own relationship experiences in childhood) enables access to the fantasy world of childhood. This examination method is also of central importance in the case of narcissistic personality disorders (see Mertens, 2005, p. 211).

Re II: When it comes to identifying the unconscious meaning – especially of jokes, of mistakes, and of neurotic symptoms – a completely different method of investigation comes into play. It enables access to the current emotional conflicts of a person.

At no point in his investigations of slips of the tongue did Freud use investigative situations that he had discovered in a therapeutic context – the situation of transference and countertransference. When investigating the unconscious meaning of a symptom, the researcher's actions are not guided by diagnosis, because they take place the therapeutic context. Even in the so-called symptom analysis, the focus is on the "unconscious meaning" rather than on the destructive consequences associated with the symptom.[6]

Although both together – the fantasy world of childhood and the unconscious meaning – make up the so-called inner world of the soul, access to it with these methods of investigation is only possible in two separate ways. This means that there are not only one but two kinds of access to the inner world. But as I already emphasised, it is mostly not possible to use both methods at the same time and place.

If, for example, the unconscious meaning of a political joke is to be investigated, the speaker in question, who is supposed to tell a joke, cannot be asked to lie down on the couch at the same time. And conversely, a patient who pursues his or her childhood fantasies in a therapeutic context cannot simultaneously tell a political joke so that the therapist can gain access to its unconscious meaning. Usually, the examination method, which is the process of transference and countertransference, cannot serve to interpret a patient's slip of the tongue at the same time.

This problem of the object of investigation becomes particularly clear when you look at the time reference and the relationship between the investigator and the purpose of the investigation, that is what is to be analysed about whom. The reference to time in the therapeutic context – the traumatically experienced relationship experiences of childhood – is very different from the reference to time in the non-therapeutic context: A currently unresolved emotional conflict situation in jokes, in mistakes, in neurotic symptoms (I will not go into dreams here).

In my opinion, this difference is reflected in the difference of the respective relationship structure: During the process of transference and countertransference, the patient makes the analyst a kind of relationship offer, which the analyst accepts and in which he or she plays a controlled role. This always concerns a figure from the patient's childhood, whom he or she has experienced, and with whom the treating analyst is also familiar from his or her own childhood. As a result, this is a subject-to-subject relationship.

In contrast, neither in the case of a joke, nor in the case of a slip of the tongue, nor in the case of neurotic symptoms, the unconscious meaning has anything to do with the person concerned making an offer of a relationship to the investigator, which the latter takes up in a controlled manner and in which he or she plays along. Rather, the respective phenomenon and the person who produced it become the object of investigation.

This does not mean that the investigator does not make a counter-transference of his own. Otherwise, he or she would not be able to understand the pattern of an emotional relationship that is part of the unconscious meaning. It is therefore all the more important that he or she maintains control of his countertransference and, if necessary, asks a third party to supervise the investigation.

This paradox is rarely discussed among psychoanalysts today for the simple reason that most of them concentrate on psychoanalytic-therapeutic work. The data collection technique of in-depth interviews does not offer a solution here. For in these interviews, transference and countertransference cannot be realised as intensively and reliably as is possible in a therapeutic context.[7]

This is a dilemma that we will not be able to solve. Perhaps psychoanalysis as a science can be characterised precisely by its paradoxes. So let me briefly mention two other remarkable paradoxes: The first concerns its critical status, since it was conceived by Freud as one of the most radical critiques of the Enlightenment – albeit by using the very means of the Enlightenment, namely science. The second paradox concerns the concept of experience in psycho-analysis. From a psychoanalytical perspective, experiences are not made by the subject, but they are what make the subject, in so far as they shape subjectivity.

There may be a way to make the insights gained in individual psycho-analytic therapies that concern the genesis of mental problems fruitful for our investigations. In our research of the depth dimension of contemporary social phenomena, we may be able to use therapeutic-clinical case reports in the sense of a seismograph of cultural upheavals. In the following I will discuss how we can take this forward in a systematic perspective.

Preconditions for a psychoanalytic cultural critique in a systematic perspective

From clinical-therapeutic case reports, we can extract the mental conflict si-tuations of childhood that are typical for our time. In each case, the ther-apeutic material and the analysis based on it already contain elements of a psychoanalytic cultural critique – albeit condensed and structurally abridged. However, explicating the elements (or aspects) of this cultural critique, which is implicitly contained in the clinical material, is an immense, if not impossible, task, even in terms of scope. Instead, I have chosen psychoanalysts who have already interpreted the findings of their psychoanalytic therapies as cultural upheavals – upheavals that affect us all. They will serve me as the basis for my interpretation when in Chapters 2–4 I examine particular cultural phenomena with regard to their unconscious dimension.

Clarifying the concept of narcissism

In psychoanalytical research into narcissism, a distinction is made between different theoretical approaches. For my research, these different approaches do not necessarily have to be compatible. Instead, I relate each of them to a specific developmental phase of childhood narcissism. The approach of my investigation presupposes the existence of a coherent self. Therefore, I cannot use the theory developed by Kernberg (1978); it deals with a narcissistic problem at a very early stage of life history, in which a coherent self does not yet exist (in the clinical context, this is the case with borderline personality disorders and psychosis).

The narcissism analysed by Kohut (1973) comes later, in the second year of life, and is therefore relevant to my research. As a reminder, these are Kohut's core theses: The narcissistic meaning of the primary caregiver for the child is illustrated by the concept of "self-objects". These are experienced by the child in such a way that they fulfil certain functions which awaken and strengthen his or her sense of self – namely, functions of protection and maintenance of self-esteem. The "optimal refusal" by the mother is inevitable, because the initial perfection that the child experiences will necessarily be impaired if maternal care fails to materialise on day.

As part of its mental development, the small child replaces this initial perfection with two narcissistic configurations: The archaic grandiose self and the idealised parental imago. Under normal conditions, these narcissistic configurations are gradually integrated into the adult personality, meaning that the child internalises them. According to Kohut, this is how joy in one's own activities and the idealised part of the super-ego or ego-ideal are created. But if the child experiences certain traumas in early childhood in connection with the self-objects and remains fixated on these configurations, both are preserved. As a result, the child's self-esteem is damaged, and the inner structure of triangulation, that is the perception of the reality of a third party, is weakened or lost.

Bassyouni worked with patients who took part in the student protests of 1968 and were suffering because of a "see-saw relationship". Such a relationship is characterised by a constant up-and-down between the two people involved: While, according to the person's fantasies, one is "up" and in a position of power, the other must be "down" and in a position of powerlessness. Bassyouni's findings were supplemented by means of the concept of self-objects. Historically, such a see-saw relationship could be associated with the living conditions of mothers during and shortly after the Second World War.

But Kohut's analysis of the self-objects is also important from a systematic perspective. I will show in the chapter on mobbing (see Chapter 2, Section 1.4) that the three basic needs of the self-object are present throughout life and can be considered normal: The need for reflection, the need for idealisation, and the need for equality and belonging. It is precisely these needs that are frustrated when a person is being bullied.

Bassyouni (1997) based her work on Mahler (1972), who focused on the process of separation and individuation of the small child, which occurs between the second and the fourth year of life. In Mahler's observations, the intra-psychic process of separation and individuation takes place when the child acquires the ability to function separately while the mother is present and emotionally available. As a result of the predominance of the new pleasurable sensations, the child can overcome the degree of separation anxiety associated with each new independent step. Each of these steps creates a feeling of narcissistic joy in the child.[8] The focus of my chapter on mobbing (Chapter 2, Section 1) is on the effects of an autonomy conflict that has not been well resolved in childhood. It is supplemented by the frustration of the need for self-objects, which I already mentioned.

The role of countertransference

Devereux (1973) in particular has pointed out that social science research always has to take the emotions into account that are produced by the scientist's experiences with the object of his or her research. They can be characterised by an unconscious process which is called "countertransference" in the therapeutic context. There, it is indispensable as a method of investigation. It is an emotional relationship that a therapist takes up in a careful and controlled manner. It originates in the patient's childhood and is familiar to the therapist from his own childhood. But in the scientific research context outside of therapy, countertransference can often become a source of, among other, anxiety and personal insecurity.

In the non-therapeutic research context, the scientist himself needs to reflect on the role of countertransference. This is especially true if, as I do in my investigations, he or she wants to uncover unconscious processes of social phenomena. In these studies, the research subject does not simply confront objective reality. Rather, reality in a certain sense is a part of the scientist because aspects of his or her own subjectivity establish contact with the mental processes taking place in the social interactions of the participants.[9]

The different types of the unconscious in psychoanalysis

Before I explain my concept of the act signatures of the unconscious, we should first agree on what exactly is meant by the word "unconscious" in the theoretical frame of reference of psychoanalysis. Freud had the tendency to hypostasise the unconscious. He treated it as if it were a unified whole and not the quality of a mental phenomenon, which can only be explained by the laws inherent to that phenomenon.

In fact, the word "unconscious" is used to describe the quality of very different psychological phenomena. The explanations of this quality are correspondingly different. Here, they are shown in an abbreviated form:

a.   What aspects of the ego–ideal cannot be reflected? If it is the result of the transforming internalisation of the idealisation of the parental figures

(Kohut, 1973), then the psychological genesis of this mental structure can no longer be reflected in this result.[10]

b.   What aspects of the super-ego cannot be reflected? This is about making a foreign will one's own. Yet this foreign will preserves its alien character as something that is not understood.

c.   The dynamic unconscious: Alterity (for example one's own feeling of powerlessness, which is warded off by the formation of a grandiose self).[11] As the conflict of "drive versus morality", by which Freud was still guided, has now shifted to the narcissistic, I prefer alterity to the traditional concept of id as the drive pole of personality. The corresponding defensive measure can be analysed as a negation of a part of oneself. It causes a non-knowledge that supports the identity of the person concerned.

d.   The descriptive unconscious: The collective knowledge of action belongs to this "preconscious system" (Freud) because it is continuously confirmed within a culture.

e.   One reason why unconscious defence mechanisms are unconscious is that they are often used like routines. Many forms of psychological defence can be related to structural elements of action, for example to projection. Through them, a negatively experienced part of the self-image is shifted to another person (or another group). With that person (or group), an aspect is then perceived as negative and rejected – which one had also rejected about one's own self-image (for example because it does not correspond to one's ideals).

f.   Displacement and condensation: We can analyse the characteristics of primary process thinking as forms of childlike thinking (see Wygotski, 1969).

g.   Dreams, jokes, mistakes, and neurotic symptoms also have an unconscious meaning. I will explain in more detail later how we can explain this quality.

All these different types of the unconscious can, under certain conditions and in their respective forms, be involved in the process of interactive action. Whenever this is the case, there are act signatures of the unconscious. I will pursue many of these meanings of the unconscious in my investigations. An important distinction, which corresponds to the methodological dilemma of psychoanalysis (see previous discussion), concerns the time frame. If an unresolved psychological conflict belongs to the time frame of the present, I will place the cultural phenomenon generated by this conflict on the first level of meaning. But if an unresolved psychological conflict is part of the time frame of childhood, I will place the corresponding cultural phenomenon on the second level of meaning. Very rarely is a conflict on the first level of meaning identical to that on the second.

First of all, I would like to explain my understanding of the unconscious meaning of dreams, failures, and so forth. This explanation is necessary because I can use it to clarify the concept of the act signatures of the unconscious.

About the unconscious meaning

The question of the unconscious meaning plays an important role when ex-amining the unconscious outside the therapeutic context. Freud's meticulous analyses of the relevant phenomena can claim to meet scientific standards (of his time). From today's perspective, they do not, but that does not mean that this symptomatological approach is outdated per se. It simply means that Freud's analyses should be adapted into a modern version, as I have suggested elsewhere (Flader, 1995).

In his investigations of dreams, jokes, everyday slips of the tongue, and the unconscious meaning of neurotic symptoms, Freud always used the same concept of unconscious meaning. As Stephan (1989) noted, Freud dis-tinguished three aspects: The associative series (which makes a phenomenon meaningful); the aspect of meaning, and the aspect of tendency or intention. The aspect of meaning enabled Freud to examine the dream as a rebus, a picture puzzle. The aspect of tendency or intention was made fruitful for the so-called interference model of slips of the tongue. For the joke and its relation to the unconscious, Freud used both the aspect of meaning (for proper jokes) and the aspect of tendency (for tendentious jokes) (cf. Flader, 2000). Finally, both aspects were also used for the investigation of the unconscious meaning of neurotic symptoms.

The entire course of action, to which an unresolved mental conflict is linked, is always represented – directly or indirectly – in the extra-therapeutic investigations of jokes, slips, and the unconscious meaning of symptoms. The only exception is the interpretation of dreams. However, Freud often did not present this course of action adequately and did not include the respective analysis of action in his explanations because he did not have a modern concept of action available. In Freud's analysis of the joke, for example, the listener plays no role. The same applies to his interference model of failures.

My suggestion to revise Freud's concept of meaning can be illustrated using an example that Freud himself investigated. In the 17th lecture on the "Meaning of Symptoms" (Freud, 1916/17), he analyses the compulsive action of an approximately 30-year-old lady who rings the bell several times a day for the parlour maid. The lady then takes a certain place at the middle of a table and gives the parlour maid either a trivial order or none at all. Asked by Freud why she was doing this, she replied that she did not know. According to her conscious self-image, she was simply the lady of the house ringing for the parlour maid. But Freud reveals something completely different about this compulsive act: The lady had repressed the memory of having been humiliated by her husband on their wedding night. The husband, who was now living in separation from her, had concealed his impotence instead of telling her about it. Out of concern for his reputation, he had put a stain of red ink on the bed sheet so that the maid would find it the next morning as the sign of his wife's defloration and his own sexual potency.

The meaning of this symptom is created by the fact that the lady has to address the humiliation again and again, and in a very specific way. On the one hand, as an example of a displacement, she transferred the stain from the bed sheet to a table and transformed it into a water stain. Every time she rings for the parlour maid, she can use the stain on the table to demonstrate to her, who now represents the public, the sign of her husband's sexual potency. On the other hand, it is in her hands to do this for him, because she could also refrain from doing so. Thus, through this action, she addresses a psychological conflict which she obviously cannot solve: She moves back and forth between anger at her husband and the desire to do something for him that is important to him.

By symptom in the psychoanalytic sense, I mean the sequence of events of the futile attempt to solve an unresolved mental problem (or a psychological conflict) through taking action. The word "symptom" is also used colloquially to refer to phenomena of social reality, even though the meaning of this word in a medical sense – as a sign of an existing dysfunction in the organism – is not appropriate in a social context. There, the use of the word "symptom" implies that the conceptual opposition of healthy and sick, which can be useful in medicine, can also be applied to social phenomena. This suggests the existence of standards of health or normality for a social institution or even the whole of society, which is highly problematic.

The theory of action of T. Parsons (1937) provides a basis for the idea that collective knowledge guides the process of social action. K. Ehlich and J. Rehbein (1979) introduced a revised theory into linguistic pragmatics by separating this theory from its functionalist background. They did this in order to examine the role of language for the various structural elements of social action. Their conclusion was that actions can be analysed as acts of speech. I have combined this theoretical model with Freud's concept of the unconscious meaning, for which Freud himself could clarify neither the role of language nor the inner structure of social actions.

Most of the examples collected by Freud as slips of the tongue are examples of acts of speech. The research approach of A. Giddens (1997), which ignores this fact and focuses on an error of memory that cannot be analysed as an act of speech, inevitably leads to problematic generalisations.

In my opinion, the meaning of a symptom comes from the fact that a double structure is created, consisting of the respective conflict situation and of the distortion of the inner structural context of action – in other words, of the collective knowledge that guides action. It is distorted in a particular way because the individual attempt to address the subjective conflict takes place in a context of social action that otherwise is completely guided by collective knowledge (cf. Flader, 2003).[12]

The fact that the person concerned is not aware of this double structure when it emerges can have a variety of reasons. In the example I mentioned, I see the application of the defence against repression as responsible. It is the negation of a part of oneself that turns into alterity – in simple terms: A woman who was seriously offended by her husband on the wedding night may repress that experience. We can also ask which psychological conflicts, which occurred in the lady's childhood without being properly resolved, played a role in the compulsive act. Why did she react to the humiliation of her husband in just this way? But it is precisely this question which cannot be answered in the situation in which Freud conducts his investigation. He would need to "put the lady on the couch".

Then again, a meticulous examination of the unconscious meaning of a symptom is not possible in a therapeutic conversation. A therapeutically working analyst must abridge his interpretation and limit himself to the result, because otherwise the therapeutic situation will be transformed into a scientific discussion forum. He must therefore necessarily interpret authoritatively. As Schülein (1999) emphasises in the presentation of corresponding thoughts by Strenger (1991), the term "interpretation", according to its inner logic, belongs to therapeutic practice. Practical interpretations are realised for the respective therapeutic treatment in such a way that they never lose their reference to the concrete situation of the individual case.

Žižek (2001) and Kristeva (1978), for example, seem to believe that they can "put society on the couch" if they interpret social phenomena of our time in an authoritative way, like a therapeutically active analyst would do.

In the case of the slips of the tongue, I suggest we should explain their unconscious meaning differently. Here, the ego of the action is doubled by the ego of a more recent version of the same action in which a psychological conflict has occurred. This has not been resolved, but only suppressed, and is reappearing in the execution of the act in question. While the subject pursues a certain goal with his action, in its execution, the suppressed desire to pursue an opposing goal comes to life again. However, only one of the internal structural elements of the action is affected by this, and only for the moment. To be able to recognise this double structure of meaning, the person concerned would have to observe himself from the position of the third party. But he or she can do this only with the help of another person. Therefore, the meaning is unconscious. A conceptual precondition for grasping this meaning is that a strict distinction is made between the conflict of action and the psychological conflict.

A conflict of goals in action can be solved by decisions. But if this is at the same time connected to a psychological conflict, then such a decision is not possible. This is what happens in the example of the president, who wants to open a meeting he is not looking forward to. He does it as follows: "I hereby declare the meeting closed." In this case, the speaker has an existing mental conflict, which already occurred earlier and could not be solved. It asserts itself in the action process and in a parasitic way; in fact, it depends on the same linguistic means by which the speaker had intended to achieve the exact opposite: To declare the meeting open. This dependence leads the linguistic act in question to fail.

The analysis of the unconscious meaning of symptoms refers to the first level of meaning of my investigations. Here, the time reference of the respective mental conflict situation is always the present (in a broader sense). The second level of meaning in my investigations is created by reference to the early childhood of the person concerned. As a consequence, forms of re-actualisation are examined.

In contrast to the usual approach (as in Freud's case), a psychoanalytic cultural critique should start from the assumption that it is the subjects themselves who, in a non-therapeutic context, produce an analogy. They do this under certain conditions which I will explain now.

First of all, I assume that the structural analogy between features of the current action context of the present and the features of a conflictual relationship pattern of childhood is part of these conditions.

Yet the unconscious content found on the second level of meaning – as I have already pointed out – is not simply the continuation of the content of the first level of meaning. Rather, modifications and other changes are to be assumed here. This is because a mental conflict, which occurred in early childhood and could not be resolved then, can be further altered in the course of the subject's development.[13]

However, it is easier to simply establish such an analogy as a scientist than to reconstruct the process in which the participants themselves can do this. The researcher reconstructing this process must, among other things, identify the contextual features in which the participants can perceive an analogy to their traumatic childhood experiences. This is a structural analogy, because the traumatic relationship experiences of childhood are very likely stored in memory as structure rather than as content.

From the data of the social fields I have selected – which include mobbing, the public debate on climate change, the leaders of the future, a model of successful management, television and film analysis, and the political dimension of the actions of vegans and vegetarians – I have identified basic patterns that recur in the data:

- The basic pattern of action
- The situation, and
- The emotional relationship between the participants and the underlying unresolved psychological conflict.

I need these basic patterns to create the conditions for recording the act signatures of the unconscious from the data. I therefore assume that transference and countertransference can also occur in a non-therapeutic context. In contrast to psychoanalytic therapy, I will not use them as a method of investigation but as a process that is subject to the so-called compulsion to repeat. This is the second of the conditions mentioned.

Now the reactivation of relationship traumas in the present is mostly not an eruptive process. It is mediated by collective knowledge. In the process of action, it is this collective knowledge which enables us to perform and understand social actions in everyday life. Such action has an inner structural context, which is represented as knowledge. This is what T. Parsons (1968) analysed for the first time in social sciences. It is supported by collective experiences that arise from the fact that those involved in interactive actions in an action community continuously confirm to each other what they know about these experiences: The course of action, the inner images, the respective motives of action, etc.

Why interactive action in particular? Interactive action in everyday life is an ideal object of research for a psychoanalytical cultural critique. It represents references to elements of the respective cultural system in which action is taken – that is values, norms, and behavioural habits. At the same time, interactive action is a suitable medium for unconsciously dealing with unresolved emotional problems that originate from traumatic experiences of relationships in childhood or from current psychological conflict of the interactants.

We need to concentrate on this social action process to meet the third of the aforementioned conditions for interpreting a re-actualisation of early childhood traumatic experiences in the present.

Further basic concepts of my investigations from a systematic perspective

My research approach is easy to explain if we conceptually distinguish between the ego and the self. The ego is the mental place where learned knowledge is updated – forms of knowledge such as language, interactive action, cultural values, and so forth. This actualisation can take place while trying to satisfy conflicting demands. Among these are narcissistic desire, sexual desires, desired images of the ego-ideal, and also the internalised demand that says: "Live your own life", to which the sociological theory of individualisation has drawn attention.

Society must build on this ego – and in doing so, incur contradictions: Diversionary tactics; an understanding of the present as a repetition of the past; the hidden forms of the satisfaction of early childhood desires, which can exist, for example, with problems of self-esteem; and so on. The ego becomes active in the service of self-esteem regulation in many different forms as well as in forms of interactive action.

What I understand by the self and its psychological development, however, depends on the narcissism concept I use.

What appears to outsiders as irrational, a disorder or deviation from behaviour, in my view documents the unconscious meaning of phenomena already mentioned. These abnormalities of behaviour are caused by the fact that the collective knowledge about social action turns into psycho-pathological knowledge. This knowledge directly or indirectly guides action on the two levels of meaning mentioned earlier.[14] On both levels, as mentioned already, we are dealing with the act signatures of the unconscious.

In the therapeutic perspective of the psychoanalyst, this knowledge of action always plays a role when the therapist uses the patient's reports to understand how his or her individual psychological problems relate to specific forms of action. But in order to be able to concentrate on the patient's psychological problem, the treating analyst cannot break down this connection into every structural differentiation of action. Yet he or she does understand it, with the individual patient in mind, based on his or her own professional experience.

Mertens (2005, pp. 179–180), for example, very clearly describes what he sees as the quintessence of disturbed narcissism:

> If one summarises … the possible causes of a disturbed self-esteem as the quintessence of disturbed narcissism, then deep down, it is *a lack of real love and recognition* that makes narcissistically disturbed people so restlessly strive for favours and recognition. As they cannot experience themselves as lovable, it is also completely inconceivable to them that other people could find them lovable. As children, they were not able to experience being loved and acknowledged for their own sake; therefore, they could not acquire this unquestioning happiness as the core of their personality.

All in all, I agree with Mertens' interpretation. The examples he gives for how the ego attempts to somehow cope with this deficiency as an adult are extremely varied.

But the treating analyst, as I have already emphasised, cannot break down this connection in all the structural differentiations of action. Otherwise, he would not be able to concentrate on the psychological problems of the patient. Based on his own professional experience, he understands it in its relation to the individual patient. In the therapeutic discussion, the connection between knowledge of action and psychological problems will in most cases only become visible through the fact that the patient is self-referential with his sense of entitlement, self-pity, self-righteousness, and so forth.

There are interesting cases, too, in which one of the structural elements of action becomes a fixed component of a certain culture. A relationship problem that is widespread within that culture gets processed through that element; it is there that it finds a fixed form. According to my interpretation, this is the case, for example, when a certain type is formed, such as the "self-actualiser", whose self-image – and the image of a reference person – has obviously been shaped by this kind of problem.

The father image can also be subject to cultural – and psychological – changes. These changes are comprehensive. I assume that a metamorphosis of the father image has taken place in our society in such a way that it now appears in many new forms, which are specialised and distributed over the different social groups and strata.

From the advice of psychoanalysts working in therapy, I can see which psychological conflict constellations of childhood can be regarded as typical for our time. And I must be aware of which of the common theories of narcissism are relevant for my investigations.

Reification and objectivity

It is clear now that the procedure I propose draws, among other things, on the theses, interpretations, and concepts of psychoanalysts working in therapy. I am aware of the fact that this procedure is open to criticism. It can be accused of not capturing actual phenomena of reality, but only the reifications of preconceived concepts. If that is the case, I will see in the phenomena only what was previously projected into them.

I consider this problem of reification to be serious indeed, especially for depth psychological interpretations. Literally speaking, reification means that a term, a metaphor, or an assumption is covertly turned into a thing and then treated as given. In the context of scientific explanations, such reification leads to pseudo-explanations. I want to demonstrate this using the example of the unconscious.

If I discover irrational or conspicuous features in a certain behaviour of a person and explain these as being typical of the influence of the unconscious on that person's behaviour, I covertly assume something as given which I would otherwise have to prove. In this case, it is the influence of the unconscious. Proof for such an assumption is often omitted.

To avoid this danger of reification, I suggested earlier to differentiate between different types of the unconscious. This requires giving a different kind of explanation about why a particular type is present in a specific case:

In fact, in the field of psychoanalysis, a so-called object cannot be adequately understood at all unless the researcher takes his own individual subjectivity as a guideline and assumes that the object of interpretation is at least structurally similar. In my view, there is no external yardstick for assessing the appropriateness of an interpretation. However, if there are many who can recognise themselves in these interpretations, they clearly are not arbitrary. The special feature of interpretations in this sense is that they cannot be reproduced experimentally, that is the concept of objectivity in this paradigm is different from that in the natural sciences.

My approach to a psychoanalytic cultural diagnosis of our time thus necessitates something that is unfortunately often missing in psychoanalytic studies of social phenomena: The precise but nevertheless comprehensible analysis of the complex content of these phenomena, specified by the structure of interactive action in everyday life, where a particular mental conflict can take place.

In short, if we want to recognise the connections between psychological processes and social action, we must first, as I have already emphasised, conceptually separate the two. Only then can we grasp how the social and the psychological interact. To this end, it is necessary to take into account the specific rules and characteristics of both the psychological and the social. It is helpful to use studies from both the sociological or psychological side on the same phenomenon that is to be studied through psychoanalysis, for example the phenomenon of mobbing or today's leadership problems.

Accordingly, my method of a depth-psychological action analysis does not follow a clinical-therapeutic perspective. As explained earlier, symptoms are not seen as signs of illness, nor is the distinction between healthy and sick used as a basis. Also, the symptom descriptions of a narcissistic personality disorder are not used for depth-psychological action analysis. Rather, I initially orientate myself on existing, non-psychoanalytic investigations of social phenomena such as mobbing.

I ask the critical question of whether certain characteristics and connections can be established about the investigated social phenomena which have so far eluded a non-psychological explanation. I then develop a proposal for how to use my research approach to make a contribution. I thus take the path of a scientific critique, which I will present in detail, especially concerning the first social problem area, mobbing, and to which I will return afterwards. I mean by scientific critique that I will show how existing non-psychoanalytic investigations exclude precisely those connections which are psychoanalytically relevant and significant for a better understanding of the phenomenon under investigation.

This is how I will also underpin the thesis that the dimension of the unconscious in the respective social phenomena is inevitably suppressed. It takes place behind the backs of the scientists and unnoticed by them, in the shape, for example, of unresolved questions.

Of course, for my investigations of the selected social problem areas, I will also take up the various concepts that I have discussed in their historical perspective and which I consider to be fruitful. In other words, whatever I consider relevant about the narcissism theories we have discussed, I will use to track down the act signatures of the unconscious in the problem areas chosen for this book.

Notes

1 As Freud stated: "We do not think it desirable that psychoanalysis should be swallowed up by medicine and then be deposited for good in the textbook of psychiatry, in the chapter on therapy, alongside procedures such as hypnotic suggestion, autosuggestion, persuasion …. It deserves a better fate and hopefully will have it. As "depth psychology", the study of the psychologically unconscious, it can become indispensable to all those sciences that deal with the history of the origin of human culture and its great institutions such as art, religion, and social order" (Freud, 1926e, p. 283).

2 I consider the interpretation of (Christian) religion as a collective daydream to be much more plausible.

3 If, as is often the case, manifestations of a blockage of narcissistic development are analysed in a non-therapeutic context (cf. e.g. Kernberg, 1978; Volkan, 2005; Maaz, 2012), then it is mostly inner images of greatness and so forth that are at the centre of the given examples of narcissistic behaviour.

4 For example, Hans-Jürgen Wirth (2011), in reference to Kernberg, points out that political leaders frequently have a narcissistic personality disorder, displaying a behaviour that can be interpreted using clinical categories. But does this view contribute to our understanding of the social and psychological dimension of politics? That remains doubtful.

5 One of the works which I criticise is that of Christopher Lasch (1979), who argues that psychoanalysis can best explain the relationship between society and the individual when it is limited to the careful study of individuals. It is precisely this view that does not clarify the aforementioned problem but omits it instead.

6 As Hermann Lang (1986) emphasises, Lacan considers Freud's claim to a universal relevance of his research – a relevance that goes beyond the medical-therapeutic framework – to be justified. He bases that judgement on Freud's extra-therapeutic investigations into the unconscious meaning of dream, wit, and so forth. In contrast, I do not find Lacan's thesis that the unconscious is organised like a language plausible. I do not consider the mechanisms of displacement and condensation discovered by Freud to be language-related structural forms. Rather, I see in them peculiarities of the way a child thinks.

7 Mertens and Lang (1991) have extensively applied the method of the in-depth interview in their work on the "soul of the company". They appear to have been optimistic that clinical categories can also do justice to problems of corporate culture.

8 Kohut himself refers to the crucial difference between his theoretical model and Mahler's results: while his own work is based on the observation of children, Kohut's theory model is empirically grounded in his experiences as a therapist in the context of transference and countertransference.

9 As Schülein (1999) emphasises, it is the personal contact with the topic that forms the basis of experience for the research subject. When I examine social interactions to see how the unconscious can manifest in them, I rely on the fact that there is a psychic resonance here.

10 I have explained this argument in detail in Flader (1995).

11 However, the metaphor of repression as the best-known defence mechanism, with its equation of space and consciousness, misdirects any attempt to explain both the use of this defence measure and the result of its use as unconscious (cf. Flader, 2000).

12 I mean the structural elements as they were named by T. Parsons: Motive – situation concept – inner images – maxims (moral standards) – and the relations between ends and means (especially when acting within social institutions) (cf. Parsons, 1937).

13 Mertens (2005, p. 204) also emphasises this difference: "But based on a storing and archiving theory of memory, psychoanalysts believed that current experiences can be easily short-circuited with experiences long past." While this means that inevitably, only half of the object is investigated, the methodological consequence does not appear to have been drawn. On the one hand, from the perspective of the observer, the unconscious appears as something that can be scientifically investigated. But on the other hand, the treating therapist is a player in the process of transference and countertransference who gains access to the world of his patient's childlike fantasies. He would call into question his relationship of trust if he were to turn the therapeutic situation into a scientific investigation.

14 It stands to reason (oral communication by Hartmut Lange) to assume that even among scientific subjects, there are those that produce knowledge which has been psychopathologically composed in this sense.

Chapter 2

Mobbing and its connection to the unconscious

1 What is mobbing? The social interaction process of an unresolved mental problem

In this chapter I will show how mobbing at the workplace can be analysed from a depth-psychological point of view as a symptom of interaction. My aim is to outline some perspectives for investigating mobbing that are not yet used in mobbing research, although they would be important for a better understanding

For such an investigation to be viable, several steps are necessary. As the first step, I will present two selected case reports which illustrate the phenomenon of mobbing. I will then draw on studies of the social manifestations and contexts of mobbing as far as they are relevant to my investigation. I place particular importance on the results of the representative statistical-sociological study *Mobbing Report* for Germany (Meschkutat et al., 2002). With the data of the report, the incidents of mobbing gain a social contour, which can be used as a starting point for a depth-psychological investigation. This includes key data such as the average duration of the process; its distribution between the sexes; the motives of the bullies suspected by those being bullied; and so forth.

This is followed by a short critical presentation of the common explanatory models in mobbing research. Only then will I explain a depth-psychological model of mobbing and its course of events in more detail.[1]

1.1 Two case reports

I will use two case reports of bullying to explain the importance of the self-esteem of the person concerned. The two cases described by Leymann (1993) are intended to show by way of example that, in addition to the social dimension of devaluation, we must also include the psychological dimension of personal mortification and further enhance our investigation from that perspective.

First, the case of Gertrud from Hamburg.

> Gertrud used to work as a model. She is very pretty and not yet thirty. She later worked as a technical designer in a construction company. She shared

DOI: 10.4324/9780429345449-2

her office with another woman and three men. At first, Gertrud didn't worry about the fact that the other four always went out to lunch together and didn't ask her along. Gradually, she realised that the others apparently did not like her. Especially the woman kept harassing her: "Better drink your carrot juice today. They're serving liver dumplings; your little waistline won't like that." And the men laughed. More and more often she had to put up with such mockery. (ibid., p. 18)

Then Gertrud tried to bring up the issue during a coffee break. This is the answer she received: "But listen, this is you who is aloof from us. Always such snotty little doll. Don't you get an ink stain on your dress" (ibid.). Again, the men were amused.

One day, she noticed that her colleagues were talking about her as if she were a man: "Has he finished the paper yet?" or "Why don't you go and ask him?" It was an elaborate mockery. They denied she was a woman and talked about her as if she were a man. After one more month of this, Gertrud quit.

According to my interpretation, this conflict at the workplace, which eventually turned into mobbing, was linked to personal mortification. Initially, it was Gertrud who started it: She, intentionally or unintentionally, slighted her colleague, who in turn reacted by deliberately humiliating Gertrud.

Through malice, ridicule, and irony she was to be devalued in her personal identity as a particularly pretty young woman. But that is not all. We understand that it was not just her female colleague but also her male colleagues who intended to devalue Gertrud. This conflict escalated; Gertrud was excluded from the group, and her colleagues consistently denied her identity as a woman through the language they used.

What could have been the motive of the bullying female colleague? Comparing herself to Gertrud, who was very pretty, I believe she may have been reminded of her own flaws, lagging so far behind Gertrud in appearance and figure. To her, Gertrud would have embodied a woman's ideal of beauty, by which she measured herself and which she (in her own assessment) failed to meet.

Without this ideal of beauty, she would probably have found it easier to be relaxed and friendly towards her new colleague. But since Gertrud was present at her workplace all the time, she (probably unintentionally) constantly touched on her colleague's sense of being flawed.

Gertrud's colleague reacted with the spitefulness we just described. According to my interpretation, her motive is not only envy but also the desire to repay Gertrud for the feeling of continued mortification she inspired. For this repayment, she used the same coin, namely stating that as an individual, Gertrud deviates from a collective valuation standard: "It is not me who is not 'right', it is you!" In this case, the colleague cleverly replaced her own deviation from an ideal of beauty (her real issue) with Gertrud's alleged deviation from allegedly valid group norms.

In her actions, she uses fictitious arguments to conceal her actual motive. This is made clear by the content of these arguments: They are formulated ad hoc and made to relate to elements of Gertrud's former profession. Gertrud gets told that should no longer stick to her diet from her professional life as a model; that she should not try to distinguish herself from her colleagues as a "snotty doll"; and that she should not pay excessive care to her dress.

Against the background of having felt mortified by Gertrud (which I assume), the colleague orchestrated a diversion. She distracted from her own feeling of inferiority as a woman – and perhaps also from her envy – by emphasising group norms from which Gertrud (allegedly) deviated.

For another example of how an involuntary mortification at the workplace can trigger mobbing actions, let us look at a second case described by Leymann. Here, the person experiencing the bullying is Lena, the only woman to work as a welder in this company.

The conflict that developed here has to do with the social role pattern of men and women, as Lena worked in a typically male profession. When two women working in the kitchen called in sick, the foreman asked Lena to stand in, but she refused. According to her own report, her colleagues then came up with the following response:

> Look, we've got a women's libber working in the company! Well, check her out! They then started to bitch about me, and the younger ones pinched my ass when I walked by. It was awful. Suddenly, you feel like there may be a job there, but you don't belong, you are a plaything for the other people. The foreman hated me. He always criticised me. (ibid., p. 19)

Lena then, similar to Gertrud, made an attempt to raise the issue with her colleagues:

> Lena does exactly what any reasonable person from a society belonging our cultural sphere would do: She tries to bring up the problem to sort it out. And Lena, like any other mature person in a similar situation, pauses in disbelief and says to herself: "This can't be possible" when she discovers that her attempt to discuss the problem meets with resistance. (ibid., p. 80)

In this case, too, Lena, at the beginning of the conflict, appears to have challenged the foreman's authority through her behaviour (probably unintentionally). The conflict started, I believe, because the foreman thought that Lena, as a woman, could easily fill in for the kitchen staff. He may have seen her refusal to do so as a challenge to his authority as her superior.

After Lena had several times failed to comply with the foreman's request, her colleagues, for their part, placed her in the social category of a "women's libber" and began to devalue her. Lena, when describing her feeling of being treated by other people as their plaything, reflects on the relationship of power and powerlessness between the bullies and their victim. She felt helplessly exposed to the attacks of her colleagues. But why did they block Lena's attempt to discuss the situation with them?

I believe that their feelings of insecurity as men played a role here. The ideal of a "real man", which Lena's colleagues probably adhered to, was already called into question by Lena's work as a welder. Her colleagues then interpreted Lena's refusal to accept the request of the foreman as refusing to do women's work as a matter of principle. From their point of view, the refusal was part of the programme of women's libbers.

In other professions, this ideal of a man's job would be considered rather unfashionable. The mobbing that Lena was confronted with was targeted at her self-esteem. It would only have been possible to discuss the situation if her work colleagues had been willing to reflect on their ideals of what constitutes proper men and women and to put this attitude into perspective at least in the workplace. Yet this obviously overtaxed them.

In this case, too, the workers' superior could have helped to make communication possible. He could have initiated a discussion to help solve the conflict. But the superior – the plant foreman – took part in the mobbing himself. He could therefore not take on this task.

I have discussed these two cases in detail because they help explain how a psychological conflict with bullies can arise in the workplace.

How did the two cases end? Both times, the initial conflict escalated – Gertrud was worn down by the elaborate mockery she was exposed to day after day and resigned after another month. Lena, who told her colleagues to stop the mobbing during a coffee break one day, met with even more hostility afterwards. Here, too, the initial conflict escalated. Lena found out that she was not being paid according to the proper wage scale for her work. After a certain time of being treated as an outcast, she became mentally ill.

Two cases are not enough to fully understand the complex events of mobbing. We need much more data.

1.2 Results of a sociological-statistical survey: The Mobbing Report for Germany (2002)

The explosive nature of bullying and a closer definition of the phenomenon

This representative study is based on an impressive volume of data which was collected in two stages. The first telephone survey was conducted from 27 November 2000 to 9 January 2001, involving 4,396 interviews which concerned a total of 495 cases of bullying.

In the second survey a standardised questionnaire consisting of 48 questions, some of which were open-ended, had to be completed in writing. Far more than 500 cases of mobbing – that had been the initial target – were analysed. In addition to the victims, the questionnaires were sent to works and staff councils, equal opportunities officers, personnel departments, and so forth. By the deadline of 9 August 2001, a total of 1,317 usable questionnaires had been sent back. A considerable number of the survey participants chose to also fill in the answer category "Other", so that a total of approximately 18,000 answers had to be coded and categorised. In addition, many people sent in documents, some of which were very personal (court decisions, medical findings, psychological reports, etc.).

The data collected shows that more than one in nine employees have been affected by mobbing at least once in their working lives. There is no area of working life that can be considered free of mobbing. Mobbing occurs in all professions, sectors, and company sizes, hierarchical levels, and activity levels (cf. Meschkutat et al., 2002, pp. 127–128.).

Mobbing affects both sexes and members of every age group. The number of female victims is significantly higher than that of men. In terms of age, those under 25 years of age are the most affected (ibid., pp. 27–28.).

The damage to the economy is considerable.[2] In Germany alone, the cost of mobbing is estimated at up to EUR 15 billion per year. In addition, there are much higher follow-up costs for the health and social security systems because of the health damages incurred by the victims (see Arentewicz, 2009).

In order to be able to collect this – and other – data, the authors of the *Mobbing Report* had to define the phenomenon of mobbing (at the workplace) in a way that was clear, practical (for a telephone survey), and sustainable (i.e. taking into account the current state of mobbing research). The following definition was chosen:

> Mobbing is understood to mean that someone in the workplace is often harassed, bullied, or disadvantaged and marginalised over a long period of time. – Are you currently or have you ever been subject to mobbing in this sense? (*Mobbing Report*, 2002, p. 19)

In his research, Leymann (1993) was the first to scientifically identify the phenomenon of mobbing in the world of work as a destructive behaviour that causes mental illness in the person affected. He defines mobbing as a "gruelling sequence of actions which only turns into mobbing through constant repetition" (Leymann, 1993, p. 21). On the basis of 300 interviews conducted with mobbing victims (ibid., p. 33f.), Leymann identified 45 different mobbing actions. He then subdivided the individual actions into five mobbing attack areas:

a   Attacks on the ability to communicate
b   Attacks on social relations
c   Attacks with an impact on social reputation
d   Attacks on the quality of professional and life situations
e   Attacks on health

Unfortunately, to the best of my knowledge, Leymann did not pursue the question of how the interviewed victims reconstructed the relevant events of mobbing in their memory in such a way as to be able to distinguish and name individual acts. It remained unexplained in these interviews, for example, why certain actions were experienced as mortifying.

From the broad spectrum of previously known and frequently occurring acts of mobbing, the authors of the *Mobbing Report*, without any claim to completeness and exclusivity, selected ten acts of mobbing for their survey. These actions are referred to as attacks and are differentiated according to the level at which they take place: Either (a) at the personal level/relationship level or (b) at the work level.

Mobbing acts – different forms, their frequency, and duration

The following list shows the ten selected acts of mobbing graded according to the frequency of their occurrence based on the telephone survey:

a   *At the personal/relationship level*

- The spreading of "rumours, untruths" was mentioned most frequently (by more than six out of ten). Its key feature is that the originators are difficult to identify.
- Frequent "taunts and teasing" were cited by just over half of those affected, and about a third of those surveyed was exposed to insults. Both actions, as the authors emphasise, can take place at the personal as well as at the professional level.
- Nearly four out of ten persons actively and directly experienced social "exclusion/isolation". The authors explain:

    "For example, they are treated 'like air', systematically excluded from work meetings or social activities such as office parties or company outings. In many cases, they are no longer addressed personally. Or colleagues who enter the office of the person concerned must later give a detailed account of their conversation to their supervisor". (Mobbing-Report, 2002, pp. 41–42)

b   *At the working level*

- More than half of the persons concerned by mobbing refer to a "wrong evaluation of work performance" as the second most important action against them. Together with "massive and unfair criticism of their work" (cited by almost 50 per cent) and the "portrayal of the victim as incompetent" (more than a third), these are attacks that can undermine not only a professional but also a social reputation. The authors of the *Mobbing Report* give the following examples from the survey:

    The work of the persons affected is continuously monitored in order to systematically prove mistakes; behind the backs of those

affected, their colleagues inform their superiors about (supposedly) incorrect performance of the work; all suggestions and
ideas of the persons concerned are ignored or criticised as a
matter of course; letters written by them are torn up without
giving reasons and thrown at their feet without comment; the
person attacked is portrayed as a failure who lacks the professional
prerequisites and whose working methods and habits are ultimately an additional burden for the other colleagues. (ibid. p.41)

- The following mobbing acts also belong to the work context: The
"refusal to provide important information" (more than half); constant
"obstruction at work" (just over a quarter); and marginalisation
through "deprivation of work" (nearly two out of ten). The authors
also point to other typical examples of obstruction at work:
Hampering the learning processes of persons still in the training
phase (e.g. by saying "Why don't you guess how that works!" instead
of answering a trainee's questions); the systematic obstruction of work
processes, for example by not forwarding necessary work documents,
sticking chewing gum on the computer keyboard, or deleting files.

According to the authors, the bullying acts carried out in the work context
have further indirect and subtle after-effects by producing social isolation and
exclusion.

It is striking that the respondents generally experience a combination of
several attacks at the social and professional levels. On average, an affected
person ticked off five of the ten given bullying actions in the written survey.

The surveys of the *Mobbing Report* also show the following:

- When comparing men and women, women are slightly more affected by
"massive exclusion/isolation" (more than four out of ten) than men (close
to a third), while men (more than half) are more affected by the action
"massive/unjust criticism of work" than women (less than half). There are
no gender differences for the other mobbing acts. However, when it
comes to the frequency of being bullied "several times a week", women
are more strongly represented (more than a third) than men (slightly more
than a quarter) (ibid., p. 63).
- It is interesting to note that from the perspective of the victims, the bullies
are believed to be aware of the overall effect of their actions.

  In the written survey, the respondents state that the mobbing against
  them was a targeted (slightly more than 80 percent) or systematic
  (almost 70 percent) action. In contrast, just under 10 percent stated
  that it was an unconscious action. (ibid., p. 60)

My study of mobbing will highlight the unconscious psychological dimension of these processes as typical of mobbing. It will have to be explained why, according to the written answers contained in the *Mobbing Report*, the vast majority of affected persons believe in a targeted or systematic action.

- As far as the frequency of the mobbing actions is concerned, the survey shows that far more than half of the affected persons are confronted with at least one of the mobbing actions frequently to very frequently (i.e. daily or several times a week). Both groups – those who experience these attacks daily and those who are affected several times a week – are confronted with almost all mobbing acts at above-average frequency. Being mobbed is a constant experience for them (ibid., p. 51).
- Twelve months is the most frequently mentioned duration of a mobbing process. On average, cases end after slightly more than 16 months. Slightly more than one-tenth of the respondents say they were exposed to mobbing for a duration of between two and three or for more than three years. But for about one third of the respondents, the mobbing process was shorter than six months. Yet it is important to realise that even in a relatively short period of time, mobbing actions often have serious consequences for the person concerned.
- The number of bullies: In most cases, three to five people were involved in the hostile acts – regardless of how long a mobbing process lasted. If the mobbing process lasted three or more years, the group of attackers was larger with six or more persons. The collected data show that when more bullies are involved, the spectrum of hostile acts increases.
- The longer the mobbing process lasts, the more people join the attacks against the person concerned: "Just under three quarters state that the bullying started with only one person and was followed by others in the course of the process" (ibid., p. 59).

A process model of bullying

The *Mobbing Report* presents a process model (ibid., p. 56) which distinguishes between several phases. No claim is made to universal validity, that is a person affected by mobbing does not necessarily have to go through all phases of the process. Only in a "classic" course of events does the conflict come to a head and escalate, usually with the result that those affected by mobbing turn into victims (ibid., p. 53).

PHASE I: CONFLICTS, INDIVIDUAL INCIDENTS

At the beginning of a mobbing process, there is usually an unresolved or badly handled conflict. It gives rise to initial apportioning of blame and isolated personal attacks against a particular person.

PHASE II: THE PSYCHOLOGICAL TERROR BEGINS

The differences become ever more pronounced. The unresolved conflict recedes into the background, while the person concerned increasingly becomes the target of systematic harassment. The self-esteem of the bullied person decreases, and he or she becomes increasingly isolated and marginalised.

PHASE III: THE CASE BECOMES OFFICIAL, AND LABOUR SANCTIONS ARE THREATENED

The development escalates. Due to the constant humiliations, the bullied person becomes so insecure that his or her work suffers considerably. He or she is increasingly considered to be so "problematic" as to be threatened with labour sanctions such as a warning, transfer, or dismissal.

PHASE IV: THE EXCLUSION

Many cases of bullying end with the person affected losing his or her job and sometimes even leaving the world of employment. Either the persons concerned give notice themselves, or they are dismissed, or they agree to terminate their employment contracts. As a consequence of having been bullied, they often suffer psychosomatic illnesses. Long-term sick leaves and sometimes a permanent incapacity to work are the results.

In this process model, the self-esteem of the affected person plays an important role in phase II. I will explain later why I believe that self-esteem does not simply decrease during that phase but is subject to a more differentiated conflict dynamic.

It is particularly noteworthy that "just over half of all those respondents, whose mobbing process had been completed, stated that they had experienced the fourth escalation phase" (ibid., p. 54). In this phase, the consequences of mobbing for the victims are so massive that the occurrence of psychological problems and symptoms of illness is the norm.

I will review this process model in more detail later. It should be noted that psychosomatic illnesses, long-term sick leave, and sometimes a permanent incapacity to work are clearly the result of mobbing. Many cases end with the loss of the job, whether through the affected person's own resignation, through their dismissal, or through their consent to termination of their employment contract (ibid., p. 54).

Who starts the mobbing

- In slightly more than half of the cases, mobbing is carried out either exclusively by superiors or with their participation. Their attacks mostly take place at the working level. Colleagues can also disrupt the work of the person concerned through targeted sabotage.

> Suddenly documents needed for work disappear; letters and telephone calls that the person concerned was urgently waiting for are withheld, and important meetings are wrongly scheduled. (Sohm, 1995, p. 30)

- The *Mobbing Report* emphasises that when mobbing originates with a person's colleagues, with either a single individual or a group (this takes place in less than half of the cases), the attacks mostly take place at the social level. Mobbing "from the bottom up" (Bossing) is very rarely mentioned.

The authors explain why the relatively high number of superiors involved in mobbing is so explosive:

> It can be assumed that attacks which originate with superiors have a particularly terrible effect on the person who is being mobbed. First, a person experiences a far higher degree of helplessness and powerlessness towards a person who is in a hierarchically higher position in the company structure and who represents authority than when mobbing starts at the same hierarchical level. Second, the chances of successfully resisting this form of bullying are considerably lower due to the imbalance of power and to professional dependence. The same is true for victims who are being harassed by several colleagues at the same time. Here too, systematic hostilities tend to be experienced as more serious than in the case of attacks by individuals. (*Mobbing Report*, 2002, p. 66)

The authors correctly point out that when a case of mobbing is considered, cause and effect are often confused – a confusion that is characteristic of the so-called myths that bullies circulate about their victim. Personal peculiarities of the person affected are redefined as the cause of the mobbing, though in fact they appear as a consequence of being mobbed. The authors of the *Mobbing Report* make the following comments:

> It is often claimed that people are bullied because they show behavioural problems or are 'peculiar' types or lack professional or social skills. (ibid., p. 89)

In the case of Gertrud, the former model also gets counted among these peculiar types. After all, she is described as a "snotty little doll". As such, she deviates from the group norms, which means that a justification for the mobbing has been found. In fact, the colleague with whom the bullying originated probably invented this myth to distract from the fact that she personally felt mortified by Gertrud. The reason was that Gertrud's presence reminded her again and again that she herself did not conform to her own female ideal of beauty (cf. Section 1.1).

Christa Kolodej (2005) also points out that superiors have a very large scope of action when mobbing occurs. They can intervene in the organisation of work processes; they can make work more difficult or even take it away; they can transfer the person affected or move him or her to a worse job. There are also many examples of a superior threatening to dismiss the person concerned. If for legal reason, he or she cannot be dismissed, the strategy may be to harass the victim in such a way that he or she resigns of his or her own accord. It is also possible that the victim is deprived of important parts of his or her work so that in the end, the continuation of employment is called into question.

Motives for mobbing

In the survey, the persons affected by mobbing were asked for their assessment of what had led to the mobbing. Those who expressed an opinion cited an average of four motives (cf. *Mobbing Report*, 2002, pp. 110–126), when presented with a list of possible reasons. Multiple mentions were possible.

- Six out of ten respondents said they became the target of attacks because they expressed unwanted criticism
- More than half of them cited competition as the motive
- Envy was also mentioned as a motive (by more than a third)
- And finally, just under four out of ten of those affected named "tension between superiors and those affected" as a motive
- A deviation from the expected performance or an individual work style can also be a motive. This is true both for the supposedly strong (more than a third) and for the supposedly weak performance of those affected (almost a quarter)

In their written responses, the people affected named an array of different reasons as the "main reason for mobbing from the point of view of those affected":

- Some respondents (almost two out of ten) stated that they represented competition for the bullies
- In more than ten per cent of the cases, envy of the qualifications and performance of the person being mobbed was given as the main reason
- Also, some of the interviewees explained the mobbing by the fact that they had put up unwanted objections at work
- In some cases, giving "unwanted criticism" was mentioned as a central reason for the mobbing

All in all, respondents gave 33 different reasons which from their point of view could have led to the mobbing.

In my opinion, this large number of reasons suggests that from the point of view of the persons affected, just about anything imaginable can be seen to cause mobbing. Some are certainly sham reasons (rationalisations) which the victims heard from the bullies and which are part of the myths that the mobbing perpetrators spread about their victim.

It is interesting, however, that what I believe to be the central aim of the mobbing actions – to devalue the victim personally – does not appear even once in this list of reasons. Then again, the authors of the report explicitly say that as a characteristic of phase II, the victims note a decrease in self-esteem. In phase III, they mention that they must endure constant humiliations. This is consistent with the consequences of mobbing (see following discussion): More than half of the respondents cite self-doubt as one of the results of having been mobbed. Therefore, the question arises: How can these effects actually be achieved by mobbing?

The *Mobbing Report* emphasises that there are no typical victims of mobbing and that no general pattern of behaviour is known to protect against being affected by mobbing. Mobbing can therefore affect anyone. Yet the question arises as to why that should be so.

Conditions at work that are conducive to mobbing

There are three factors that shape the organisational culture of a company, and their interaction is key to creating an environment that is conducive to mobbing: Work organisation, design of work content and workflows, and leadership behaviour. Deficits and errors in this area have a considerable share in the development of mobbing (ibid., p. 123).

When considering which conditions in a company are conducive to mobbing, it becomes clear that the analysis of the *Mobbing Report* – as well as the usual attempts at explanation produced by mobbing research – is based on a different research paradigm than the one I base my work on. They aim at a causal explanation that covers as many individual cases as possible, whereas I am oriented towards a structural analysis. My goal is to identify a basic pattern that becomes visible in individual cases.

But let us first continue to follow the *Mobbing Report*'s research approach. In the survey, almost two-thirds of respondents confirmed that the atmosphere at work was bad at the time of the mobbing. Superiors, as mentioned earlier, were not willing to engage in a discussion (more than eight out of ten respondents agreed to this, which makes it the second highest score). Also, respondents described their superiors as conflict-averse (almost half of the respondents) which makes for a further deficit in leadership behaviour.

The authors of the *Mobbing Report* summarise these surveys as follows:

> The general conditions at work that are favourable to mobbing include a poor working atmosphere, deficits in management behaviour, stress and

work pressure, lack of clarity in the organisation of work, lack of transparency in decision-making, and fear of losing one's job. An increased risk of mobbing can also be identified in companies where reorganisation measures are carried out. (ibid., p. 126)

Similarly, Kolodej (2005, pp. 54f-55) cites professional performance requirements, competition in the workplace, and existential fears as factors conducive to mobbing. Yet we should note that these references to (assumed) motives and reasons still give no satisfactory answer to the key question: How can the initial conflict at the workplace, which occurs in the first phase of the process, set in motion a process which turns the person affected into a victim of mobbing and during which mobbing gains a dynamic of its own?

Consequences of mobbing for those affected

The survey of the consequences of mobbing – differentiated according to the hierarchical position of the bullies – confirms the hypothesis of particularly massive effects. Just over half of the interviewees said that they became ill after having been mobbed by their superiors. Mobbing with the participation of superiors resulted in illness for six out of ten respondents (ibid., p. 86).

Not a single person among those affected by mobbing was spared the consequences listed in the survey. This even applies to cases where hostile acts occurred less frequently than several times a month. Clearly, mobbing has a very serious impact on work and performance behaviour.

In the written answers, the respondents agreed to an average eight of the following 16 points:

- More than two-thirds of respondents were "demotivated" by mobbing and reacted to it with "strong mistrust"
- "Nervousness" and an "increasing feeling of insecurity" were cited by about six out of ten
- For more than half, mobbing led to "lack of concentration" and "performance and thinking blockades" (at the working level)
- More than half also stated that they suffered from a "state of anxiety", "doubting their own abilities", "withdrawing", "developing feelings of powerlessness" and "quitting internally"
- More than four out of ten felt "irritated/aggressive" as a result of the mobbing, and in a quarter of the cases those affected had "diffuse feelings of guilt" (e.g. because their ability to perform at work was deteriorating)
- With regard to the state of health, the written survey shows that mobbing had an effect on the physical and psychological well-being of almost all of those affected; slightly more than a third suffered from short-term illness, while about one in three fell ill for a longer period of time. The authors explain that point in detail:

The persons affected cite a broad spectrum of medical conditions, which they attribute to mobbing, from typical stress symptoms such as sleep disorders, headaches, and migraine attacks to shortness of breath, paralysis, and neurodermatitis, to serious chronic illnesses such as depression, diseases of the stomach and intestinal tract as well as cardiovascular diseases and cancer. (*Mobbing Report*, 2002, p. 79)

Women as well as men become ill, but the proportion of women is higher. While every second woman affected falls ill, slightly more than one in three men are affected.

In severe cases, the mental and physical suffering caused by mobbing resembles the post-traumatic stress symptoms of torture victims (see Maercker & Rosner, 2006).

Lawyer Ralf Müller-Amenitsch, who has been providing legal assistance to victims of mobbing for years, gives a very vivid description of his experiences with clients who often suffer from post-traumatic stress syndrome:

This leads to flashback-like memories of the situations in which they were shouted at and humiliated. They then experience the same devastating emotions as in the humiliating situation. This happens without any external cause, triggered only by thinking about the workplace. I have observed this on several occasions with clients who did not even dare to open mail from their employer. They were trembling and staring anxiously as they handed me a letter from their employer to have me open it. These are very memorable experiences that show that those affected need urgent, empathetic, and humane support. Without knowledge of the circumstances of the illness, a dangerously trivialised impression of the harmfulness of mobbing to health often arises. (Müller-Amenitsch, 2009, pp. 3–4)

According to the *Mobbing Report*, about three out of ten respondents stated that they had voluntarily changed jobs within the company. Women (with a share of four out of ten) changed jobs about twice as often as men.

- Almost a quarter of those surveyed ended their employment relationship by giving notice; the proportion of women here is almost twice as high as that of men. The authors suspect that the willingness of men to endure mobbing situations for a longer stretch of time than women is responsible for these differences – on the one hand, because many of them (even today) need to be their family's breadwinner, so that leaving the job voluntarily is out of the question; on the other hand, because they try to live up to their ideal of a man who should be able to cope with pressure.
- Following the mobbing, more than one in ten of the respondents was unemployed, which is a serious professional and personal setback.

- The consequences on the person's private life and on his or her family were also very varied. Respondents mentioned "imbalance", "social isolation", "quarrelling in the family or partnership", "a general strain", "financial problems", "weakness and listlessness", and other consequences.
- It is noteworthy that six out of ten respondents stated that the mobbing did not have any consequences for the people doing it. Especially for superiors, there appeared to be no consequences: Superiors had by far the highest rate for "no consequences for the bullies". However, they often benefited less from the mobbing than other persons (colleagues) who used bullying as an unfair competitive strategy (*Mobbing Report*, 2002, p. 92).

Ways and strategies to cope with being bullied: Resistance

People affected by mobbing rarely behave passively. Some try to talk to the bully; others seek support from third parties. If countermeasures, offers of reconciliation, and so forth are not useful, the mobbing continues and the affected person is increasingly forced to develop strategies that enable him or her to somehow endure the situation (ibid., p. 93).

> It is an essential part of a mobbing process that it is made difficult for the persons affected to defend themselves against the hostilities. The harassment is often trivialised by the bullies, relegated to the fantasy realm of those affected, or denied. (ibid.)

Brigitte Huber (1993) has pointed out that superiors who harass their subordinates in various forms tend to put forward understandable reasons, that is to present these harassments as logically comprehensible measures.

The written survey, which asked the persons affected about their ways and strategies of coping with the mobbing, produced the following results, among others:

- In "direct resistance", the most frequent attempt (nearly three out of four) was to "ask to discuss the situation". This is what Gertrud in our example tried to do (see previous discussion). More than half of the persons affected "massively talked back"; almost one in two "asked the bully for the reasons for his or her behaviour" or "asked him or her to refrain from the behaviour", which is what Lena did in the previous example. About every third person "offered suggestions to the bully for a solution". Only rarely did the affected persons try to "turn the tables" and do the mobbing themselves.
- In the vast majority of cases, the resistance strategies did not meet with success. Only a few respondents said that they had been successful. Just over a tenth of those questioned reported that they had not even tried to resist because they felt it was hopeless or they were afraid of losing their jobs.

- Because the persons concerned did not believe that they could get help internally, and because in many cases internal support really was insufficient to solve the mobbing problem, almost all of the respondents turned to contact persons outside the company. The majority spoke to their partner or family, to friends/acquaintances, or to the family doctor. Many also sought help from psychologists/therapists, trade unions, or lawyers (respondents could give multiple answers). When asked about who "could help me", the psychologist/therapist received a particularly high approval rate (more than half), almost on a par with the partner or family.

- According to the authors, the internal coping strategies described by the affected persons show a broad spectrum of helplessness: "Ignoring the situation", "concentrating on work", "avoiding the bully", "building up inner strength", "trying to hold out somehow", and others (ibid., p. 102).

- In retrospect, more than seven out of ten respondents – regardless of whether they fought back or not – believe that they had no possibility of preventing the mobbing. In terms of individual reactions, just under half stated that they would react differently today. In retrospect, the majority of respondents would fight back earlier and more massively. About a quarter would give up their jobs more quickly to escape the mobbing. Another quarter would call in a lawyer and take legal action under labour law. Only one in 13 of those surveyed thought that involving a superior and/or making the case public would be a sensible strategy. What a slap in the face for superiors!

- The main reason for the end of the mobbing was given by more than half of the respondents (whose case had already been closed) as "termination" or "dissolution of the employment contract". A more detailed look shows that in almost a fifth of the cases, the mobbing ended because the persons affected resigned by their own initiative. More than a tenth were dismissed by their employer, and slightly more than a tenth signed contracts to end their employment.

- The survey shows clearly that most mobbing processes only end in phase IV, usually because the persons affected give up their jobs (voluntarily or because they get fired), get transferred, or leave the labour force. But there is also a significant number of terminations and transfers that already take place in phase II.

- Almost all of those affected took the view that one countermeasure should be for companies to take mobbing more seriously. Among other observations, they said that improving internal communication within the company was a key means of combating mobbing (ibid., p. 106). The most frequently mentioned concrete measure at the workplace was to hold training courses on the subject of mobbing. Outside the company, a good three-quarters of those surveyed called for mobbing advice centres to be set up.

1.3 Common explanatory models in mobbing research

Mobbing research has come up with different answers to the question why mobbing can have such disastrous consequences. For any explanation, the typical sequence of events in the process of mobbing offers an important orientation. There is broad consensus in research on what constitutes a typical sequence, and the *Mobbing Report* takes the current results into account. In the written survey, the interviewees were first given an explanation of this typical sequence of phases. They were then asked to state which of the phases they personally experienced and how long each of these phases lasted.

At this stage, the impression may have arisen that the results of the *Mobbing Report* largely exclude the subjective dimension of the offence only because the data cannot be reliably collected using the techniques employed here (telephone interviews and questionnaires). In fact, this subjective dimension of humiliation, which I consider to be the central characteristic of mobbing actions, is also excluded from the various explanatory models. I will now go into these in more detail.

> The stress-medical definition says that mobbing is a social process that acts as a so-called stressor and leads to biological stress reactions in the body. The experience of being mobbed puts the person concerned in a constant state of tension between defence and retreat. This upsets the hormonal balance of the body: Stress hormones "flood" the brain, impairing its function, and the body develops psychosomatic signs of illness. (Arentewicz et al., 2009, p. 13ff.)

1   The stress-medical explanatory approach that Leymann applied to his interview data in Sweden can be characterised as follows:

From this point of view, an individual who has certain performance capabilities is faced with an environment that makes demands that he or she wants to meet. Should the individual's potential no longer be sufficient, an imbalance arises. Then stress is experienced that can be transferred to other employees, that is by taking it out on them. The result is psychological violence in the form of mobbing (cf. Leymann, 1993).

> With people whom one does not know well (such as new colleagues), one ordinarily assumes that their behaviour is rooted in their personality, in their character. One pays hardly any attention to the social situation of the other person. The same applies to people to whom one is hostile. (ibid., p. 78)

2   According to the frustration-aggression concept (cf. Scherer, 1979), individual aggressions arise from frustration. Such frustration is understood as a disturbance in the satisfaction of individual needs. The strength of an

aggression becomes a function of the extent of the disturbance of satisfaction. A bully may be frustrated, for example, because he or she cannot meet the relevant professional performance requirements according to the person's own or someone else's judgement; or he or she is frustrated because of a need for social recognition which has not been sufficiently satisfied.

3   Attribution psychology is used by Leymann (1993) to explain the formation of myths (on the part of the bullies) about the mobbing victim. Leymann uses an example to explain his concept:

In the process of the creation of myths about the victim, Leymann considers the myth of self-infliction to be central. Using the example of the welder Lena, to which I referred earlier, Leymann explains this process: Lena's colleagues did not pay attention to her reasons for doing something; they based their judgement solely on what they observed in her behaviour:

> The colleagues and superiors ... of Lena, the welder, judge only the visible behaviour. But they do not relate this behaviour to the provocations that Lena has to endure. At the most they say: "Well, she's playing hard to get. Like the princess on the pea. It's silly." (ibid., p. 77)

I do not consider this explanation to be very convincing. In my view, it is more plausible to analyse the myths in the context of the bully's mental conflict situation – that this is how he or she tries to distract from their inner conflict. For example, in the case of Gertrud, the former model (Section 1.1), the myth formed about her was the result of a shift intended as a diversion: By assigning Gertrud the title of "snotty little doll", the woman behind the mobbing created a criterion that made her victim differ from the group norm. She did this to distract attention from herself. This was the only way she could get her male colleagues to join her in the mobbing acts. In fact, according to my interpretation, she was jealous of Gertrud who embodied an ideal of female beauty to which she subscribed but could not herself attain. Unintentionally, Gertrud repeatedly reminded her of her own perceived inadequacy.

4   Hardly anybody who is interested in the process dynamic of actions, social groups, institutions, and so on will disagree with the basic idea of the systemic approach, that the whole is more than the sum of its parts. Can a group-dynamic approach to mobbing provide better understanding?

From a group-dynamic perspective, one would assume that the exclusion of a colleague from the working group fulfils a function that is important for the cohesion and identity of this group. The group can turn the excluded colleague into a scapegoat by projecting subliminal feelings of fear and insecurity onto this person (see Kolodej, 2005, p. 76).

Kolodej associates the systemic approach with the view that the assignment of social roles – such as that of perpetrators and victims – only becomes apparent as the mobbing process progresses. She also suggests replacing the term "victim" with the term "affected person". This proposal is justified as follows:

> Victims are usually associated with an inability to act. In the course of the dynamic mobbing process, a person who is affected by mobbing will also experience an increasing incapacity to act. Ultimately, he or she even will even doubt their professional qualifications and social skills. The person's self-confidence dwindles as the process progresses. This is precisely why a mobbing intervention must support and strengthen self-confidence, action, and content competences. (ibid., p. 71)

I consider both this proposal and its justification to be problematic. Why should we blur the distinction between the language used for investigation and the language used for intervention when only a closer examination can shed light on the complex interrelationships of mobbing? Without such insight, will the results of the planned support and strengthening of the victims' self-confidence not remain dubious?

Why should we, as Kolodej suggests, speak of victims of mobbing only when physical and sexual violence (ibid., p. 72) are involved? After all, she herself provides a description of the psychological injuries suffered by the victims. In my opinion, this blurring of conceptual differences and ambiguity means that the factual asymmetry (in the possibilities for action of perpetrators and victims) is simply ignored. In fact, I do not know of a single case in which a victimised person has used the same destructive actions that were employed by the perpetrator.

It is true that the interpersonal dynamics of mobbing cannot be explained as a one-sided causal effect. Instead, perpetrators and victims react to each other through interaction. However, this is nothing unusual and cannot justify why the power gap that exists in mobbing should not play a role.

Kolodej (2005) uses the escalation model developed by Friedrich Glasl (1992) to point out that mobbing should be understood not as an existing conflict but as its escalation. "The crucial leap from conflict to mobbing takes place with the personification of the conflict. The conflict is no longer based on factual differences alone, but on attacks on the personal integrity" (Kolodej, 2005, p. 89).

Glasl's model presupposes equally strong opponents – a condition that is noticeably absent in the case of mobbing. In none of the available case studies about mobbing has there ever been an "exchange of blows" between the persons doing the mobbing and the persons who were mobbed.

In the systemic view, psychotherapists emphasise that one should not concentrate on one individual as the key to any problem; rather, the aim is to focus on the whole system (e.g. in the case of a child with behavioural problems, this would be the system of the family). But what is meant by "system" in the case of mobbing: The respective corporate culture of a company, the economic system of our society, or even society as a whole? The respective corporate culture may indeed be relevant here. But we would not be able to give a satisfactory explanation of the inherent dynamics of this phenomenon if we were to shift the problem structure of this interaction process away from the people involved and onto the respective corporate culture.

And what insights do we gain into the conditions under which mobbing occurs if, for example, we declare it to be a "symptom of our economic system" – insights that go beyond the circumstances that promote mobbing?

For the group of work colleagues that join in the attack, mobbing can fulfil the function of relieving internal strain. But from my perspective, something more than an internal relief function for the group is necessary to explain the special kind of destructiveness that these attacks have.

> Bullying is an often subtle form of violent behaviour in which damaging action patterns are repeated and carried out over a long period of time by one or more pupils, with an imbalance in strength between the perpetrator (bully) or group of perpetrators (bullies) and a defenceless victim. (ibid., p. 267)

5   An approach based on behavioural psychologicy: Herbert Scheithauer and Heike Dele Bull (2010) start from a definition of "bullying" (the authors always use this English term) which is very revealing:

This definition implicitly contains an important distinction: In cases of mobbing at the workplace, this form of harassment always remains below the threshold of what is punishable by law. But we must expect that bullying at school can also take forms of physical violence (e.g. beating, shoving). In this respect, the definition makes a valid point.

At the same time, this explanatory approach does not consider the attack on self-esteem to be the central feature of bullying – in school as well – as I suggest. Instead, the authors are guided by an image of man, which they call constructivist: "Constructivism emphasises the active interpretations of the discerning subject, the process of the current construction of meaning and significance" (ibid., p. 270).

This view excludes any subjectivity from the very beginning of the in-vestigation. We can also say that such constructivism has a destructive effect on the subject, insofar as it excludes from the scientific investigation any element of the past, any biographical development, and any form of re-actualisation of unresolved psychological problems of childhood. This approach focuses only on the here and now of a behaviour that can be presented as observable. Such behaviour then can be reduced to the realisation of certain competences – which makes them measurable.[3]

Since, according to the authors, previous prevention programmes have proved to be mostly ineffective, they developed the so-called fairplayer.manual, which recorded the competencies of 138 pupils of different school types aged between 13 and 21 in a pilot study. The goal of this "fairplayer.manual" is to encourage pupils to take action against mobbing, to improve their social skills, and to prevent mobbing and other school violence.

For the study, the implementation of the "fairplayer" measures was integrated into the school lessons and supported by the teachers or the members of the research team. Crucially, however, it was the pupils who were the target group of this programme. The teachers merely accompanied the implementation in class. As a result of this programme, the number of mobbing victims decreased. The pupils also scored significantly higher on the scale of "prosociality".

One might dismiss this kind of scientific research as an expression of a longing for objectivity to be fulfilled through methods of measuring. However, one must be aware that such an approach is the complete opposite of the prevention measures proposed and encouraged by experts on school bullying.

Just as the superior in the company is directly responsible for intervening right at the beginning of any mobbing, so the teacher in the school has a special responsibility: "The first preference is for the teachers to take action against bullying. This is why peer mediation, i.e. conflict resolution among peers, is not considered by experts to be an adequate measure against mobbing" (Schäfer & Herpell, 2010, p. 154f.).

However, the "fairplayer.manual" presents itself as a modern version of peer mediation based on behavioural psychology. In fact, it is the complete absence of fatherly authority on the part of the teachers who make this prevention and support programme so suitable to the present day – and at the same time so unpromising. Instead of investigating why there are so many teachers who do not live up to their responsibility of intervening in mobbing at school, this behavioural psychological approach relies from the outset on the pupils and their willingness to cooperate as well as on their empathy and moral awareness.

The fairplayer programme aims to turn children into subjects who only seek harmony, but this is a goal that cannot be achieved against the psychological background of bullying. The reason is that the approach fails to recognise the actual psychological conditions under which bullying occurs, and teachers have the duty to intervene in the early stages of bullying and to act as a model for the pupils for dealing with conflicts arising at school. Emotionally, the support and prevention programme of the "fairplayer.manual" abandons the pupils to themselves and the abilities they already have – the same macabre situation that many families in our society find themselves in and which is now simply repeated in school. The role of the teacher as a third party, who with the help of such a programme should learn how to intervene, is simply removed.

In summary, the aforementioned explanations leave us somewhat perplexed. They cannot answer important questions that arise in the context of mobbing.

- Why is it that the person getting mobbed – especially in phase I of the process – often fails in his or her attempts to get the bully to talk to him?
- Where does the enormous aggression, even anger, of those who are called "mobbing perpetrators" in the *Mobbing Report*, in phases II, III, and IV of the process actually come from?
- Why is there no empathy with the victim on the part of the bullies?
- Why do many of these actions take place in a covert manner?
- Why is the action of the bullies often characterised by a creeping destruction of the living and working conditions of the person concerned?
- How is it possible that the bullies do not even shy away from breaking the law?
- How can the arrogance and self-assurance of the bullies be explained?
- Why do the superiors in charge intervene so rarely in these events?
- What kind of power is exercised here? And why is this position of power accepted by the person who is being bullied?
- The various attacks must have an underlying psychological conflict that ties them together. How can these conflicts and the corresponding contextual characteristics of mobbing be understood in terms of a structural context?
- Why do victims of mobbing need such a long time to believe that they are the target of attacks?
- Why do mobbing victims often remain passive, even once they have realised that they have become targets of attack?
- Why does bullying not end on its own? Why does it usually only end when the victim gives up and leaves the scene?
- If – in a later phase of the process – bullying often amounts to the destruction of the victim's social identity, then the question arises: How can this last consequence of bullying be explained?
- How can we explain the broad spectrum of clinical pictures – ranging from typical stress symptoms, respiratory distress, paralysis, and neurodermatitis to chronic diseases – which were attributed to mobbing by the interviewees in the *Mobbing Report*?

1.4 Mobbing from a psychoanalytical perspective

In my approach, I agree with the statement of Leymann (this includes Arentewicz et al., 2009) that mobbing initially has nothing to do with the character or personality traits of the participants – even if in one of the later phases of mobbing there may be a negative change in the personality of the mobbing victim.

I do, however, emphasise a feature of the mobbing actions that so far has not been considered at all or only marginally by mobbing research: Whether the perpetrator is aware of it or not, his attacks are directed against the self-esteem of the victim. My research therefore assumes that we will only grasp the full drama of mobbing if we systematically include this subjective dimension in the investigation.

The following short case report given by lawyer Ralf Müller-Amenitsch emphasises the connection between the damage to the self-esteem of the person affected and the resulting psychological damage:

> A social education worker was damaged in her self-esteem by her direct superior through unobjective criticism (loud shouting, public dismissal of her alleged lack of professional performance in front of a team of colleagues) to such an extent that she developed a severe trauma and could no longer imagine working under this superior without suffering insomnia and panic attacks. (Müller-Amenitsch, 2009, p. 12)

With the approach I have developed here, I will try to provide answers to some of the questions listed earlier. In doing so, I will follow the process model on which the *Mobbing Report* is based. According to this, at the beginning of a mobbing process, there is usually an unresolved or badly handled conflict. In contrast to the *Mobbing Report*, however, I assume that this is usually an un-resolved psychological conflict of the attacker and that the attempt to solve this conflict is the motive of the attacker. For this first phase of the process, I will distinguish between different types of psychological conflicts.

I will then examine in more detail the question of how it is possible to go from the first to the second phase of the process, in which psychological terror sets in and the person concerned becomes the target of systematic harassment.

Both Leymann and the authors of the *Mobbing Report* emphasise that one can only speak of mobbing when certain destructive actions of various kinds are directed against the person concerned repeatedly and over a longer period of time. However, we can only find a plausible justification for this statement if we look at the subjective dimension of the mobbing actions mentioned earlier.

This also applies to the third phase, in which the person being bullied becomes so unsettled by the constant humiliation that his or her work suffers. The mobbing victim is finally considered so "problematic" that he or she is threatened with disciplinary actions. This escalation of the initial conflict in the second and third phases of the process can, in my opinion, only be adequately understood if we take both into account: An unresolved psychological conflict constellation of early childhood, which is widespread and still effective today, and basic narcissistic needs, which cannot be satisfied because of the mobbing.

1.4.1 The first level of meaning: The current psychological conflict of the perpetrator in phase I

I assume that at the beginning of the mobbing process, there typically is a conflict: An unresolved current emotional conflict of the person doing the mobbing. By means of the mobbing actions, he or she tries to cope with this in vain and without being aware of it.

I distinguish the following types of psychological conflict, by no means exhaustive:

CONFLICT TYPE I: DUE TO AN EXAGGERATED EGO-IDEAL, A PART OF THE
SELF-IMAGE ARISES WHICH DOES NOT CORRESPOND TO THE IDEAL AND
IS THEREFORE EXPERIENCED AS NEGATIVE AND PROJECTED ONTO A
CO-WORKER

The following case from the professional world will serve as an example:

> A client of African origins, who worked for a large German automotive group, had the following problem: Although he held a PhD, he was repeatedly reprimanded by his superior for his German, which was not accent-free. He was also transferred to an office in which the desk chair was positioned in the middle of the walk-through area of two passage doors. The result was that the person concerned had to interrupt his work every few minutes, get up, and move his chair to the side to allow other employees to get through. (Müller-Amenitsch, 2009, p. 8)[4]

First of all, in accordance with my analysis of the first level of meaning, I want to find out to what extent the mobbing actions during the first phase of the process are based on a current psychological conflict. We can then interpret the characteristics of the actions – especially the bully's – as attempts to cope with this conflict.

One can clarify the central aim of these attacks by the superior – the intended mortification of the self-esteem of the person concerned – with the psychoanalytical concept of the ego-ideal (see Lampl-de-Groot, 1962). How this ego-ideal is re-presented in the self-esteem of the adult can be summed up by the phrase: "The way I am is just right." The yardstick of evaluation is the person's own ego-ideal, which represents how the person concerned would like to be. If his actions, his way of life, his social relationships deviate strongly from this ideal, he feels "wrong".

If this type of conflict is present, the message of the attacker for the person concerned in a verbalised form would be: "It is not I who should feel wrong. It is you!" That is what I assumed in my interpretation of Gertrud's case study (see Section 1.1).

So here we have a projection: It is a psychic form of defence in which a part of one's own self-image that is rejected as conflictual gets attributed to another person as his or her "flaw". It is shifted onto the image of this person and thus removed from the self-image.

Due to the performance pressure at the workplace and the demands of the social group of work colleagues, an internal contradiction of this kind can easily arise in the superior who in the previous example was doing the mobbing. Even criticism voiced by employees can be irritating for superiors who are under particular stress. They can then become unsure whether they can meet the performance requirements. After all, six out of ten respondents cited in the *Mobbing Report* point to undesired criticism as a motive for being bullied.

If such high work demands are made that the person concerned is afraid of not being able to meet them, he or she should reject them. If the person fails to do so, he or she may develop a distressing feeling of insecurity and wrongness in his or her contacts with the employee. This can happen especially when the employee "somehow" deviates from the group norms and values. In the case study mentioned earlier, this is the case for the manager with African roots.

The attacker can try to cope with this unpleasant feeling by turning the negative part of him- or herself outwards and attaching it to another person. The attacked person will then, I suspect, be somewhat perplexed by the de-valuing attacks.

It will probably not occur to him or her that the motive of the attacks could lie in an (unconscious) attempt of the attacker to cope with his or her own insecurity, which the attacked person causes.

The otherness of the person being bullied – in this example the skin colour and the accented German – is often mentioned in research as a reason for bullying. Before I explain the other types of conflict, I would like to briefly comment on this discussion.

THE OTHERNESS OF THE VICTIM

We can see from the *Mobbing Report* that especially attacks on young employees who are still in training happen in a form that is related to this conflict type (on the part of the bully). If employees or colleagues do not comply with widespread social norms and values, they are particularly at risk of becoming victims of mobbing, for example immigrants, asylum seekers, homosexuals, and people with disabilities or with infectious diseases. In many cases, these same groups of people are still discriminated and disadvantaged in the workplace. Strengthening their rights is the aim of the Allgemeine Gleichbehandlungsgesetz (AGG), the German anti-discrimination law, which I will explain later.

Kolodej (2005), who explains group-dynamic aspects of mobbing in more detail, also points to this origin:

> Especially persons who question the existing system of group norms run the risk of becoming victims of mobbing. Such group norms can manifest

in various ways. They can mean that all social activities must be taken part in, that a certain level of performance must not be exceeded or undercut, that innovations must not be introduced too quickly, or that the person generally does not conform to the social norm codex. (ibid., p. 76)

Fortunately, according to Kolodej, physical threats occur relatively rarely. However, the author (ibid., p. 32) rightly points out that sexual harassment of women in the workplace occurs much more frequently than is publicly known. According to a survey conducted in Austria (cf. Meschkutat et al., 1993), 36.6 per cent of the 1,411 women surveyed stated that they were "exposed to sexual assault every few days".

Even if this is an important pointer, further analysis of mobbing actions will show that sexual assaults, which do not only occur in everyday working life, but also in family life or during leisure activities, do not match important other characteristics of mobbing actions.

Arentewicz very generally ascribes the psychological dimension that should be part of any investigation of mobbing to "human weaknesses":

> The envy of those who have (always) felt less-favoured; rivalry with colleagues over the favour of the boss; securing one's own position at the expense of others, being offended when a younger colleague, whom one has perhaps even trained, is promoted; the fear of not being able (anymore) to cope with the demands – especially when the company is restructuring and new tasks are pending. (Arentewicz, 2009, p. 21)

For my approach, the "human weaknesses" described here need to be identified more precisely. We must understand that the objective otherness of a colleague is not sufficient in itself to lead to mobbing. It is only because of the bully's psychological problem situation that the victim's otherness turns into a flaw.

CONFLICT TYPE II: IMPULSES TO FIGHT BACK AGAINST EXCESSIVE WORK DEMANDS ARE PROJECTED ONTO THE VICTIM

Here, too, a negative part of oneself is projected onto the victim. And here, too, the person doing the mobbing has an exaggerated ego-ideal. But in contrast to conflict type I, the bully here feels an impulse to fight back against the excessive performance requirements. But he or she "must" not give in to this impulse. He or she must fend it off psychologically – by projection onto the mobbing victim.

Quite possibly, this may be made easier for him by the fact that the victim does not correspond to the group norms and values in terms of clothing, way of speaking, or haircut. Yet he or she does not belong to the aforementioned group of typical victims of mobbing.

CONFLICT TYPE III: ATTACKS AS REVENGE FOR A NARCISSISTIC MORTIFICATION SUFFERED BY THE ATTACKER

The attacker has been (unintentionally) narcissistically mortified by the victim and now pays back in kind (as in the case of Gertrud, for example).

I assume that for her colleague, Gertrud embodied an ideal against which she also measured herself. From that comparison, a painful feeling of personal inadequacy arose. Since this had to be fended off psychologically, the colleague attacked Gertrud. As if it had been Gertrud who was responsible for the feeling of inadequacy, the colleague now tried to mortify her again and again.

Gertrud tried in vain to discuss the situation with her colleague. Instead, the conflict escalated, and Gertrud drew the inevitable conclusion and resigned. I suspect that she had less difficulty than others in taking this step because she was not so badly hurt by her colleague's attempts to mortify her. In this respect, she did not accept that the bullies should hold a position of power over her. Perhaps her professional background as a model played a role here, as well as extra-professional, private experiences: Gertrud's femininity had been confirmed so often in other places that the intended insult, "In reality she is a man and not a woman", could not shake her self-image.

Table 2.1 aims to summarise (without claiming to be complete) the similarities and differences between the three conflict types:

CONFLICT TYPE IV: ATTACKS ON A COLLEAGUE CHOSEN AS SCAPEGOAT

European history has always known disasters – such as the plague, climate change, or lost wars – for which no objective explanation could or would be found; instead, a scapegoat was sought to blame.

When a team (in a company) is confronted with the fact that its own work performance falls short of expectations and that the failure of a project may be imminent, one possible psychological defence against the fear of punishment is to look for (and find) someone to blame – a scapegoat. The concept of a scapegoat entails that an open and direct assignment of blame be made to the person concerned. This is presumably done primarily by those individuals who will later join in the mobbing, but also, and more importantly, shared with the superior.

However, the attempt to exonerate one's own responsibility is a separate issue from the choice of scapegoat. A negative image of the scapegoat will usually have pre-existed, and the scapegoat strategy thus becomes linked to interpersonal defence of type I. Here, too, the motive of the attacks is an attempt to cope with one's own feeling of insecurity and wrongness by attaching the negative part of oneself to the attacked person.

Table 2.1 Mental conflict types

	Type I	Type II	Type III
1.	The mobbing victim bears signs of otherness: He/she has a flaw	The mobbing victim bears signs of otherness: He/she is a rebel	The mobbing victim embodies the ego-ideal of the bully: He/she is a provocation
2.	The mobbing perpetrator has for a long time fended off the mental conflict of not being able to satisfy his/her ego-ideal. He/she is afraid of being a failure	The bully has an inflated ego-ideal but wants to meet the high-performance standards he/she faces	The victim embodies the ego-ideal of the bully, from which the latter deviates
3.	The bully projects a negative part of him-/herself onto the victim, because that one's otherness is a constant reminder of his/her own negative self-image	The bully has the impulse to fight back against the excessive demands for performance, but resists this impulse	The bully has a negative view of parts of him-/herself and feelings of insufficiency
4.	Mobbing attacks are directed against that part of the victim that the bully is trying to fend off in him-/herself	The bully projects the negative part of him-/herself onto the victim and attacks, what he/she is trying to fend off in him-/herself	Mobbing attacks serve as revenge for the suffered narcissistic insult

CONFLICT TYPE V: THE ATTEMPT TO GET AN EMPLOYEE TO RESIGN TURNS INTO A CASE OF MOBBING

The aggressor, in this case a superior, sets the mobbing process in motion because he wants to get the person concerned to resign from his job, as dismissing the person would be difficult under labour law. Since this strategy is generally considered unfair and the superior's position of authority can protect him or her, an open discussion will be difficult here as well. In the event that the manager feels challenged by the mobbing victim because he or she feels that his or her own authority is being questioned, a further development may occur which corresponds to the type I mentioned earlier: The victim has inadvertently touched a pre-existing sore spot concerning the professional authority position of the bully.

1.4.2 The constant repetition of mobbing and the difficulty of discussing the situation

WHY DOES MOBBING NOT COME TO AN END; WHY MUST IT BE REPEATED SO OFTEN?

How is it possible that the mere presence of a colleague or employee who is different can be enough to unsettle the attacker? One of the psychological conditions of these attacks is that the person doing the mobbing does not just project.

Rather, he or she goes a step further, fighting what he or she fights in himself/herself (conflict types I, II, and IV), or else he or she repays the victim with equal coin for the mortification (conflict type III).

We are dealing with forms of a so-called interpersonal defence, that is a form of psychological defence for which (at least) one other person is needed. Depending on the part of the conflict (the conflict constituent) projected onto him or her, the mobbing victim (X) takes a different unconscious meaning for the attacker:

> X is "bearer of a flaw" (which X objectively does not have) (Type I)
> X is a "rebel" (in reality, X probably isn't) (Type II)
> X is a "provocation" (which X does not want to be) (Type III)
> X is a "scapegoat" (X is wrongly blamed for something that X has not done) (Type IV)

The psychological problem that the bully has with this form of defence is the insecurity of it. One can also say that it is the nature of this type of defence that employing it causes insecurity. Every time a person uses it, he or she perceives of something in the mobbing victim as "real", which otherwise is only present in himself or herself (unconsciously) as an impulse or a vague feeling. The reason is that the mobbing victim embodies the exact same issues that the attacker rejects about himself or herself. The "flaw", for example, stands for his or her own feeling of job insecurity or fear of failure; the "rebellion" for his or her existing inner impulse to fight back against the excessive performance requirements, and so forth.

To cope with this in the long run, the attacker will have to find social backing and stabilisation for the projection that he employs as a defensive measure. However, this form of institutionalisation is not possible for reasons of labour law and other (cf. Mentzos, 1988). Interpersonal defence cannot be institutionalised at the workplace or at school, in contrast to the institution of marriage, for example.

The person doing the mobbing is left with only his personal, non-institutionalised efforts to counteract the uncertainty of his interpersonal defence. This, I believe, is the deeper reason why the attacks occur again and again, that there is no end to them: The existing emotional conflict of the attacker does not only remain unresolved, but it is repeatedly refreshed.

AN ACT SIGNATURE OF THE UNCONSCIOUS IN THE MOBBING PROCESS

As explained in Chapter 1, Section 1.2, we have here the first level of unconscious meaning which concerns a current mental conflict situation. The meaning here is the double structure of a mental conflict situation and an action-oriented attempt to cope with it.

Table 2.2 Act signature of the unconscious – type I

The aim of the mobbing action	The devaluation of the victim
The inner image of the person being mobbed	He or she is being experienced as the bearer of a flaw. This is threatening, because the flaw unconsciously represents the negative part that the attacker is fending off in him-/herself.
The motive of action	The attacker fights in his victim the same aspects that he/she tries to fend off in him-/herself. But it comes back to life again and again due to the victim because the interpersonal defence of the attacker cannot be institutionalised.

Since on the part of the bully, the processing of the mental conflict takes place involving specific internal structural elements of action, which are re-presented in the action knowledge, these elements are also shaped accordingly. From a collective knowledge gained from experience, which guides social action, the bully begins to develop a psycho-pathologically composed knowledge that guides his attacks.

This act signature of the unconscious is represented in type I as follows (Table 2.2).

WHY ARE THE ATTEMPTS OF THE VICTIM TO SPEAK ABOUT THE SITUATION WITH THE ATTACKER SO OFTEN UNSUCCESSFUL?

The example of Gertrud illustrates this difficulty in communication – the difficulty the bullies have when asked to publicly verbalise their own narcissistic injuries.

According to the *Mobbing Report*, three quarters of the respondents tried in vain to engage the people responsible for the mobbing in a discussion. Gertrud, too, made such an attempt.

If the person being mobbed seeks a discussion with the attacker, then his or her own self-image must be distinct from the negative image that the bully conveys to the victim about his or her attacks. Otherwise, the person who is being bullied would find it impossible to "fight back massively by means of language", "ask for the reasons for the behaviour", and "ask the attacker to refrain from the behaviour". In other words, a person affected must be able to distinguish between the intention and the effect of the bullying actions at this point in the mobbing process.

This obviously applied to Gertrud. The interesting question in her case is: What could the work colleague, who felt mortified because of Gertrud, have said to her in such a debate that would have resolved the conflict? Could she have openly expressed her feeling of mortification, for example, by saying: "Frankly speaking, I feel mortified by your beautiful appearance?" Since, according to my interpretation, she measured herself against the ideal of beauty which she saw embodied in Gertrud, she had to fear being mortified gain. Gertrud, according to her fears, might have reacted by comparing the two women in terms of her own ideal of beauty. For example, Gertrud might give the answer: "I can understand you quite well, in comparison with me you really aren't very attractive as a woman."

If someone fears this kind of an answer, it becomes difficult, if not impossible, to verbalise the feeling of being mortified – at least to the person who caused this feeling. Such a debate would then simply reinforce the devaluation that was already felt.

Such a situation makes it all the more important for the managers of a company to intervene in time. It is their responsibility as a "third party" in a conflict that threatens to escalate into mobbing. A manager should try, for example, to create suitable communication conditions for those affected so that they can address the psychological side of their conflict.

Using Gertrud's example, we can identify two reasons why this is so difficult. The first reason is that in our society, there is no cultural code for the public communication of narcissistic mortifications. Our performance-oriented Western society does not want to know anything about such mortifications in public. On the contrary, it has produced cultural codes that determine the character and selection of which mental states can be publicly communicated. Positive conditions include, for example, one is quick-witted, self-confident, in a good mood, and celebrating for the sake of celebrating.

Our society is apparently characterised by a lack of language with regard to describing the state which we call "narcissistic mortification". Those affected feel "small", "not in a good mood", "somehow bad", "powerless", and the like. It is difficult to find the right expressions in our language for a concise description of this feeling.

The lack of a cultural code for these communication contents is probably also a reason why the *Mobbing Report* presented a choice of observable events (and not of feelings of devaluation) to the respondents in its list of ten possible mobbing actions.

The majority of those interviewed for the *Mobbing Report* assumed that the attacker has rational or strategic intentions instead of following an unconscious attempt to deal with narcissistic mortifications. This fact may be partly due to the lack of such a cultural code.

The second reason is that it is indeed not easy to communicate to another person that one's self-esteem has been hurt, especially at work. It is all too easy to fear that the other person will react as negatively to such messages as one is inclined to do concerning one's own self, because such messages are not compatible with the collective ideal of public behaviour. What is needed is a relationship of trust in which this anxiety is reduced to an extent that some of the narcissistic offenses can finally be admitted. But such a relationship of trust does not exist, especially in a competitive professional situation.

A BASIC PROBLEM OF THE SOCIOLOGICAL-STATISTICAL SURVEY: THE SUPPRESSION OF SUBJECTIVITY

Any sociological-statistical survey necessarily omits the psychological dimension of mobbing acts. The listed actions, subdivided according to the factual and relational level, are described exclusively from a perspective of observation. This means that data for a survey must be countable. Thus, the dimension of subjectivity is largely suppressed. The reason is that for a sociological investigation, the subject is always a social subject, that is a competent player. In contrast, a depth-psychological investigation will put the main focus on subjectivity.

Many researchers have excluded this psychological dimension of mobbing because it is not directly observable and therefore appears to them as subjectively random. The authors of the *Mobbing Report* also hint at this problem. They criticise Leymann's classification of mobbing actions as incomplete, logically inconsistent, and redundant of certain actions.

This criticism is plausible in so far as there can be no such thing as a complete and final list of mobbing acts. The authors of the *Mobbing Report* are right to make no claim to exhaustiveness with the ten mobbing acts they selected. There is no end to the diversity of what mobbing attacks can be based on in terms of concrete incidents, situations, or behaviour of the person affected.

Yet this does not affect the fundamental structure of the social act of devaluation. The authors give the following explanation:

> "An additional problem is that in principle, any action can be interpreted as hostile that is perceived as such by the recipient. This observation shows how difficult it is to make a selection – with the aim of ascertaining their extent – of attacks that can be described as mobbing actions. It is impossible to compile a complete list of all hostile acts occurring within the human behavioural spectrum …. (Mobbing-Report, 2002, p. 21)

I have already referred to the simple distinction between the intention and the effect of harassment during the mobbing process. If the person who is being mobbed does not make this distinction, it will be difficult for him or her to ask the attacker for a discussion. This, however, makes it clearer which elements of the mobbing actions take place only in the emotional context of the victim and which do not.

However, demonstrating an intention to mortify another person's self-esteem with suitable forms of attack is not something that is open to individual feeling or interpretation, and the same is true for the understanding that the person attacked has of such an intention. The identification of intention is part of the understanding of a social act and its focus.

Accordingly, it is not difficult for the victim to recognise an intention to devalue by means of mobbing actions – even if in the initial phase of the mobbing, victims often do not recognise the originator(s). They may even believe that they have no enemies at work. But if a victim, in the further course of the mobbing process, becomes aware of the attacker(s), and if the attacker knows of this awareness, then the selected types of mobbing actions are guided by reciprocal knowledge. The attacker recognises the personal weak points of the person being bullied, who in turn is aware of this recognition (cf. ibid., p. 44).

It is a question of practical relevance whether this intention to devalue a victim has the desired effect. In this case, the question is whether it really causes severe narcissistic mortification. This truly is a question of individual feeling. The effect of the mobbing actions only sets in when the victim accepts to carry out the devaluation on his or her own self which the attacker has performed on him or her.

THE DYNAMICS OF MOBBING: PHASES II AND III IN THE MOBBING PROCESS

As a reminder, in the second and third phases of the process (according to the model of the *Mobbing Report*) the person affected by mobbing becomes the target of systematic harassment – psychological terror sets in. While in the beginning, it was about one person committing calculated, individual actions, the attacks on the victim's self-esteem are now carried out by several colleagues. At this stage, different mobbing actions are combined and carried out both at the professional and at the personal or relationship level.

Due to the constant humiliations, the mobbing victim has become so insecure that his or her work suffers. Even during the first phase, the devaluing attacks had a destructive potential. Now this potential is massively expanded. How can this be explained?

The devaluing attacks, which are based on various psychological conflicts (see previous discussion), all have the same result: The attacker's open or hidden wish that the attacked person should "disappear" is not being fulfilled.

Therefore, the bully will intensify his mobbing actions and look for support from his colleagues. He will develop fake reasons for his actions and point out the alleged "deviance" (in behaviour or professional performance) or a "problematic" otherness of the person being mobbed. These are the myths that are propagated about the victim as in the cases of Gertrud ("snotty doll") and Lena ("women's libber"). Such myths can help a superior to win over his or her colleagues to take part in the mobbing.

The actions of these colleagues can be determined by the same defence mechanism of projection that I have analysed: They – possibly out of fear of becoming victims of this superior themselves – turn the mobbing victim into an embodiment of a negative part of their own self which has then become externalised.

However, we have not yet found a sufficient explanation for the escalation of the initial conflict, neither for its devastating effect nor for the enormous potential of released aggression.

It has been said that in the second and third phases of process, the devaluing attacks will by sheer number and intensity gradually wear down the victim of mobbing. Yet this observation does not provide answers to the many questions that have not yet been answered in mobbing research, which I listed earlier: The enormous anger of the attackers; the persistent belief of the bullied persons that the devaluing attacks may stop of their own accord; the sad role of the superior who should intervene but usually does not do so; and so forth.

What answers we can find to these questions depends on the theoretical perspective from which we investigate different phenomena. My suggestion is that we distinguish three of these perspectives here:

- A perspective of interaction sociology
- The psychology of Kohut's self-objects
- A psychoanalytical perspective, in which the re-actualisation of traumatic relationship experiences made in childhood is reconstructed

I will present the first two perspectives only in some aspects that I consider relevant to the issue here. The mobbing of phases II and III will then be examined in more detail from the third perspective.

ASPECTS OF A PERSPECTIVE BASED ON INTERACTION SOCIOLOGY

Intentional devaluation in the workplace is possible because in our culture professional performance is highly valued, in combination with belonging to a community (the company you work for), the professional colleagues you work with, and a supervisor you have to get along with. The workplace thus becomes a place of multiple high valuations for someone whose job is secure, who gets on well with his or her superiors and colleagues, and whose professional achievements are generally appreciated.

The fact that these positive valuations are so important for everyone involved is linked to a fundamental social need arising from a person's identity: The need to be confirmed in one's identity by others.

Such confirmation takes the form of attributions, such as "good mate" or "capable employee", which others decide on and which people are happy to accept (cf. Strauss, 1974). But if this kind of confirmation does not take place, or, even more dramatically, if this identity is deliberately attacked, the person concerned will be drawn into a social conflict which is difficult to solve. On the one hand, out of pure self-preservation, this person will try to adopt a more distanced attitude to his or her superior and the colleagues at work who are mobbing him or her. On the other hand, however, he or she will continue to feel a strong social need for recognition.

If this social need becomes overpowering, it can also happen that the person affected carries out the devaluation intended by the bully on his or her own self, in whole or in part. If this happens wholly, the distinction between intention and effect (see previous discussion) becomes invalid.

Here, of course, individual differences must be taken into account concerning the affected persons, because different people will deal with the bully's intention of devaluation in very different ways. But in every case, they will struggle to prevent this intention from having the effect that the attacker is aiming for.

The authors of the *Mobbing Report* rightly point out how difficult it is for those affected to defend against the mobbing. They cite quite understandable reasons for this, such as the power gap that exists between the bullying superior and the employees affected; the fear of losing one's job as breadwinner of the family; and the difficulty of those affected to identify the originator of rumours or untruths that are spread about them.

Only one thing is certain: The victim is largely helpless in the face of this hostile power.

This position of power that the bully holds is not only due to the fact that as the victim's superior, he or she can claim authority and dominance in committing the mobbing actions. As the *Mobbing Report* emphasises, a group of colleagues, who join together in the mobbing, will also occupy a position of power vis-à-vis their victim.

Carrying out the mobbing puts the attackers in a position of power and dominance because through their actions, they claim to be the authority that decides whether or not an employee complies with the group norms and ideals in his or her behaviour, professional performance, and so forth. This is true even though in most cases, such opinions about the victim are merely used to a hide a different motive of the attacker, as we have seen in the case studies of Gertrud and Lena.

If these colleagues really do believe that they are in charge of guarding these norms and values, we can understand why they do not have any sense of committing an injustice when they sanction the victim for the alleged violation, especially by imposing social isolation.

The conflict is further intensified by the fact that in the further course of the mobbing, an inherently contradictory social status is ascribed to the victim: The status of a person who no longer has any status within the company. Excluded from the community of work colleagues and unfairly judged by the superior in his or her own work performance, the person affected is often left with only the status of a person who has taken sick leave, if he or she does not resign or transfer to another department.

To put it bluntly, the victim of mobbing is threatened with social death at the workplace.

THE PSYCHOLOGY OF KOHUT'S SELF-OBJECTS

If we assume that in the present day, the desired good feeling of positive self-esteem is a problem for most people, the effectiveness of mobbing actions becomes clear: They target that very problem.

The different types of mobbing can be used to differentiate which aspect of the victim's self-esteem is under attack. The affected person experiences a devaluation of himself or herself on the following levels:

I   "You want to be particularly efficient, hard-working, and reliable in your work? You are none of that. On the contrary"

II   "You want to be a responsible breadwinner for the family or someone who earns good money? If you lose your job, you can't be that anymore"

III   "You want to be a civilised, friendly, kind colleague? You are just the opposite; we do not want you here because …"

IV   "You want to be a highly valued, appreciated employee in this great company/department? You're not at all"

From the perspective of Kohut's self-psychology (1973, 1981), the harassment endured during mobbing permanently frustrates the basic narcissistic needs that everyone has, including as an employee in a company:

a   The need for reflexion: One's own positive assessment of one's work performance may be reflected in corresponding performance appraisals by the supervisor, which is a cause of pride (I)

b   The need for equality and belonging: If it is satisfied, it engenders a sense of earning "good money", like many others do, as well as a sense of community (in the group of work colleagues) (II and III)

c   The need for idealisation: In the company or with one's direct superior or colleagues, one feels that one is being well treated (IV)

To define what Kohut understands by the term of self-object: It is, starting in childhood, the dimension of our experience of a caregiver, which is linked to the function of this caregiver to act as support for our self. According to Kohut, the need for it lasts a lifetime. It can be considered normal.

The psychological development of our self is closely linked to this: If the need for reflexion is sufficiently satisfied – the early basic pattern for this is the infant's reflexion in its mother's eyes – then this leads to a feeling of self-esteem, self-respect, and appropriate self-assertion.

If the need for idealisation is sufficiently satisfied by protective and re-assuring reactions of the self-objects, this leads to the ability of self-reassurance. The adequate satisfaction of the need for equality and belonging leads to the development of a sense of community and pride.

During mobbing, the satisfaction of all three basic needs through self-objects – with individual deviations – is withheld and denied. Since only their adequate satisfaction – even in adulthood – leads to self-esteem and self-assertion, the withdrawal of this satisfaction from the victims in phases II to IV of the process is necessarily experienced as a massive attack on their self-esteem.

Some of the data in the *Mobbing Report* support or directly confirm this interpretation: More than half of the respondents, according to the authors, reported that they suffered from anxiety states, that they had lost their self-confidence and doubted their own abilities (*Mobbing Report*, 2002, p. 77).

When mobbing acts are combined at the professional, personal, and relational levels, they can drain the sources of self-esteem that exist at work. To put it bluntly, mobbing puts the victim into a kind of void in the company. In this void, the victim can no longer experience the self-objects that are important to him or her at work.

The constant repetition of this harassment makes all the experiences with important self-objects that the victim could otherwise have at work impossible. This is true for experiences with the company or department which would otherwise make an employee feel well-looked after because they provide protection and reassurance. This is equally the case for the circle of colleagues who would otherwise perceive the person affected as "nice" and civilised and enable him or her to develop a sense of community and pride. Finally, it also applies to the direct superior in whose performance appraisals the employee can see his or her reflexion as a competent specialist.

It seems normal that a person affected by mobbing becomes ill in the end as a result of these constant mortifications. This makes the question all the more urgent: Why do – as the *Mobbing Report* says – so many of those affected hold out for so long? Why do they not give notice in time or apply for a transfer to another department?

Again, many individual differences can be assumed. I will briefly mention three possible reactions of the victims, which I will interpret from this perspective.

It is possible that a victim is particularly stubborn in his or her need for idealisation. "It just doesn't want to get into his head" that there is no superior who will put an end to this nightmare. But the mobbing continues, and the victim endures.

It is also possible that the victim seeks out what one might call "islands of strength", to which he or she can temporarily escape to regain the strength needed to get through the mobbing.[5]

Finally, according to the *Mobbing Report*, the majority of respondents find help outside the company from psychologists/psychotherapists or from spouses (*Mobbing Report*, 2002, p. 98). This is based on the need for idealisation: The person affected seeks an experience with self-objects who can provide protection and reassurance.

The same phenomenon can thus be illuminated from two sides, in terms of both interaction sociology and depth psychology. Both yield results, and the two can complement each other. Mobbing ultimately deprives those affected of what they need to maintain their professional identity or of the professional conditions needed to maintain their self-esteem. From one perspective, social death threatens; from the other, a void, meaning that at work, the victim can no longer satisfy his or her "normal" needs for a relationship with self-objects.

All in all, it is perhaps the depth-psychological/psychoanalytical perspective which is more productive in the case of mobbing. It can answer some of the questions that so far have remained open in mobbing research. The reason is that the depth-psychological conflict which we assume to be at work here in some ways goes deeper than the social conflict. It can explain certain peculiarities of mobbing actions by connecting them with the re-actualisation of traumatic relationship experiences in childhood.

I mean peculiarities such as the enormous aggressiveness of mobbing; the attacker's belief that they are above the law; their non-existent empathy with the victim; the illusionary hope of those being bullied that a superior will finally put an end to the nightmare; and so on.

A great advantage of this perspective is that both sides, the person doing the mobbing as well as the person affected by it, are seen to be involved in the re-actualised childlike relationship pattern. They take up different but related positions.

In the following I would like to show how we can recognise these connections.

HOW TRAUMATIC EXPERIENCES OF CHILDHOOD RELATIONSHIPS CAN BE RE-ACTUALISED IN MOBBING

We can combine two different approaches to analysing the conflictual genesis of the "see-saw relationship", in which two people alternate between the position of power and the position of powerlessness. The first is that of Mahler, who describes the difficulties with the childhood developmental phase of individuation. Kohut with his psychology of self-objects offers the second approach: A fixation on the narcissistic configuration, that is on the grandiose self and on the idealised parental imago. I will use both approaches to make the characteristics of mobbing in phases II and III understandable.

I would like to emphasise, however, that I do not assume that such a re-actualisation takes place always and under all circumstances during mobbing. It is quite possible that a mobbing victim is not affected by it. That person's actions will then be solely (or mainly) determined by the fact that he or she, as the victim, is being deprived of the satisfaction of his or her normal basic needs. The sources of his or her self-esteem and self-confidence at work are being drained.

However, it is also possible – and in my experience, this is the case in most cases – that as mobbing proceeds and takes on a momentum of its own, both elements play a role and can be mutually reinforcing: The threatening vacuum (and the reactions to it) and the re-actualisation of traumatic relationship experiences from childhood.

TRAUMATIC RELATIONSHIP EXPERIENCES FROM CHILDHOOD AND
CHARACTERISTICS OF BULLYING: STRUCTURAL ANALOGIES

On this second level of meaning, we will interpret the characteristics of mobbing actions as a consequence of the re-actualisation. I assume that the participants themselves create a structural analogy between the characteristics of their mobbing interaction and the characteristics of a childhood trauma, which, despite many individual particularities, many people experience. It is the (unconscious) recognition of this structural analogy by the participants which leads to a revival of the conflictive emotional relationships of childhood in the present. The current process of mobbing is thus (unconsciously) experienced as a repetition of the past.

Let us first note the typical characteristics of mobbing interaction identified so far. Some of these characteristics I took from the *Mobbing Report*; others are the result of my interpretation:

Already at the beginning of the mobbing, the relationship between the attackers and the person affected is characterised by

- a serious communication problem or even a blatant communication disturbance (cf. *Mobbing Report*, 2002).

In addition to this characteristic, five other contextual and action characteristics of bullying have been mentioned:

- The enormous power differential (superiority/inferiority) that exists between bullies and their victim. It is defined above all by the fact that the positions cannot be exchanged.
- The third party – the superior – who should intervene usually refrains from doing so (cf. *Mobbing Report*, 2002).
- The attacks are usually aimed at mortifying the self-esteem of the victim.
- The attacks are often carried out in an indirect manner, so that the bullies remain hidden (cf. ibid.).
- Social isolation ensues: Exclusion from the group of employees (cf. ibid.).

With these six characteristics of mobbing, the persons involved can unconsciously establish a structural analogy to the characteristics of a psychological conflict constellation of early childhood that was traumatically experienced. It is a conflict constellation which could not be properly resolved in childhood. Like a poorly healed wound, it can, under certain conditions, re-open again and again. I consider this to be an important difference between phase I and phases II and III of the mobbing process: For the majority of those affected, we can only explain the later phases of the process if we take into account the connection to conflict experiences in childhood. This is not necessary for the analysis of mobbing acts in phase I.

My thesis is: If mobbing develops its own momentum, that is from phase II onwards, the majority of victims experience a re-actualisation. For them, the devaluing attacks are derived from forms of attacks committed from a position of power which, due to their experiences of childhood, is represented by the mother. It is the mother who decides whether a little child feels comfortable, develops, and thrives.

If mobbing actions are ultimately intended to deprive the victims of the conditions necessary for maintaining their self-esteem at work, then these forms of attack can be derived from the inner image of an overpowering, "evil" mother. The mobbing actions are aimed at pulling the rug out from underneath the victim's feet, so to speak.

The mobbing victim also "knows" this psychological conflict constellation from his or her own childhood. I therefore assume that an unhealed psychological wound, which is preserved in the memory not only of one individual but of many people in the present day, can break open again at the workplace in the course of the mobbing, and this on both sides.

Before adding the schematically depicted characteristics of the traumatic childhood experience to our list of mobbing characteristics, I will briefly summarise the relevant findings based on therapeutic clinical case reports.

AN AUTONOMY CONFLICT DATING BACK TO CHILDHOOD

Findings from therapeutic practice can help us identify emotional conflict situations and developmental blockages that belong to the collective unconscious of our time. Only against this background does it become possible to interpret the dynamics of mobbing (from phase II onwards).

My interpretation focuses on an autonomy conflict which was not well resolved in childhood. Of course, there are other psychological problem constellations associated with early childhood trauma which may be relevant for a better understanding of the phenomena of mobbing. But my selection is doubly justified: According to analysts working in therapy, this psychological problem is indeed widespread today. At the same time, even a single traumatic relationship pattern of childhood and its connection to social action in the present can already be so complex that we need to concentrate on one aspect only.

In decades of therapeutic experience, the child therapist Wolfgang Bergmann (2003) identified various patterns of parent–child relationships, which he regards as characteristic of our time. A typical pattern is the emotional appropriation of the child by the mother or both parents.

The psychoanalyst Christiane Bassyouni (1990) in her many years of therapeutic work found a relationship pattern based on a narcissistic problem from which her patients (and their partners) suffered. She attributes this to an early mother–child relationship which superficially is very different from the one Bergmann focuses on: According to Bassyouni, the pattern of a see-saw relationship has its origin in early traumatic childhood experiences with an empathy-disturbed mother (cf. Flader, 2004).

I now assume that these two very different relationships with the mother – Bergmann's and Bassyouni's – have psychological consequences for the developing child that are quite similar. Both can cause a psychological blockage of development. It becomes very difficult for the small child to resolve the psychological autonomy conflict and to take the first steps towards individuation (cf. Mahler, 1972).

The child has the need to take the first steps of his own and to detach his self, which is still fused with the image of the primary caregiver (the mother). He or she needs to oppose this self to the mother, who is experienced as overpowering. But this need is countered by the child's fear of losing the mother's love. This fear becomes overpowering when the mother repeatedly stops these first steps of the little person, be it because she misunderstands them as a childlike defiance (as a result of an empathy disorder) or because she cannot allow the child even the smallest distance from herself (as a result of a mental over-absorption of the child).

As a result, the symbiosis in the dyad with the mother does not get resolved properly, that is the child's self is not clearly separated from the mother's inner image. The small child experiences the mother's behaviour as aggressive; yet it is forced to identify with this behaviour as the mother again and again stops the child's attempts at individuation. Only this act of identification makes it possible for the child to psychologically ward off the enormous anger that the mother's behaviour has triggered. This is necessary because the child fears to lose the mother's loving attention if it gives in to its anger.

The negative consequences for the developing child are amplified by the widespread gradual disappearance of fatherhood in the psychological sense. I assume that the unconscious emotional processes that are of interest here are characteristic of Western culture and have found their societal expression in mobbing. I therefore believe that these research results can be transferred to other countries in the West.

In addition to societal conditions, there is an intra-familial relationship dynamic that accelerates this disappearance of fatherhood. The symbiosis in the dyad with the mother has largely been preserved because the conflict over autonomy could not be resolved (or not well). As a result, in the third or fourth year of life, when the father should come into play as a third party, the child has a very different experience from what Freud described with the model of the Oedipus conflict: The father is either experienced as a threat to the happy, paradisiacal two-in-one and must therefore be fought or at least marginalised; or he is commiserated with and seen as a poor wretch. He is commiserated with because the child assumes that he wants to belong to the happy symbiosis that unconsciously exists between the mother and her child but is denied this desire.

If this conflict constellation of early childhood – which begins in the second year of life – is re-actualised in mobbing, then we can assume that this is true for both sides: For the perpetrator as well as for the victim. Both are unconsciously connected to each other by the same conflictual theme; but in doing so, they naturally take up two opposing positions of action: That of the attacker and that of the attacked.

Neither side can reflect on this because both have employed the defensive measure of repression. This remains in place even when the element that has been repressed returns, with the consequence that there is a lack of knowledge about alterity. While a bully, for example, believes to be representing a group norm, he or she actually carries out an unconscious earlier instruction of the mother. She prevented him from taking the first steps, which he or she now believes that the mobbing victim is taking.

I do not think that the very early childhood conflicts that took place even before the child began to acquire language are preserved in its memory. A mental conflict structure is dependent on language to be preserved in memory. However, we can assume that the parents' relationship patterns will continue to shape the psychological development of the child. This is also indicated by the examples that Bergmann cites in this regard. The primary caregivers of the growing child will continue to stimulate the unresolved conflict of autonomy of early childhood in new and modified forms in later phases of development, and thus consolidate this conflict structure in the child's memory.

I will now illustrate schematically to what extent an analogy can be established between the action and contextual characteristics of mobbing and the traumatically experienced constellation of the unresolved autonomy conflict of childhood. This is unconsciously done by the participants themselves (Table 2.3).

One could object here that these analogies are far-fetched, for example that the social isolation of the mobbing victim as established by research cannot be seen in analogy to the traumatic experience of early childhood, when the child is threatened with its own perdition.

However, we must not forget that this threat of perdition is one of the elements whose unconscious meaning we want to uncover: What does it mean, for example, for the unconscious mind of those involved when the bullies express their wish that the mobbed person should "disappear"?

I see this re-actualisation made possible by the structural analogies mentioned earlier. Like for phase I, I also assume for phases II and III that we can analyse a double structure in the known phenomena of mobbing. But here it does not consist, as in phase I, of a current psychological conflict situation of the bully and his actions, with which he is attempting to address his current conflict situation. The double structure is now created by reviving on both sides the psychological conflicts of early childhood which both have experienced and to which both react differently in their actions when they try to cope with this conflict situation in the present.

Table 2.3 Schematic representation of the structural analogies and the double structure of mental conflict and act signature

Structural analogies and the double structure of mental conflict and act signature	
Mobbing in the workplace	The unresolved autonomy conflict of childhood
A serious communication problem or even a striking communication disruption	The communicative connection is interrupted during the conflict situation
A great discrepancy in power (superiority – inferiority)	For the child, the primary caregiver is the guarantor of life
The third party, who should intervene, does not usually do so: The superior	The third party is excluded from the dyad
The attacks are mostly aimed at reducing the self-esteem of the person concerned	Attempts to partially separate the self from the mother are prevented by the mother
The attacks are often indirect, so that the authors remain hidden	The "evil" mother, who is experienced as overpowering, does not threaten confrontation, but the child's basis of life
Social isolation takes place: Exclusion from the group	There is a threat of exclusion from the happy symbiosis – the descent into perdition looms

The re-actualisation of the unresolved conflict of childhood and the way it is reworked do not happen eruptively, like a volcano, but rather in the inner structural context of the mobbing actions and the reactions of the mobbing victim to the harassment. Even more than in phase I, the collective knowledge about actions, which is an original general knowledge gained through experience, is now being transformed and distorted. It becomes a psycho-pathologically composed knowledge which henceforth guides the course of bullying (cf. Chapter 1).

This is similar to Freud's "return of the repressed" in that it typically occurs in the medium used to support this defence (cf. Flader, 1995). And in the case of mobbing, this is the destructive action or rejection by the mother that was experienced in childhood and which is now directed against the victim. Yet the not-knowing – the consequence of the defensive measure of repression – protects both sides from a very unpleasant memory and from having to reflect on their actions, because it supports their identity: What they do, they – seemingly – only do as employees of a company.

This psycho-pathologically composed knowledge serves as a basis for experiencing the present as a repetition of the past without becoming aware of it. The double structure of the unconscious sense that now takes shape in action is in fact a doubling of the ego of the person concerned: The ego of the action – which also includes, for example, the endurance of a victim of mobbing – is doubled by the ego of the conflictual relationship pattern of childhood, which is re-actualised – if we can already speak of an ego there. Such a doubling makes it impossible for those affected to reflect on the resulting simultaneity of the non-simultaneous in their actions. They could only do so if they were able to observe their actions from the outside, from the position of a third party. Doing this on your own is not possible; for this, everybody is dependent on outside help.

As it is psycho-pathologically composed, this knowledge continues to guide action and produces modes of action of the person concerned which from the outside appear illogical, strange, unorthodox, self-destructive, irrational, and the like. Also, such behaviour has destructive consequences, as is the case with mobbing, which cause considerable material and psychological damage. Quite a few of the actions of those involved must appear to outsiders as irrational or blinded. I have listed them in the list of open questions that research on mobbing has not been able to answer sufficiently so far, for example the phenomenon of the unbelievable anger of the attackers; the peculiar fact that mobbing actions will not stop on their own; the complete lack of empathy with the terrible situation the victim is in; the strange passivity of many mobbing victims; the frequently occurring difficulty of identifying the at-tackers; and so forth.

For phases II and III of mobbing, I therefore distinguish between a total of four perspectives of investigation:

- The positions of action between the attacker and the victim
- The characteristics of action and context
- The re-actualisation of the conflict constellation of childhood (an unresolved autonomy conflict as the psychological conflict on both sides)
- The interpersonal defence against this unresolved psychological conflict

On both sides, the re-actualisation takes place via the structural elements of action which on both sides are presented as knowledge.

1.5 Act signatures of the unconscious in phases II and III of the mobbing process

I would like to emphasise once again that the following is not a real analysis of the actual course of events in an individual case. Rather, I am developing a depth-psychological interpretation that is intended to reveal possible con-nections through the act signature of the unconscious.

In doing so, I will make use of a method that corresponds to Kohut's as-sumption that one typical element of memory consists of "telescoping ge-netically analogous experiences" (1973, p. 74). I propose to use two interpretation schemes just like two lenses of a telescope. This will do justice to the fact that an autonomy conflict that was not properly resolved in childhood can be re-actualised in two ways: Based on a very early form, that is between the end of the first and the second or third year of life, and based on a later form in the third and fourth year of life. The underlying psychological conflict remains the same, but its socio-psychological differentiation is greater at the later stage of the child's development.

The differentiation between the two lenses is important because in mobbing, several participants may only re-actualise the latter form of conflict constellation. I will call this form "lens A". It is a psychological conflict structure which builds on the original unresolved conflict of autonomy but is shaped by a later development phase of the child. I assume that this conflict structure of the third party (the father) will first become critical for the dynamics of the mobbing process. Then I will examine form B, which concerns mobbing as seen through the lens of an unresolved autonomy conflict of earlier childhood.

These two lenses give us a sharper view of a specific detail of my analysis. They help to examine a particular phase of childhood and differentiate accordingly. Lens A (mother–father–child) focuses on knowledge about the developed childhood; lens B (mother–child) focuses on knowledge of the very early childhood.

1.5.1 The third party in the mobbing process (lens A)

THE ATTACKERS

The mere fact that the mobbing victim is still around (his or her refusal to disappear) can be perceived as a provocation by the attackers. It calls into question the superiority, indeed the power of the "us" group. Therefore, the pressure must be increased to make him or her disappear.

From the perspective of lens A, mobbing perpetrators are characterised by a complete lack of guilt and a willingness to break the law. From their position of superiority, they also always believe that their actions are right and good, and thus above the law. Therefore, any sense of wrongdoing is absent. Unconsciously, they "only" carry out the will of the idealised mother. It is in her image that the company is (unconsciously) experienced. The bullies feel that they are the guardians of group norms and values that are part of the idealised mother. As a result, they can neither put themselves in the position of the mobbing victim nor do they have any sympathy for his suffering.

By enduring and therefore resisting, the victim may embody the attackers' own inner wish to rebel against the group norms and values. This is a continuation of the projection of wishes on the victim which we assume happened during the initial phase of the mobbing process.

If the bullies also re-actualise the symbiotic connection with this idealised mother, then the blissful, paradisiacal aspect of the symbiotic relationship in the dyad takes centre stage for them. They then perceive the colleague they are mobbing as a disturbance because he or she threatens this symbiosis (from the bullies' point of view). The victim does not fit in with the "us" in his or her behaviour, religious views, or similar aspects. The reason is that he or she brings something from the outside into the bullies' realm of experiences, which seems strange to them and for which there is no place in the symbiotic relationship with the mother. This foreignness can – and this should be emphasised again – manifest in very different ways. Yet all these manifestations have in common that they threaten the "us". The symbiosis with the idealised mother does not accept anyone who is outside it. This is where the anger of the attackers finds its justification.

From a social point of view, this highly aggressive side of the symbiotic connection with the inner image of the mother threatens the victim of mobbing with the withdrawal of social recognition and with social isolation. From a psychological point of view, the threat lies in the irreversible loss of the maternal affection that the little child needs to survive. At the same time or alternatively, the victim faces a fall into nothingness.

One particular feature of this form of attack is rarely mentioned: Its indirectness. We can associate this characteristic with the helplessness resulting from the fact that often the victim does not know what is being done to him behind his back.

If confrontation takes place openly and directly, it is not to be regarded as mobbing. None of the case reports on mobbing that I have seen describes a verbal exchange that is mutual. When a mobbing victim tries to talk to the bully, the bully is unwilling, but the victim does not know why.

Both sides profoundly misunderstand the other side's behaviour. While the mobbing victim, in his or her own perspective, was never on the "outside", for the attackers, he or she was never on the "inside".

The two sides of the devaluing attacks – the satisfaction of the need for a triumphant union with the idealised mother and the interpersonalisation of the psychological defence – have one thing in common: They are both unfulfillable. The former fails because of the psychological reality, the latter because of the social reality. There is special psychic deficiency at play here which I already mentioned in the introduction in a different context.

Like any narcissistic desire, this need of the attacker aims to eliminate a deficiency – and the very attempt to do so only ever produces the deficiency anew. Lacan has drawn attention to this (cf. Lang, 1986). According to him, this deficiency has its origins in the introduction of language. The sensory immediacy that the small child feels in contact with the environment is irretrievably lost when the symbolic order of language comes between subject and environment. From that time, the linguistically mediated world of imagination exists between subject and environment. It cannot be ignored even though that is what narcissistic desire strives for. Thus, the bullies will never fulfil their desire to restore the triumphant unity with the mother because they cannot help but strive for it through linguistic actions (or actions that are translatable into language). And because the meaning of those actions is socially (and linguistically) mediated, the lack of immediacy that the child once experienced persists. The triumphal union with the mother is not restored.

As far as the interpersonal defence is concerned, which the bully tries to establish through his use of the mobbing victim, the same explanation applies as earlier: No stable interpersonal defence can be achieved through mobbing. For this, the victim would have to play along, that is he or she would need to accept the image that the attackers have of him or her and give up any inner distance to this image. But the psychological staying power of the victims depends on maintaining this inner distance.

Bullying itself produces its non-fulfilment and thus spurs the bullies to try again and again to achieve fulfilment after all. If their mobbing finally achieves its goal and the victim "disappears", then their psychological defence has become invalid. Table 2.4 shows the structural elements of mobbing from the position of the attacker.

THE VICTIM OF MOBBING

The person affected will probably be deeply disappointed at the lack of support from the superior and other possible contact persons at the company (cf.

Table 2.4 Structural elements of mobbing (from the position of the attacker; lens A)

Motive	To secure the power of the "us" group, a disturber is attacked. In a re-actualisation of the blissful symbiosis in the dyad with the mother, the mother is defended against an external threat.
Inner images	The bullies believe themselves to be guardians of the group norms and values represented by the idealised mother (the company); the "us" gives them an experience of greatness. While they feel at one with the mother, the mobbing victim is a wretched third party who is excluded from the grandiose symbiosis of the dyad.
Situation concepts	The mobbing victim is on the "outside"; the perpetrators are on the "inside".
Maxime (Moral)	The complete lack of awareness of any wrongdoing goes hand in hand with the willingness to break the law.
Relation between ends and means	The progressive devaluation of the mobbing victim has two goals: It allows the bullies to maintain power and enjoy superiority, and it preserves the grandiose unity threatened by the disturber (interpersonal defence).
Goal of action	The goal is to secure the unity that is perceived as grandiose and to reject one's own rebellious wishes, which the victim seems to embody.

Mobbing Report, 2002, p. 96f.). He or she will find out that more and more colleagues are keeping their distance. Quite a few will actually side with the attackers. The person will feel completely isolated as he or she is faced with a superior power which is behaving as if it was the guardian of the group norms and values, which the victim supposedly violates. The harassment accelerates.

With the continuous attacks during the first phase of the process, the bullies make their goal unmistakably clear: "Get out of here!" But the victim usually does not fulfil this wish – he or she remains at the workplace.

This endurance and perseverance can be individually motivated in a variety of ways. Some may see themselves as fighting a battle and will not resign of their own accord or ask for a transfer to another department because this would be tantamount to personal defeat. Others are uncertain of finding a new job and fear becoming unemployed.

The idealised mother, under the influence of this particular phantasm, takes on the role of personnel management in the course of the mobbing process. This is associated with a dyadic conflict structure: Either a single colleague faces a group of bullies or a superior is looking for allies when he attacks an employee because his mobbing acts (supposedly) represent group norms.

The mobbing victim now faces the power of the "us" group. Therefore, the fear of the outside, that is of what is outside of the company, prevails. For if the company is (unconsciously) experienced in the image of the idealised mother, then there cannot be any life (and work) "outside". Being "outside" entails the threat of social death which touches on earlier fears of death.

This can explain why there are victims of mobbing who for the longest time cannot even imagine that they have enemies at work.[6] They continue to experience themselves as belonging. And so they will continue to do their work in the best way they can – in the hope that the mortifying attacks will stop at some point, that the idealised mother will finally intervene.

Why it can be so difficult for a victim to identify his or her attackers also becomes understandable in this context. Apart from the fact that the perpetrators often hide their attacks to protect themselves, these interpretations offer another answer:[7] As the victim fears to lose the vital relationship with the idealised mother (i.e. the company), he or she finds it difficult to accept the very existence of a bully. The victim often cannot imagine that for the other people at work, he or she has turned into an enemy who is "outside". He or she still hopes that at some point, the harassment will stop on its own. The victim does not know that by remaining at work, he or she is continuing to rattle the psychological defence of the bullies.

After all, it is not uncommon for a victim of mobbing to blame him- or herself for having become a victim: "I forced her to behave so aggressively." This reaction, too, is understandable if we assume that the victim accepts the group norms and ideals (and the underlying power position of the idealised mother). The victim wants to continue to belong; he or she needs the affection and social recognition of the other people at work. Since the "evil" side of the mother image comes into play, it becomes difficult for the victim not to accept the corresponding psychological position as a victim.

How illusionary the hope is that the harassment will stop at some point becomes understandable when we take a closer look at the psychodynamics of mobbing. According to my interpretation, this is responsible for the fact that in this phase, the bullies become unable to stop their attacks of their own accord.

Regardless of what motivates the mobbing victims to hold out at their workplace, there is a danger that the permanent mortifications will eventually have an effect: The person affected will begin to perform the various forms of devaluation (of his or her own work performance, exclusion from the community of colleagues, etc.) on him- or herself, at least temporarily. Then, it is helpful to look for resources that can stabilise the victim's self-esteem – for example situations of success at work, in the family, or in hobbies. Otherwise, self-doubt and uncertainty about whether the bullies "aren't in the right after all" can easily arise. This is countered by the affected person's own positive self-image. Nevertheless, it will become more and more difficult and exhausting to maintain such a positive self-image against the external image created by the bullies.

Re-actualising the symbiosis with the mother will increase the mobbing victim's fear of the "outside". He or she is very afraid of losing the positive attention of the mother, of dropping out of the vital symbiosis of the maternal dyad, and, ultimately, of being pushed into nothingness.

The victim remains passive; he or she waits and waits – quite illusorily – for an intervention by a higher authority. This expectation will be severely disappointed because the higher authority usually does not intervene. The "signals that the victim sends out to this idealised parental imago remain unheard" (cf. Kohut, 1973, p. 86). In addition, there is often little self-consolation that can be employed against the effects of narcissistic mortifications.

Against this background, it is easier to understand why the victims of persistent mobbing become so seriously ill both mentally and physically. They find themselves unable to compensate for the effects of narcissistic mortification, which is the core objective of mobbing. Also, they can do nothing to counter it. On the action level, they must constantly make and maintain the distinction between intention on the one hand and effect on the other. The reason is that mobbing actions only have an effect when the victim adopts the image that the attacker has of him or her. So, on the psychological level, the mobbing victim must constantly defend against the pull that results from the combination of contextual features and their structural analogy with traumatic childhood experiences and current circumstances of the professional situation. Without outside help, he or she will hardly be able to cope with this heavy psychological burden.

Table 2.5 shows the individual structural elements of bullying from the position of the victim.

Table 2.5 Structural elements of mobbing (from the position of the victim; lens A)

Motive	If mobbing is experienced as a kind of fight, then a retreat (through resignation from the job or the request for a transfer) would be tantamount to personal defeat. There is hope that the mobbing will soon stop of its own accord. Possible forms of fear (of losing one's job, of being "outside", of falling into nothingness, etc.) prevent the victim from taking action.
Inner images	At first, it is difficult to identify the enemy. The tendency not to distinguish between the intention and the effect of the repeated attacks on the victim's self-esteem cause self-doubt. There is the fantasy of being under the protection of the idealised mother. But because it is unclear how one can defend oneself successfully, feelings of powerlessness arise. Quite possible, the victim begins to feel guilty.
Situation concepts	One's job takes on a contradictory meaning: On the one hand, it is the place of continuous mortification; on the other hand, it represents the protection of the "inside" under the roof of the idealised mother.
Maxime (Moral)	"Don't take any crap! You've done nothing wrong! Believe in justice!" Or: "Be obedient!" (in relation to the idealised mother).
Relation between ends and means	The earlier performance at the workplace is continued as far as possible. Quite possibly, the victim tries even harder in the hope that the psychological terror will soon stop of its own accord. It is also possible that new resources are found to confirm the positive self-image (at work, in hobbies, in the family, etc.)
Goal of action	Perseverance and endurance: To endure the suffering inflicted (unjustly) until help arrives.

THE SUPERIOR

If a superior who intervenes in mobbing were to do so from the position of the third party, then, in the conflict structure assumed here, he or she would become a "disturber" for the bullies – just like the mobbing victim. In reality, however, the superior who takes this position would be doing precisely what he or she should be doing: Accepting the responsibility that institutionally comes with his or her position. Yet the interviewees of the *Mobbing Report* leave no doubt about the fact that this does not happen often.

Asked about their own strategies in retrospect, only one in 13 respondents of the *Mobbing Report* said that it was a good strategy to involve their superior or to make the mobbing public (cf. *Mobbing Report*, 2002, p. 100). When asked about the situation in the company at the time of the mobbing, respondents very frequently said that their superior was not prepared to discuss the situation.

Among all possible answers, this received the second-highest agreement (ibid., p. 125).

In the *Mobbing Report*, the respondents also said that they turned to the works/staff council (68.7 per cent) and to colleagues who were not involved in the mobbing (62.3 per cent) when seeking support within the company. These attempts were also mostly unsuccessful.

The fact that a mobbing dynamic can develop in the first place can be interpreted as an expression of the group dynamics of a leaderless group. In such a group, nobody really takes responsibility, takes a standpoint, or is ready to take part in an aggressive confrontation, that is prepared to draw aggression upon him- or herself. The information about the weak father, which comes from clinical-therapeutic case reports, finds its equivalent in management positions of companies.

In my opinion, there are two mutually reinforcing elements at work here: On the one side, the managers themselves often find it difficult to accept a triadic conflict structure: this is to say, manager, the bully, and the victim; on the other side, the phantasm of leadership derived from the symbiosis does not give room to the authority of a third party, since the latter has been marginalised or completely excluded.

Once the mobbing dynamics come into play, it becomes more difficult for the managers who are formally responsible to intervene in time. Managers may also simply be afraid to take on the growing group of bullies.

In the event of mobbing, there is a particular style of leadership which, in my interpretation, has its roots in a highly aggressive side of the inner mother image. The kind of power at stake here becomes clear if one compares it to a paternalistic style of leadership. Modern concepts of corporate culture document the current tendency to replace traditional leadership with a leadership corresponding to the phantasm of the idealised mother. Special emphasis is placed on human sympathy, the well-being of employees, conflict resolution through mediation, and so forth. I will discuss this in more detail in Part II, Chapter 2.

However, there does not yet seem to be any general awareness of the new potential for aggression which is present alongside these positive values. Mobbing research makes this very clear. The conflict analysis offered by Kolodej (2005, pp. 97f.) gives no indication at any point of the difficulty many people have today in accepting the triadic conflict structure and not avoiding it. To avoid misunderstandings: I believe that a paternalistic leadership also has a potential for aggression that can have a destructive effect. The crucial point is that as long as this paternalistic leadership style existed – and it partly still exists – there was a general awareness of this aggression potential. This does not apply to the leadership style derived from the symbiosis in the dyad, whose highly aggressive side becomes visible over the course of mobbing. More and more often, persons who occupy the father position in the family either fail at handling the triadic conflict structure in their emotional development or shy away from this conflict structure because they find it too strenuous. They then fall back on the dyadic conflict structure.

The new form of aggressiveness that can arise in a company – such as mobbing – is often overlooked. By dismissing the traditional principle of authority, the psychological infantilisation linked to it can be avoided. But new, archaic forms of infantility take their place, and that is also often overlooked.

1.5.2 Mobbing in the context of an unresolved autonomy conflict in early childhood (lens B)

THE BULLIES

In this earlier conflict structure, the bullies believe that their victim is threatening their psychological defence against the individuation attempts that took place in their childhood.

The structural analogy established here goes back to the conditions under which the conflict situation arose in childhood: The victim demonstrates today the same behaviour that the bully had attempted in vain in his or her childhood: To be different, to take his or her own path, not to correspond to what the overpowering mother expects. This image of the mother from early childhood now corresponds to the dominant reference group at work.

The mother's actions that were experienced in early childhood consisted of rejecting or hindering the developmental steps that the child wanted to take in connection with individuation. It is, as explained earlier, a painful process in the life of the infant, who on the one hand wants to gain some distance from the mother but at the same time is very afraid of losing her (cf. Mahler, 1972).

In early childhood, the child deals with this conflict with the mother by abandoning and psychologically warding off the fact that it had to abandon its efforts to do something on its own. The child does that by identifying with the position of the forbidding or rejecting mother. The colleague who becomes disturbing because he or she reminds the adult bully of these past experiences must be fought because he or she threatens the bully's psychological defence. This means that the bully was a victim in early childhood. Here, we also have an explanation why there is no empathy with the mobbing victim: The bully, in his or her unconscious mind, must not, under any condition, behave the way this colleague does.

For the bully, the victim's persistence in wanting something different from the dominant group represents an aspect of his or her own self, which against his or her own keen wishes, the bully was forced to ward off as "bad". In this respect (according to my interpretation) this is a form of an interpersonal psychic defence – more precisely, the attempt to erect such a defence.

In order to maintain this psychological defence, the bully attacks the employee whom he or she experiences as disturbing from the position of an "evil" mother. The aim of these attacks – to threaten of social death and

ultimately eradicate the co-worker – corresponds, according to my interpretation, to the means of a "bad mother", who actually reigns over the life
and death of her child. The withdrawal of her love, if the little child does not do
what the mother wants it to do, is experienced as a threat. It can cause fear of
death. And since there is no confrontation in this dyad – a particularity of the
early childhood which does not have experiences regarding the third party – the
attacks happen in an indirect form.

The interventions experienced in the early childhood will have caused
enormous anger in the young child, who felt that his own attempts at autonomy and demarcation from his mother were being obstructed. This anger,
which was split off or suppressed in childhood, can now, in a kind of identification with the bad mother, be directed against the work colleague who
triggered this psychological pattern of conflict.

According to my interpretation, the dynamics of mobbing can continue
even if professional third parties (psychologists, works council members, etc.)
become involved in the conflict. It seems that many of the consultants,
mediators, and so forth involved follow the maxim: "Never identify with the
victim!"

This can lead to violations of the law because the people in charge do not
know how to solve the problem in any other way. In the phantasm of a
leadership connected with the idealised mother, labour law, for instance, can
simply be disregarded.

The self-assurance of the bullies and their remarkable presumptuousness
towards the victim, which I noted when looking through lens A, is also experienced through lens B. In their unconscious imagination, the attackers are
still in the position of magnificence and superiority that they enjoy in their
union with the idealised mother.[8]

By establishing an identification with the forbidding mother, they repeat in
the position of this highly aggressive mother the refusal and rejection which
they themselves experienced in childhood. In this position of superiority over
the mobbing victim – suggested by the recourse to group norms – a fantasy of
power can be enjoyed without raising any self-doubt among the bullies.

Of course, the mental conflict from childhood, which the bully attempts to
resolve through mobbing, cannot be solved in this way. Indeed, it gets triggered again and again by the mere presence of the work colleague who has
become a victim. The bully's own rejected desire for autonomy is stimulated
again and again by the fact that the victim shows by his or her behaviour that
otherness is possible.

Therefore, the victim must be made to disappear. And this is why mobbing
is so dangerous once it has developed its own momentum: It will not stop on
its own. The bully will normally only stop the harassment once the victim has
given up (gets transferred, falls ill, leaves the company, or ultimately agrees to a
dismissal). According to the *Mobbing Report* (2002, p. 105), mobbing processes
usually only end in the fourth phase of the process and only once the victim

Table 2.6 Structural elements of mobbing actions (from the position of the attacker; lens B)

Motive	Rejection and punishment of the child who wants to develop something autonomously
Inner images	The bully identifies[9] with the inner image of the "evil" mother; moreover, he or she enjoys the position of imagined superiority – after all, the bullying victim is in the position of the negative self-part that was once split off
Situation concept	Punishment in the position of the "evil" mother, who pushes her child away
Maxime (Moral)	"Moral" of the symbiosis in the dyad with the mother
Relation between means and end	These are acts of attack aimed at destruction, albeit in an indirect and mostly covert form
Goal of action	The goal is to cast the victim out into nothingness via social death

has given up. Table 2.6 shows the structural elements of bullying actions from the position of the attacker.

THE VICTIM OF MOBBING

The victim sees him- or herself at the mercy of an untouchable power against which he or she is utterly powerless. There is a threat of falling into nothingness through social death in the workplace.

I suspect that the relation between ends and means of action, which we normally use as a matter of course because particular means fulfil a particular purpose, is not readily accessible to the victim at this time. Clearly, he or she could end the suffering through rational action – for example by applying for a transfer to another department. But the victim is almost entirely unable to plan rational action of this kind without outside help.

One might object that it should be possible to see these phantasms as unreal, that it should also be possible to foresee the threat of exclusion from the community and social death if the person affected does not take the initiative to transfer to another department or even resign. For this, however, the victim would have to take a position outside the course of events. Without the help of a third person who provides orientation, the victim of mobbing cannot see that the acts of devaluation will not stop of their own accord.

This third person is unlikely to be the superior – in companies, it is usually hard to find a superior who does not act like a weak father.

The victim, as I interpret it, ultimately falls prey to mobbing because he or she unconsciously experiences the conflict in the mobbing process as analogous – albeit in a modified form – to the unresolved autonomy conflict of early childhood: The desire to make his or her own way was countered by the fear (nourished by the mother) of losing her affection, which in the early development of the child would have meant losing life altogether.

If this unresolved conflict of childhood is repeated in the mobbing process and the mobbing victim thus comes under its influence, he or she will not be able to solve the psychological conflict at work, however modified it may be. The only option is to hand in notice or ask for a transfer to another department.

The various coping attempts mentioned by the interviewees in the *Mobbing Report* drastically document the wide spectrum of psychological and/or physical suffering of the persons concerned (ibid., p. 88).

In mobbing, when it develops its own momentum, the social and psychological conflicts are combined. The need for social recognition with a simultaneous need for self-assertion is joined with the (unconscious) desire to hold on to the blissful unity with the mother while at the same time experiencing the fear of putting this at risk. The combination of both conflicts makes it so difficult for those affected by mobbing to take the decision to leave their department or even the company on their own. Table 2.7 shows the structural elements of mobbing actions from the position of the victim.

I am aware of the fact that this representation is quite schematic and that many of the possible individual variations are not considered. Also, I would like to point out once more that these act signatures of the unconscious are a result of my interpretation; this is not an attempt to depict actual mental processes. Nevertheless, I think that these action psychograms can offer practical orientation for the victims as well as for people involved in dealing with mobbing more generally.

In conclusion, based on my research on mobbing, I would like to formulate five motives for why a superior, despite being responsible, does not intervene in an imminent mobbing incident:

Table 2.7 Structural elements of mobbing actions (from the position of the victim; lens B)

Motive	The fear of losing the vital unity with the idealised mother conflicts with the desire to do things autonomously (and, for example, request a transfer to another department). The fear prevails.
Inner images	The victim of mobbing blames him-/herself for not fitting in. The victim sees him-/herself at the mercy of an untouchable power against which he/she feels powerless.
Situation concept	Being punished in the position of the "bad" child who tried to take autonomous steps.
Maxime	The kind of moral in the dyad with the mother that says: "I'm staying with you as you are".
Relation between ends and means	This rational element is not available to the victim.
Goal of action	He/she endures in order to avoid psychological death.

- He or she fears attracting aggression from both sides
- He or she fears the power of the group which presents itself as the guardian of group norms and values
- As a third party, there is no role for him or her as a reference person in the mobbing process
- In the psychological sense, he or she is not a father but a son who is working stubbornly on his professional advancement and has internalised the maxim: "Never identify with the weak!"
- He or she is also a bully

A SHORT SUMMARY

I will now summarise the interpretation results with regard to the interpersonal defence, which is meant to support the already existing psychological defence of the bully. Yet it fails to do so reliably.

- In phase I, it begins apparently quite harmlessly. A colleague at work – without intending to do so – triggers a psychological defence that already exists within the bully. This colleague is then attacked because he or she embodies what the bully must also attack in him- or herself.
- The mere fact of the disturber's endurance is experienced as a challenge to the power of the "us" group and triggers the already existing inner conflict dynamics of the bullies. They, too, occasionally experience an inner rebellion of this kind, which has now become embodied by the mobbing victim. Therefore, the attacks must be continued throughout phases II and III. In the first case, mobbing was a two-person event; now it has become a group phenomenon. Myths are spread about the victim which conceal the actual motives of the attack (cf. II, Chapter 1.1).
- The re-actualisation of the symbiosis from the dyad with the mother adds a new element: The fact that the victim endures the attacks can also be experienced as a threat to this unique dyad. Here, too, we see an interpersonal defence that cannot become stable.
- Conflict Structure B: For the bully, the victim comes to embody of his or her own attempts at autonomy in childhood. The already existing psychological defence against these attempts is endangered by the presence of the victim. Therefore, the victim must be bullied.

1.6 About solving mobbing problems

For the bully, repeating mobbing acts reproduces the inadequacy which those acts were meant to eliminate. This inadequacy is twofold: It affects satisfaction as well as the bully's psychological defence (see previous discussion).

1.6.1 Countermeasures in the company

My approach provides a basis for interpreting mobbing experiences. Victims can make use of it, but so can bullies and anybody else who is willing to confront the inner dynamics of the phenomenon in order to better understand it. Those who feel drawn to my interpretations because they recognise themselves in them contribute to the kind of objectivity that can be achieved in analyses in this area.

Mobbing is still taboo in many companies. This is also a consequence of a fact mentioned earlier: Our society has virtually no cultural code for the public communication of narcissistic mortifications. With my interpretations, I hope that those on both sides who are voiceless – the attackers as well as the victims – find a way out of their isolation and begin to communicate with each other.

The usual explanatory approaches of mobbing research do not even come close to explaining the enormous destructiveness of mobbing. Therefore, the proposed countermeasures remain in the sphere of the well-intentioned. I see the main problem of these countermeasures in the fact that they suggest that this conflict situation can be influenced. In reality, it evades any technical intervention, any mediation, and any social or legal regulation because it is of a psychological nature.

I have pointed out the destructive potential that acts of mobbing have from the outset. As the conflict escalates, this potential is released and causes the various clinical pictures that the persons affected attributed to mobbing in the *Mobbing Report*. I have mentioned them already: Stress symptoms, shortness of breath, paralysis, neurodermatitis, and chronic diseases (such as depression and gastrointestinal diseases) (ibid., P. 79). However, the narrow perspective taken by mobbing research fails to make the connection to clinical-therapeutic case reports, although these can provide information about widespread emotional conflict situations. This is why the proposed countermeasures appear to be largely ineffective.

In general, the optimism about the feasibility of preventing mobbing is striking. For example, Kolodej (2005) takes the view that a company should ensure a debating culture that includes an open attitude towards conflict:

> This requires the existence of appropriate ways to hold discussions within the company: established company arbitration boards, company agreements on the subject of mobbing and sexual harassment in the workplace, special contact persons within the company, and the possibility of using external consultants to resolve conflicts. (ibid., p. 61)

The psychodynamics of mobbing, especially the widespread evasion of the triadic conflict structure, is not affected at all by these measures. Siblings can also quarrel to their heart's content, and nothing prevents them from evading the psychological authority of the third party.

It is not realistic to assume that guidelines, committees, and works councils can create conditions in which managers accept their responsibility and prevent mobbing before it escalates. Instead, how can a supervisor, whose leadership competence includes accepting this responsibility, intervene successfully when the first signs of mobbing become visible in his sphere?

The statement: "In the case of conflicts and especially in the case of mobbing, there are no uninvolved, neutral viewers, no matter how much these people would like to be" (Arentewicz et al., 2009, p. 21), indicates an important fact, but one that also cannot be adequately captured through an approach based on stress medicine.

Anyone who wants to intervene in mobbing – a superior or a member of a works council – should, if possible, do so in the early phase of the mobbing process to avert further damage. From my investigation, certain indications of an incipient mobbing – that is phase I of the process – can be deduced. There can be signs of arrogance on the part of the bullies when asked about their colleague because they feel superior to him or her. Linked to this, the bullies will show a complete lack of compassion for the victim and his or her well-being. There will also be a communication barrier in the sense that both sides no longer talk to each other.

The superior or member of the works council will find it difficult to put him- or herself in the shoes of the victim if he or she follows the maxim: "Never identify with a victim!" With the help of this maxim, feelings of insufficiency can be kept in check and hidden from others. However, this attitude is counterproductive to understanding what happens during mobbing. The superior or member of the works council needs to touch on his or her own experiences of devaluation and personal mortification in order to be able to understand the game being played here.

It is certainly not easy to implement this approach in a company. But the representatives of the various bodies responsible for dealing with a case of mobbing should be able to understand this perspective. This may be helped by understanding that a destructive pattern of conflict resolution has developed in mobbing, based on a psychological problem that is also effective in other areas of society.

1.6.2 A concept for a workshop

Together with the social pedagogue and mobbing advisor Monika Hirsch-Sprätz and lawyer Ralf Müller-Amenitsch, I developed a concept for a workshop for managers who need to recognise the challenge presented by mobbing. It focuses on empowering managers to identify the beginnings of mobbing, to discuss it with those affected, and to assist the potential victim.

As a measure to combat mobbing, almost all the respondents of the *Mobbing Report* took the view that companies should take mobbing more seriously. Among other things, they called for improving internal communication as a key means of combating mobbing. When asked about the concrete measures their companies had instituted to combat mobbing, respondents mostly mentioned training courses. Outside of the workplace, a good three quarters of those questioned are in favour of setting up mobbing advice centres.

Arentewicz et al. (2009) point to the conflict resolution process in mediation and coaching. In simple terms, it is not the paternalistic leadership principle that applies here, but the help of a mediator or coach, who brings the parties to the dispute around the table and seeks solutions that meet the various interests of the parties involved.

This view is in line with my view of today's "expert", who is the result of a metamorphosis of the traditional father image.

How can a third party intervene successfully – be it in a conversation that the superior has with those involved or a conflict resolution forum set up by the company? Briefly, there are three functions that can be helpful for somebody acting from the position of the third party:

DIFFERENTIATE

What is reality, what is fantasy in the statements of both sides, for example? Who actually is the bully, who is the victim? Which justification is only being professed, what is the actual motive?

CHOOSE

What is relevant for understanding the mobbing case, what is irrelevant? What is the key point?

SEPARATE

How can both sides stand back without creating a disadvantage for either side?

Counsellors working in mobbing advice centres should complete training as psychotherapists. Only then will they be able to address the complex psychological processes in a way that really helps the mobbing victims.

Given the complexity of the problem, it makes sense to design and implement multi-professional advice for the people involved in mobbing (victims and perpetrators): Legal and depth-psychological advice as well as systemic organisational analysis. At the Berlin-Brandenburg Mobbing Counselling Centre, such an approach is planned in conjunction with a training course for counsellors for mobbing victims.

1.6.3 Legal recourse: The role of Germany's anti-discrimination law

In terms of legal advice and representation of mobbing victims, Germany's General Act on Equal Treatment (AGG) of 2006 is a step forward. The primary aim of this law is to strengthen the rights of members of social minorities by making discrimination and disadvantages caused by mobbing an offense.

This was achieved, among other things, by shifting the burden of proof to favour those affected by mobbing. If the party being bullied can provide evidence that suggests mobbing, under the AGG, the other party now bears the burden of proof that there was no violation of the mobbing provisions. Until then, the situation of mobbing victims was almost hopeless:

> Those affected by mobbing are faced … with a burden of presentation and proof, under which they have to prove that their individual problem somatisation, i.e. their constant headache, insomnia, anxiety, or back pain, are caused by the mobbing incidents. An almost impossible task". (Müller-Amenitsch, 2009, p. 4)

In principle, the AGG applies only to members of a social minority. However, Müller-Amenitsch, based on case studies from his legal practice, points out that under certain circumstances, mobbing victims who do not belong to a social minority can also be covered by the AGG. This is true in cases where the mobbing has already progressed so far that the victims have become permanently ill. The main reason is the generous statutory definition of the disabled under the law. Müller-Amenitsch gives the following example:

> A social pedagogue was so mortified in her self-esteem by her direct superior through unobjective criticism (loud yelling, public castigation of her alleged lack of professional performance in front of a team of colleagues) that she developed a severe trauma and could no longer picture working under this superior without suffering insomnia and panic attacks. (ibid., p. 12)

Since the employer did not react to her complaint about the mobbing and the demand for a "suitable workplace far away from her superior that would be appropriate to her suffering", a complaint was also made under the AGG that accused the employer of "discriminating against disabled people through omission" (ibid.). The employer's failure to take appropriate measures to further integration plays a role here because it represents one of the typical disadvantages covered by the AGG. Further legal steps by both parties followed. The integration office, which was called in, then provided important evidence:

> The decision of the integration office, in which it was officially stated that the employer had not made use of all the possibilities to enable employment appropriate to the suffering, was used as an indication to demonstrate that there was discrimination by omission. Under these

circumstances, a significantly higher severance payment than usual at the end of the employment relationship, which the client had requested in the meantime, could be obtained. Without the AGG scenario, such a severance payment would not have been possible. The employer would have left the person affected in the job that caused the illness until a permanent illness had led her to resign without severance pay or to leave due to unreasonable absenteeism. (ibid., p. 13)

It may seem like a cynical legal tactic if a victim of mobbing only has a real chance in a legal dispute if he or she is permanently ill as a result of advanced mobbing, or if he or she can be covered by the AGG due to an already existing disability. However, it should be remembered that it is the current legal situation which recommends this procedure to the lawyer if the mobbing victim does not belong to a minority exposed to discrimination.

I believe it is possible that in the legal regulation, the burden of proof can be shifted even further in the future. This becomes all the more likely the more society becomes aware of the inner dynamics of mobbing and the psychological conditions of its destructiveness – the existing dyadic conflict structure, the various psychological conflict situations with the different meanings of otherness, and so on. But I doubt that the law is an appropriate instrument to prevent mobbing. The psychological conflict situations, which I assumed in my interpretation of the unconscious meaning of mobbing, cannot be resolved through legislation.

Notes

1 Some of the theses and interpretation results presented here I already outlined at a lecture at the Institute for Psychoanalysis, Psychotherapy, and Psychosomatics Berlin (IPB) in 2013.
2 According to a survey carried out on behalf of the European Foundation for the Improvement of Living and Working Conditions, 12 million workers in the European Union have suffered from bullying at work over the last 12 months (from the date of the survey).
3 By the way, the measurability of assumed competencies and skills seems to be an important factor for the acquisition of research funds.
4 It would be interesting to know whether we can use the negative performance assessment by the supervisor to demonstrate a type of childish thinking that Freud called deviation and condensation. Wygotski (1969) analysed this form of thinking as complex thinking. In this case, the supervisor may have understood the slight accent in the pronunciation of his employee as a condensation of his own existing shortcomings or as deviation of these own shortcomings from the employee's pronunciation. To provide a more detailed picture, however, we would need a recording of these conversations, which unfortunately I do not have.
5 Oral communication by Ursula Sarrazin.
6 Oral communication from Ms. Hirsch-Sprätz – certified social pedagogue, supervisor, mediator, lecturer, and counsellor for conflict management and head of the Berlin-Brandenburg Mobbing Counselling Centre.

7 Hirsch-Sprätz points out how important it is for mobbing counselling that the victim learns to identify his or her enemies and becomes aware of the aggression directed against him or her.

8 The psychoanalyst Irene Roski (oral communication) pointed out that a sadomasochistic need structure can be particularly important for the bully in the sense of sexual satisfaction. I see this as an important addition to my research, which focuses on the narcissistic issues of mobbing.

9 The term "identification" is misleading here. It presupposes a self of the child, which has yet to develop – just like the existence of a stable demarcation from the object. More appropriate here is perhaps the term of catching up with the mother, which can reestablish the interrupted connection with her in the sense of a symbiosis (unity of two).

Chapter 3

Depth-psychological aspects of the public debate about climate change

1 A psychoanalytical approach to climate change awareness

One of the phenomena of our time that poses a particularly serious threat to humanity is global warming, euphemistically known as climate change. I will not go into the highly complex interactions of physics, economics, politics, and sociology involved in this phenomenon. In my analysis of the public debate on climate change, I will take the work of Leggewie and Welzer (2009) as the starting point for a psychoanalytical approach.

Their work seems to me particularly suitable because it is not only highly informative and well informed about the current discussions in this field. As far as psychological considerations are concerned, the two authors represent a theoretical view of cognitive psychology which is completely opposed to the psychoanalytical perspective while also being empirically focused on action. It is precisely this theoretical distance between my approach and theirs that makes it easier for me to distinguish the specifically psychoanalytical interpretation from that of cognitive psychology and thus to show its relevance.[1]

I would therefore like to demonstrate how important it is to pay sufficient attention to depth psychological aspects of both the public debate on climate change and the socio–psychological conditions of climate change itself, at least in Western culture.

I will then deduce several theses from this analysis, examining the question of why it is so difficult today for scientists to make a lay audience understand the disturbing results of their research on global warming.[2]

1.1 A psychoanalytical interpretation of the book The End of the World as We Know It (C. Leggewie/H. Welzer, 2009)[3]

The authors of this book devote a great deal of attention to a fundamental question: If so many people are well informed about environmental problems and impending disasters, how can one explain that the necessary consequences are not drawn from this knowledge to help avert the threats? Worse, why are

DOI: 10.4324/9780429345449-3

there so many people who act in a way that blatantly contradicts their own convictions? To find explanations for this contradiction, the authors take a sociological as well as a psychological perspective.

From a sociological perspective, the authors draw attention to Erving Goffman's research (1972). He showed that in modern societies, the different social situations and role expectations make it necessary to provide a corresponding flexibility of interpretations and actions.

> Reasons and causes for actions that have their origin in a person's socialisation or biography are usually subordinate to situational perceived requirements and adopted solutions. The idea that people must always follow the same morals and strategies regardless of situational conditions proves to be dysfunctional in view of the multiple requirements that people must fulfil in modern societies. In fact, someone who acts in accordance with the coherence requirements would be regarded as totally inflexible, if not a pathological case. (Leggewie/Welzer 2009, p. 75)

From this point of view, it would be impossible to consistently translate one's knowledge of the threatening consequences of climate change into everyday action. To ignore all the other requirements which need to be met by action would lead to complete, possibly even pathological inflexibility.

What strategy can be used to resolve a contradiction such as the one between climate-related convictions and one's own actions? The authors present the thought experiment of a person who keeps a climate diary and used it to record the actions by which he or she has violated his or her own climate-related convictions.

> You will notice that every time you need to write about an incident in which you violated your own principles, you immediately have a justification at hand. This covers why you had to use a taxi just now (deadline pressure), why you had to turn up the heating (had a bad cold only last week), or why you drove the 500 metres to the supermarket by car (you cannot leave the children by themselves for long). (ibid., p. 76)

Goffman's concept of role distance, to which the authors refer here, is based on role action being flexible. As far as phenomena of consciousness are concerned, this approach is quite plausible, because one's own actions in a social situation must always meet a variety of requirements: They must agree with the interpretation of given rules, the definition of situations, the consideration of concrete expectations of others, and so forth.

The assumptions made by Goffman, however, are the very same that are called into question by psychoanalysis. The ego is simply not "master in its own house". The subject of an action cannot dispose of the psychological conditions of his or her action. The discoveries made by Freud in the context of the slips of the tongue and of neurotic symptoms, among others, point to this (cf. Flader, 2003). Leggewie and Welzer state that the reasons and causes for actions that can be localised in a person's socialisation or biography are generally subordinate to what that person sees as being required by the situation and the solutions he or she adopts. Thus, they equate the perspective of the subject of action with the perspective of a reconstruction of the psychological conditions under which reasons and causes for actions can also become effective in the adult world. After all, these traumatic experiences were experienced during childhood.

The approach I have adopted here, which is to look for act signatures of the unconscious where traditionally a return of the repressed would be assumed, follows this perspective of investigation. As I have mentioned several times, the point here is that in very specific social contexts, with the appropriate characteristics, the subjects can unconsciously perceive an analogy between these characteristics and the traumatically experienced patterns of emotional relationships from their own childhood. If they establish such an analogy, then we can expect a re-actualisation of childhood relationship patterns.

If this re-actualisation takes place during the process of social action as well as in the collective knowledge of action that guides these actions, then this collective knowledge of action serves as a basis for experiencing the past as being repeated in the present. As a result, the knowledge guiding action is transformed into psycho-pathologically composed knowledge, which is betrayed by conspicuous features, forms of irrationality, and non-conformity, which I understand as the act signatures of the unconscious.

I have explained this phenomenon in detail in the chapter on mobbing (cf. Chapter 2, Section 1).

From a psychological perspective, Leon Festinger's concept of cognitive dissonance (Festinger, 1964) might apply. This concept is used to explain how contradictions between one's own actions and one's convictions about the climate can be resolved. The fact that such contradictions can occur is rooted in the actuality of the phenomenon itself.

> A phenomenon such as climate change is capable of triggering considerable cognitive dissonance. The threat is becoming clearer with each passing year, while global quantities of emissions are growing ever faster. In 2007, the figure was three percent higher than in 2006, and the increase in 2008 will be comparable. (ibid., p. 78)

The concept of cognitive dissonance refers to a level of action that ignores the same psychological processes which I consider relevant in terms of depth psychology. The question is: How can a depth-psychological approach explain a contradiction such as the one that exists between a person's conviction about climate change and his or her actions? In my opinion, we need to take a much more fundamental approach here than the two authors suggest. The heart of my argument is that all of us already have a particular psychological relationship with what is commonly called nature.

At this point I cannot go into the complex cultural-philosophical developments that have shaped the relationship with nature in different ways. I would just like to draw attention to the analysis of an equation that all of us create, if mostly unconsciously. I am referring to the equation of "Mother Nature" and the experiences made in early childhood with the primary reference person, usually the mother.

I consider the following features of a structural analogy in the context of nature and mother to be relevant:

a   Source of care and security
b   Ubiquitous reality
c   Continuous alternation of opposing conditions (such as day and night, cold and warm)

It depends on the child's type of relationship with a good mother and the aspects of a bad mother how we shape our relationship with nature as adults. Of course, there are many differences between individuals.

Based on a perceived analogy, we give back to nature what we experienced as a child in our relationship with the mother.

According to Kohut, a person can hold on to the narcissistic configurations of early childhood even as an adult. They will shape the later relationship with nature if the "optimal frustration" by the mother of the small child's desire for perfection has not been successful.

Johann Wolfgang von Goethe can be considered a prominent example of this phenomenon. On the one hand, he seems to have held on to an archaic grandiose self even as an adult, which helped him in his poetic work; on the other hand, he also showed how nature can be idealised if it is seen as more than the sum of all visible living things. In Goethe's pantheistic view, nature conceals a divinity that is reflected in all living things. As an adult, he probably shifted the idealisation he once applied to his mother to nature and preserved it there.

This form of idealisation of nature matters little for Western culture today. But the idealisation of the parental figures has not disappeared from our culture. It has shifted to something different, probably because nature is no longer experienced as a source of food and security. For example, social values that seem universal and human work performance are idealised today.

But still, as far as nature is concerned, it is important to note that Western culture unconsciously clings to the archaic grandiose self, from which the belief is derived that nature can be subjugated. It is well known that Goethe in his time vehemently resisted the development of the scientific belief that nature can be mastered. Throughout his life he considered his theory of colours to be his most important work, probably because he tried to establish an alternative research into nature.

Mendel has put forward the thesis that as society develops, the traditional principle of authority is gradually being replaced by the principle of efficiency. As far as nature is concerned, we witness many forms of indifference to its laws, which we can attribute to the principle of efficiency. Few people who dump a plastic bag in the countryside will consider the enormous amount of time needed for this plastic to decompose.

It is therefore possible that today, nature is being paid back for what the small child once suffered at the hands of the primary caregiver, the mother. This includes the anger that the mother once aroused when she tried to stop the child's first attempts at taking its own steps. Although this anger was warded off (suppressed) by the small child so that he or she could survive psychologically, it can later return in a modified form, taking the shape of indifference, if not aggressiveness towards nature. We have already looked at the difficulties which children today can have with the individuation phase previously (cf. Chapter 2, Section 1.4).

An initial explanation of why this connection is unconscious, that is necessarily removed from reflection, can be found in the concept of the return of the repressed. But the doubling of the ego also plays a role here. The adult ego, which looks at nature, is kept in service to another ego which was present in early childhood. This second ego wishes to take revenge on nature for what the primary caregiver once did to it.

Even if we take all these mental difficulties of narcissistic development into account, we come across another important difficulty. In Western culture, the reference to a higher authority, in whose name one might insist on nature conservation, has generally become fragile. Legendre (when referring to Lacan) pointed this out emphatically. It is a reference which seems to largely have disappeared today.

In all probability, we must accept that we cannot achieve rational action based on rational reasons alone. We need to refer to a higher authority to endow and support climate protection with some kind of authority and to act rationally towards nature in our own interest. But the only forms available today as substitutes for the missing reference are images of future developments or forecasts, such as the ones that are primarily provided by science.

If my interpretation is correct, then many people can certainly live with the contradiction that Leggewie and Welzer try to explain: While they are convinced about the threat of climate change, their actions in everyday life that often contradict this conviction. Why should contemporaries resolve the contradiction mentioned by the two authors when it is much more pleasant for them to follow their own needs? Moreover, they often fail to recognise that there is an unconscious need for punishment and an anger within them that contradicts the lofty values and social obligations that make up their conscious convictions. One of the discoveries of psychoanalysis is that as adults, people do not organise themselves from the outset in a way that is appropriate for life as an adult, but that traces of their developmental history from childhood are always preserved in their actions.

This repetition of early childhood patterns also occurs in the form of aggressive actions, with the consequence of making the many appeals to the responsibility of individuals towards their natural environment ineffective. The success of such appeals usually presupposes a sense of guilt on the part of those addressed, which is incompatible with an attitude of indifference and ruthlessness. Rather, an anger (which remains unconscious) must be assumed, which stems from this early relationship with the mother and which can be directed against nature.

The authors point to the enormous debts that governments incurred during the financial crisis of 2009.[4] This debt policy comes at the expense of later generations, which amounts to a cold-blooded breach of the "contract between generations" (ibid., p. 56). With regard to today's 15- to 25-year-olds, the authors conclude that this generation's future is doubly impaired:

> Younger people will not live under the same conditions under which their parents and grandparents started out, neither in social terms nor in terms of the environment shaping their future. The unspoken but rigorously practised motto is: "Our children should have it worse than we do". (ibid., p. 62)

In my view, this unspoken motto more likely reads as: "We want to be children too!", just as future generations are also children. This motto would be justified by the psychological flaw we are already aware of: People whose souls were starved when they were children, or who were unable to take steps of their own because of an overbearing mother, unconsciously deduce from this the claim that now they should be allowed to "finally be a child for real".

If this motto means that one takes the position of a child to try and influence the next generation, this interpretation has a certain plausibility.

In this context, it is worth recalling Legendre's thesis that society today is heading towards a state in which there are only mothers and a great number of sons and daughters. In this sense, the position of the father is being made to disappear, not only in the family, but also in society.

For the most part, decision-makers find themselves in the position of sons and daughters without being able to reflect on this. As a result, it must seem outlandish to them in psychological terms to feel responsibility towards the next generation. How can someone who (unconsciously) is in the position of the next generation feel responsible for the future fate of those who really are the next generation? It is possible that they may intend for the younger generation to be worse off, but the most probable attitude, given this psychological condition, is a simple lack of interest. For these decision-makers, it matters not at all what the life of the younger generation will be like in the future.

Appeals of reason, especially those addressed to the political elite, are directed at people who are unwilling or unable to occupy the position of father, or who themselves had a weak father in childhood. Although they may publicly advocate measures to protect the climate, they secretly often admire the business elites who call for more growth and thus increased profits because they are exclusively oriented towards the requirements of their professional system of action. The potential consequences of their decisions to accelerate climate change do not enter the equation.

One might object that in my interpretation of Legendre's work, I have just emphasised that we can avoid thinking in terms of black and white in the context of the traditional father image, which is largely absent today. I do believe that a metamorphosis of the father image has taken place in society. It now takes the shape of an expert, a form which no longer betrays its origins.

Experts can still fulfil a father function today, but they are specialised and oriented towards the expectations of particular groups and social classes.

Yet this same role creates a dilemma for today's nature conservation: Protecting the climate is something that concerns all of us and which we all should take part in. But how can this be elevated to the rank of a general public responsibility, which everybody respects through their actions, if it is the experts who admonish us to take on this responsibility?

A psychoanalytical approach can help us to understand why an ultimately destructive attitude towards nature is impervious to all moral appeals and rational arguments. I will use the example of "the automobile man", which the authors discuss, even though they do not take this psychological angle into account.

> Due to its symbolic power, its huge effect on infrastructure, and its industrial-political significance, the car is the central iconic object of industrial societies.... Systemically, its central position, especially in the USA and Germany, is based on the fact that car manufacturers, including upstream and downstream companies, bring in a large chunk of the gross domestic product and serve as economic barometers. Against all reason, cars and trucks have remained the main means of transport for people and goods. (ibid., pp. 88–89)

The authors explain why the car is so strongly anchored in our cultural identity:

> Capitalism satisfies the need for meaning through consumer opportunities, and the car provides fun, power, distinction, freedom, comfort, fetish, technology, and sound – in other words, the maximum of consumable meaning. That is

why nobody wants to abolish it, even though it should long have been a thing of the past. (ibid., p. 91)

The authors do not mention the unconscious but essential significance of the technically sophisticated, highly motorised car in an industrial society. I am referring to the narcissistic satisfaction that owning and driving one's own car provides. In this interpretation, we find ourselves at the first level of meaning, which refers to a mental problem in the present time. I believe we can detect an act signature of the unconscious at this level of meaning, too.

Driving a car can give you the feeling that it is driving by itself. If the driver is experienced, it nearly becomes a part of him or her. From this perspective, the car is a self-object in Kohut's sense (1973). Unless the car suddenly fails to perform in any of the aspects that drivers take for granted, they can feel as if the car was an extension of themselves and that they are at one with it. According to Kohut's self-psychology, such a self-object is not a form of mental immaturity but something that exists as a matter of course. Why should motorists give up this narcissistic satisfaction?

In addition, another narcissistic need is reflected in this same feeling: the early narcissistic configuration of the grandiose self, which quite a few motorists, if they prefer highly motorised cars, can maintain. Only this second meaning makes it understandable why wonderful freedom and enormous power can be associated with a car. The user — interestingly enough, it is mostly men — must feel unfree and powerless often enough that the car gives him the illusion of being free and powerful. In other words, in this context the car is exactly what its user is not but wants to be.

The idea of a complete abolition of the car completely ignores the fact that the car, given its double capacity to satisfy needs, contributes to the fact that motorists can maintain their mental balance. If, for rational reasons, one would take the car away from them — and with it the satisfaction of needs — then at least some thought would need to be given to providing a replacement. However, the authors do not address this issue. Nor do any other social groups and environmentalists make any suggestions to that end.

Another point made by the authors is the relationship between politics and climate change. Leggewie and Welzer very succinctly call for changing the political representation in our democracy to ensure that the needs of the next generation are taken seriously.

What is most lacking is a mode of representation that the American philosopher Jane Mansbridge has called 'surrogate representation'. If you apply this to the climate issue, it means that politicians need to address voters outside their own circle, i.e. from all over the world and future generations, instead of just keeping an eye on fulfilling their election promises and getting re-elected. A decision made today based on short-term calculations binds future generations, which naturally cannot be consulted. Yet they are irreversibly being forced into taking particular actions because of the consequences of this decision. (ibid., p. 224)

The authors hope that this fixation on the present day – and therefore the neglect of responsibility vis-à-vis future generations – can be overcome by developing a we-identity. "If we do not have a we-identity with the perspective of a vanishing-point that lies in the future, it will not be possible to develop a new cultural project that can tackle, let alone solve, the problems and crises that have long since piled up" (ibid., p. 234).

On the basis of a we-identity, people could make statements like: "Among us, nobody is stupid enough to drive through the city in an off-road vehicle." But as this we-identity does not yet exist, the authors hope that "we are looking for a new story to tell about ourselves" (ibid., p. 235).

These practical orientations for cultural change appear somewhat feeble. Yet they are based on psychological considerations. The authors ignore the psychological conflict constellations of the unconscious, which I have described earlier. Why, for example, should people be able to develop a we-identity if isolation as an individual is normal for them? Developing a common narrative about oneself, even if there is a story that one has experienced together, is a purely cognitive construct as long as concrete ways of experiencing this story are not included.

The authors cite many impressive examples of citizens' initiatives, self-help groups, and so forth. They give rise to the hope that the necessary radical restructuring of industrial society can be realised because many people identify with this restructuring (ibid., p. 235). But the authors' definition of normative and identity-building goals for the future ("What kind of society would you want to be part of in the future" (ibid., p. 229)) is too far removed from the collective psychological conflict situations that I have analysed in detail.

After briefly summarising my analysis of the work of these two authors, I will develop some further considerations.

We (unconsciously) do to nature what was done to us in early childhood by the primary caregiver. This thesis presupposes, among other things, a structural analogy between nature and the mother.

If we follow this analogy, we become aware of a problematic relationship pattern which arises from a blockage of narcissistic development in childhood. It causes people to take out on nature what they themselves experienced or suffered in a failed relationship with their mother in early childhood. On a scale from indifference to vandalism and destructiveness, we are dealing with elements of personal attitude and professional action through which this relationship pattern can have an impact on society. The people involved usually act without reflecting on this correlation.

This attitude will only change for the better once the underlying traumatic experiences of early childhood become rare. Children need to grow up in a relationship with a "sufficiently good mother" (Winnicott) and a father who sufficiently fulfils his father functions. But is such a development likely in the Western world?

The fantasy of the grandiose self, which is behind the idea of the scientific mastery of nature, is also anchored in Western culture (cf. Richter, 1979). What is new, however, is that the scientists who are concerned with climate change and its consequences have developed a concept of nature and its complexity that relativises the fantasy of the grandiose self of controlling nature. Climate is seen and analysed as a self-regulating system, and such a system can no longer be adequately explained with the outdated concept of causality.

1.2 How can scientists explain the disturbing results of their research to a lay public?

Well-informed and knowledgeable physicists and other scientists do not share in the optimism that "science will fix it". Rather, they doubt whether Homo Sapiens is really sapiens and can stop or at least slow down climate change – which is mostly caused by humans – in time.

What follows from this for the public presentation of research results, which scientists want to make accessible to a lay public? Let us take the layman's perspective first to look at public presentations.

Well-informed physicists draw attention to the complexity of the physical processes of global warming. In contrast, the general consciousness of people in a lay audience is dominated by the belief that, as far as their own behaviour is concerned, they do not have to take such processes into account. This is well matched by a form of rejection concerning the physicists' research results and their scenarios of possible future catastrophes. Intelligent members of other professions are particularly prone to this rejection. "Scientists behave as if they were a modern caste of priests who want to scare us with the apocalypse", they say. But how is this argument structured? In using this argument, the layperson makes certain presuppositions which, although not verbalised, are nevertheless often understood by the listener.

First, the layperson draws an analogy between the physicist's object of research, which is the Earth as a system, and the omnipotence position of God. This analogy is also used to compare the representatives – both those of physics and those of God Almighty – with regard to their professional activities. Just as priests preach about the idea of God on earth in all its consequences, so do climate specialists preach when they publicly communicate their research results.

On the basis of this equation, rejecting the scientists' warnings about impending catastrophes corresponds to rejecting a doctrine of God and the practical rules set by that doctrine for how to live one's life.

Scientists speak about a global threat, even if local effects can be widely different. They also call for practical measures to avert this threat. But the lay public perceives these calls as an intrusive meddling with the personal fates of individuals. The motto "Everyone is the architect of his own fortune", which is very popular among certain professional groups, means that such measures are rejected as interfering in a personal lifestyle. Yet this attitude completely overlooks the fact that it is not the physicists who make it necessary to analyse the Earth's system but the climate.

Let us now look at the public discussion from the physicists' perspective. They wish to make the results of their research, which are indeed disturbing, accessible to a lay public. Just how easily this mediation can fail is illustrated by an assertion often been repeated in the media: "We know that global warming is man-made. Therefore, humanity can control it and avoid its potentially devastating consequences!" If we examine this assertion a little more closely, we can see how questionable it is.

The term man-made corresponds to the perspective of a scientist who is used to differentiate between nature and humanity because they both follow different laws. Here, however, the question arises: Does the premise on which this statement is based really lead us to the logically possible conclusion that global warming can be controlled by humans? In fact, two very different concepts of humanity are used for the two parts, the premise and the conclusion. In the first case, humanity it is the generic subject, in the second, humans are the subject of action, that is the bearer of appropriate actions that can serve to control climate change.

This conceptual difference is easy to understand when you consider that it was not humanity that started off the process of global warming at the beginning of industrialisation. Nor is it humanity that is now called upon to translate the disturbing research findings of physicists into concrete action. This action is determined by economic, political, psychological, and other conditions, which can be completely different. This subject of action simply does not have the character of a uniform subject. Rather, it consists of the subjects of the politicians in the parliaments, the political parties, the economic interest groups, and many more who are involved here.

How can intelligent scientists make an assertion of this kind? It is probably due to the fact that they know that global warming affects the whole of humanity, which is why they are trying to design a collective subject which can take action to protect the climate. Of course, one wonders where such a subject would be located.

In addition, we also need to realise that physicists who wish to present their research results on global warming to the public face several dilemmas. Let me explain three of them.

The dilemma of the social position

What should be the social position of a physicist presenting his results in public? Should he or she appear as an expert on the subject who engages in science didactics? If so, he or she would largely ignore the disturbing nature of the results and would not point out the fact that the problem of global warming actually concerns absolutely everybody in some way or other. Should he or she admonish the public? That would mean running the risk of not being taken seriously. Should he or she appear as a messiah, who is convinced that humanity will be saved by scientists? As mentioned earlier, many lay people will react with rejection if climate researchers take up this social position.

The dilemma of adopting a perspective

Are scientists aware of the resentment, touchiness, and possibly even feeling of rejection that can govern a layperson's response? Should they address these emotions?

We must bear in mind that most scientists have not been taught what to do when presenting their research results to a lay audience: Every thesis they put forward should answer questions that are already present in the minds of their audience but do not get asked. However, as scientists, they will (rightly) say that this is not their task. Yet the fact that they do not provide those answers means that they often fail to address the interests and expectations of a lay audience.

The dilemma of the so-called we-identity (Leggewie and Welzer)

How can scientists convey the truth of the statement "We are all in the same boat" to their audience? The imagery of the boat is appropriate because it also explains the goal of environmental research: namely, to have experts provide the information needed to steer the boat past the shoals. But this image is also wrong because it presupposes a helmsman who, like a collective subject, is responsible for using the information he or she is given about shoals out there. But where might you find this helmsman?

It cannot be the scientist because he or she is a specialist in charge of a particular field of research. To represent the whole, one would need to refer to a superior authority, in whose name restrictions and waivers can be enforced. So far, this authority does not exist.

I assume that at least the leading physicists have reflected on the problematic aspects of a scientific tradition based on what I have referred to as the belief in controlling nature. Even if they do not allow their own scientific actions to be guided by the archaic grandiose self, this can still influence the process of public presentation of their research results. After all, these physicists belong to a group of scientists who are contributing to the salvation of mankind, making it understandable if they adopt messianic gestures for their public appearances. However, they do have to deal with the fact that quite a few of their listeners will reject them and say: "I will not let you save me!"

In my opinion, a truly sustainable we-sense or we-identity can only be established if both sides – scientists and laymen alike – adopt the appropriate psychological position in view of their shared concern and responsibility towards the next generations. From this position, they would be psychologically prepared and able to assume responsibility towards their own children.

What is not effective is to appeal to politicians to finally realise that their decisions compromise the lives of the future generations. Such attempts generally meet with failure because they are not directed at where the "symbolic exchange of positions" (Legendre) between the generations is blocked: the strong need of the people in charge now to still be allowed to be children. After all, the unspoken motto of these politicians is "We want to be children, too!", just as future generations are children. This motto is rooted in the psychological deficiency we have already analysed. People, who were starved of affection when they were children, or who were unable to take steps of their own because of an overbearing mother, are shaped by this experience. Unconsciously, they claim the right to "finally properly be children".

If vocational training existed for future politicians, it would need to include a compulsory social year in a retirement home, a kindergarten, or a similar institution. Perhaps this would provide decision-makers with an experience of practical responsibility for people in need of protection and care – an experience from which they would benefit in the context of political decisions affecting future generations.

1.3 Recent psychoanalytical approaches to climate change

In 2013, the eminent British psychoanalyist Sally Weintrobe published an anthology on climate change based on an interdisciplinary conference held at the Institute for Psychoanalysis in London three years earlier. To shed some more light on the important issue of climate change from a psychoanalytical perspective, I will first look at Weintrobe's introduction and own contribution and then at an input by John Keene from the Institute for Psychoanalysis. Their most important insights have implications for political action, especially for communicating climate change issues.

The following topics were discussed at the conference:

- What are the reasons behind the widespread denial of climate change?
- How do we deal with our feelings about climate change?
- Why is it so difficult to acknowledge our dependence on nature?
- Which identifications trigger conflicts?
- Is there a need to grieve before we engage in a positive way with the new conditions which we find within ourselves?

1.3.1 Denial and disavowal according to Weintrobe

Sally Weintrobe (2013) sees psychoanalysis as a theory of the mind. As such it has three focal points. The first focus is on what we experience: our affects, our wishes, our anxieties, and our sense of ourselves and who we are. The second focus is on the mental processes we use to organise our experience and defend ourselves when an experience feels intolerable or causes us too much anxiety. Finally, the third focus is on how we represent our experience of ourselves and of our relationships with figures in the outside world, internally, meaning within the psyche (Weintrobe 2013, p.6).

The concept of psychoanalysis as a theory of the mind helps to identify those elements of psychological defence that are mainly directed against the anxieties arising from climate change. Sally Weintrobe combines research into the psyche with an analysis of speech communication. Indeed, she convincingly distinguishes three forms of denial in relation to climate change:

1   Denialism: Here, we see campaigns which are financed by actors who pursue their own commercial and ideological interests. Their goal is to produce doubts about climate change and its consequences, that is about the trust in climate science itself (ibid., p. 7). Above all, this concerns the prognostic capacity of climate science. According to those campaigns, climate scientists make statements that are "only" 90 per cent certain. As they fall short of 100 per cent certainty, they are branded as unscientific. In fact, the opposite is true: Climate scientists can only square a 90 per cent certainty with their scientific conscience because anything else would be unscientific. This applies in particular to the presumption of a 100 per cent certainty in their forecasts. According to Von Wright (2008), the opponents confuse inductive-probabilistic and deductive-nomological viewpoints. While the latter explains why an event was necessary once the basis was given and the relevant laws were accepted, climate science is a case of the inductive-probabilistic view because it allows for the possibility that an event might actually not have taken place. It merely justifies certain expectations of its occurrence.

2   Negation involves saying that something that is, is not. Negation defends against feelings of anxiety and loss. In psychoanalytical treatment, it plays an important role in feelings of mourning (ibid., p. 7).

3   Disavowal is based on the paradox of knowing and not knowing at the same time. Mere negation does not destroy the truth. Disavowal, however, is a much more serious and intractable form of denial. While negation is a temporary form of defence and can be a first step towards accepting the painful reality of climate change and its consequences, disavowal destroys the truth in a variety of artful ways. It can lead us further and further away from accepting the reality of climate change. The more we systematically avoid reality by making it insignificant or distorting it, the more anxiety builds up unconsciously. This is what makes disavowal so dangerous.

Weintrobe harshly criticises modern science:

> Models [in current research] tend to assume a unitary non-divided self. Nearly all research confines itself to looking only at behaviour that can be measured. The zeitgeist is currently that if it cannot be directly seen and measured, it is not legitimate, and we do not want to know about it.... Within this framework, issues of subjectivity and meaning – not measurable or losing meaning when measured – can be "safely" ignored. Deeper structures are also not measurable. (ibid., p. 13)

Politicians, Weintrobe adds, are equally at fault. Politicians who encourage us to adopt sustainable behaviour are popular. Yet these same politicians want to spare us the emotional difficulties associated with climate change. They do not want to know what climate change means to us, or what we are doing about the anxieties it is causing us. They also do not ask what aspects of reality are so difficult to bear for some people that they use defensive strategies. But real leadership should be based on a deeper understanding that while people are conflicted and want to avoid difficulty, they need to face reality and experience their feelings of anger and grief over what they have lost. That, however, is precisely what modern politics fails to do (ibid., pp. 13–14).

THE TWO MAIN FORMS OF ANXIETY

The model underpinning Weintrobe's understanding of anxiety is based on a psychoanalytical insight into human nature: We are inherently in conflict between different parts of ourselves, and much of this conflict takes place at an unconscious level (ibid., p. 31). The biggest conflict we face in life is between two essential elements of ourselves: a part that embraces reality and a narcissistic part that hates reality. I would like to briefly explain the basic concepts of the models Weintrobe is guided by.

In her approach, Weintrobe follows Melanie Klein (1940), who in turn built on Freud's pioneering work on "Mourning and Melancholy" (1917) to recognise that fear is at the very heart of our effort to confront reality. Klein argued that the narcissistic and the reality-based part of the self both experience anxiety. The narcissistic part is anxious that it will not survive if reality is accepted; the realistic part is afraid that the narcissistic part has caused damage and may imperil its survival. Both anxieties relate to survival. Klein also pointed out that for the part of the self that loves reality to be more powerful than the part that hates reality, emotional support is needed to bear anxiety and also to endure difficult feelings like guilt, shame, and loss.

The nature of these two types of anxieties can be illustrated by a conversation between a friend of Klein's and her three-year-old granddaughter Katie. Katie was facing a serious change at home with the arrival of a new baby. "Grandma", Katie said, "I've decided to marry Daddy and we are going to have lots and lots of babies". "I see", said the friend, "but what about Mummy and new baby Gemma?" "Oh, that's alright. They are only dwarfs", the child said (ibid., p. 34).

Katie's omnipotent phantasy allows her to reduce her anxiety over having to share her parents with the new baby. The part of herself that used to believe that she was the adored and special centre of the family – will it survive? In response, Katie found a magical solution: She now is a "big lady" and concludes a powerful couple's alliance with her daddy. Her feeling of being small is projected onto Mummy and the new baby. But new anxieties emerge – for example, what will Mummy do about all of this?

PARANOID-SCHIZOID ANXIETY AND DEPRESSIVE ANXIETY

According to Klein, the narcissistic part of the self has characteristic defence mechanisms: mental splitting, idealisation, and projection. Klein calls the anxieties and defences which relate to the narcissistic part of the self "paranoid-schizoid" – schizoid, because Katie uses mental splitting to reduce her anxiety. This is different from the anxiety experienced by that part of the self which loves reality: According to Klein's characterization, that anxiety is depressive, not in a clinical sense, but because it is loaded with sadness, guilt, and shame. It is also associated with the anxiety that the narcissistic part has caused harm. For this part of the self, there is more love, concern, and realism (ibid., p. 35).

Having these conflicting anxieties is entirely normal, Klein says. Working them through begins in early childhood and continues throughout life. We also need emotional support to make the self that loves reality more powerful than the self that hates it. Katie is loved by the adults in her life who understand her anxieties and desires. These adults intuitively understand what is behind her defence mechanisms.

As adults we often think and feel the same way as Katie without realising it. The only thing that clearly distinguishes us from her is that as adults, we are better at concealing our own irrationality. Sally Weintrobe does not distinguish between children, about whose behaviour in the family she was informed, and children who are her patients. In particular, she considers the depressive position which is associated with disavowal to be a result of the child's psychologically problematic development independently of whether that child has the status of a patient.

COMMON DEFENCES AGAINST ANXIETY

Weintrobe distinguishes three quick fixes, which are irrational and can also occur together to try to reduce anxiety (ibid., p. 36).

1   Social groups as well as individuals can feel magically large and powerful.
2   The feeling of being powerless and unloved can be projected onto others. Katie projects this feeling onto her mother and the new baby.

3   Denial is a commonly used psychological defence. There are, generally speaking, two different sorts. Negation is a first step on the way to mourning illusions and acknowledging reality. Disavowal, in contrast, can become delusional. With disavowal, irrationality can become predominant and escalate.

In a normal development, mourning begins with negation, then goes to anger and finally to grief and the acceptance of the loss. Negation helps us to process the initial shock of loss when it is too much to bear (ibid., p. 37).

To be able to mourn, we vitally need the presence of supporting figures who do not judge us too harshly, who are warm in their feelings for us, and who can forgive us and accept our human frailty. These figures are not just the actual people in our lives – parents, teachers, and superiors – but also the figures who are part of the world of relationships that we represent in our internal worlds and carry with us, mostly in unconscious forms. The degree of support from these internalised figures influences how much we are able to mourn and face reality.

Thinking is not just having an intellectual and rational understanding of a reality that causes us pain and anxiety; it is the reality felt and owned by the self – not an activity, but a process involving mourning and facing the anxieties that come with inner change

DISAVOWAL AS NON-RECOGNITION OF REALITY

Disavowal involves radical splitting and a range of strategies that ensure that reality can be seen and not seen at one and the same time. Disavowal is often described as turning a blind eye, but this description does not go far enough in distinguishing disavowal from negation. There are two key differences: First, with disavowal, our more wish-fulfilling narcissistic part may have come under the sway of the more entrenched arrogant attitude that can exert a powerful hold on the psyche. Second, disavowal can be part of a more organised and enduring defensive structure, whereas negation is typically a more transitional defence against anxiety (ibid., p. 38).

Disavowal is part of a pathological organisation. Disavowal aims to block mourning at the stage before sadness, grieving, and reconciliation, and in this sense may be seen as a form of arrested, failed mourning or melancholia, as Freud (1917) described it (ibid., p. 39).

Triumph is an important part of disavowal. The arrogant, omnipotent part of the self feels very clever for being able to "solve" painful problems so instantly. The delusion that nothing is lost because loss itself has no meaning is perhaps the ultimate triumph.

While negation denies the truth, it does not distort its shape so much. Disavowal, however, can result in confusion and an inability to think with a sense of proportion. The splitting that occurs with disavowal also leads to a breakdown of proportionality in thinking. Anxiety is minimised, guilt and shame – emotions that also cause us great anxiety – are minimised, and all this is achieved through omnipotent thinking.

ANXIETIES ABOUT CLIMATE CHANGE

When investigating survival anxieties about climate change, Weintrobe differentiates between anxieties that are experienced through the reality-based part and those that are shaped by the narcissistic part of the self. Those anxieties that stem from the denial of climate change through disavowal are becoming increasingly prevalent.

First, let us look at the depressive anxieties regarding climate change which are shaped by the reality-based part of our selves. We are confronted with losing the Earth as a dependable bedrock which makes life possible for us and our children. More specifically, we are facing the results of a climate tipped into instability. The terrible anxieties we face about this are akin to the small child's anxieties of losing the mother he or she utterly depends on (ibid., p. 42).

When we are small, fears about losing the mother are exacerbated by fears that our greedy demands on her have damaged her. We can tend to see and treat her as an ideal "breast-and-toilet" mother, there endlessly to supply our needs and demands and to absorb our waste.[5] Climate damage can also revive our earlier childhood fears of damaging the mother, for instance through greed.

We should now consider the anxieties regarding climate change which are shaped by the narcissistic part of our selves. In current consumerist societies, we are actively encouraged to express our sense of identity through our material possessions. Losing these can therefore mean losing our sense of identity. Weintrobe believes that what we dread giving up is not so particular material possessions or particular ways of life, but our way of seeing ourselves as special, and as entitled, not only to our possessions but also to our "quick fixes" of the problems of reality. This underlying attitude, just one side of human nature, is strongly ingrained in current Western societies. We know that in giving up an unsustainable consumer lifestyle, we are threatening the identity of this part of ourselves, one we are mostly not aware of but will fight tooth and nail to protect (ibid., p. 43).

A CULTURE OF DISAVOWAL OF CLIMATE CHANGE

Currently, there are signs that we are in the grip of disavowal when it comes to climate change, with all its effects of distortion of the truth. This means that we are dealing with a particularly serious and thorny form of denial.

If we look at the predisposing factors to disavowal, we can see that they fit current realities about climate change very well (ibid., p. 44):

1   The reality has become too obvious to be simply denied with negation.
2   There is anxiety that the damage is already too great to repair.
3   There is felt to be not enough support and help to bear the anxiety and suffering that knowledge of reality brings.

Clearly, climate change is progressing, and its effects are becoming ever more visible. But unless greater support for facing reality is given, and unless group identification with a stance of arrogant entitlement is challenged to a greater extent, we can expect disavowal to be the prevalent defence against the "too-much-ness" of the reality. Inaction on climate change therefore does not only lead to soaring levels of CO_2 emissions. It may lead to spiralling disavowal.

From her analysis, Weintrobe draws three main conclusions:

1   Avoiding the subject of anxiety does not make people's anxieties about climate change go away. The defences used to minimise anxieties drive them underground, where they are not worked through and can escalate.
2   People need genuine emotional support to bear their anxieties, and this is particularly the case when the defences used to minimise them involve disavowal.
3   It is important for people to bear their anxieties, because when they do not, their thinking deteriorates and irrationality, lack of proportionality, hatred, and narcissism are more likely to prevail (ibid., p. 46).

SOME IMPLICATIONS FOR POLICY

In fact, according to Weintrobe, people need ordinary, real, un-idealised leaders to help them to face and engage with very difficult realities about climate change. It is vital to come to understand our own anxieties about climate change as best as we can before seeking to engage with others about it. If we do not, we are in danger of projecting our anxieties onto the people we want to engage, passing them on, as it were. This makes it more difficult for people to think in a rational way. Unwitting projection of this kind may have been a part of some of the early, "catastrophising", stridently doom-laden communications about climate change (ibid., p. 45).

It is very important that we understand as much as possible how disavowal works in our culture in order to work collectively to resist it. Anxiety, Weintrobe concludes, is the biggest psychic barrier to facing the reality of anthropogenic global warming.

1.3.2 John Keene's views about Mother Earth

In his contribution to Weintrobe's book, Keene (2013) argues that we are transferring a problematic image of the mother to the Earth. He believes we are treating the Earth as a "breast and toilet mother" – as something that only exists to cater to our needs and absorb our waste. Keene is deeply convinced that essential psychoanalytic categories need clarification of their conceptual foundation to scientifically identify and distinguish their scope from other scientific approaches.

Public discourse is currently dominated by the tradition of the Enlightenment and thus by rational thinking. Therefore, we are always surprised to realise that this way of thinking does not always prevail. This is precisely where the categories of psychoanalysis can help us if their scope is defined correctly.

Environmental research, Keene says, is not of much help where climate change is concerned. When relating to the environment, our ancestors only knew "friend or foe" and the "now" (Keene 2013, p. 145). From the psychoanalytical point of view, developmental theories are more interesting:

> The feeding situation provides a model based on bodily experience for how we take in and form ideas about the physical world.... Like the mother, the Earth – or so aptly, 'Mother Earth' – is experienced as utterly enormous in relation to our individual activities and therefore often believed to be quite immune to our puny demands on her. (ibid., p. 146)

In earliest infancy, maternal provision for urgent needs and a holding environment is taken for granted until it lapses. Keene recognizes the "environment mother" as contributing to a sense of the world as sustaining and there for us to use without undue concern. We can see her as the bountiful and limitless "breast mother" that we can forever take for granted. The author points out that these fantasies may be based on the firm belief that natural resources, for example particular fish, are bountiful and need no protection.

Ordinary children, Keene says have to deal with varying balances of good and bad experiences in a state of maximum psychological vulnerability. The earliest way of managing this is for the infant to regard the good experiences as coming from a wholly good person, and the bad experiences as coming from someone who is the source of pain and frustration. This separation and splitting of good and bad helps to avoid the anxiety that the good mother will be destroyed by the bad mother or by the infant's own needs or demands.

In the child's imagination, the anxiety of evacuating is also difficult to deal with. This happens in the same way that the infant evacuates its waste: The mother takes away the little child's "poos" and "wees". A "good-enough mother" (Winnicott) can detoxify this waste by identifying with the child's anxieties and soothing it. The author convincingly states: "I believe that these repeated encounters contribute to the complementary belief that the planet is an unlimited 'toilet-mother', capable of absorbing our toxic products to infinity" (ibid., p 146). Thus, the perception of pollution is mediated through familiar evolved cues of smell and appearance. Attitudes towards the environment are further complicated by old attitudes to the mother's body.

BION AND THE GROUP PERSPECTIVE

Testing reality is difficult because people prefer to keep to ideology and to hunt for culprits. Due to the author's style, the following passages are somewhat difficult to understand. Keen is inspired by Freud to apply categories of psychoanalysis to phenomena outside the therapeutic discourse. This is how he also incorporates his own experiences which cannot come from Freud. The author does the same with the relevant studies presented by the British psychoanalyst Wilfred Bion, who concentrated on group situations (Bion 1961ff.). Nevertheless, I will briefly explain Bion's perspective on groups because we can make use of them regarding in climate change.

Joined-up thinking, according to Bion, is largely aversive and difficult to achieve. It is emotionally much easier to live in a world of simple certainties and the voyeuristic pleasures of scandals and personal triumph or weakness. This splitting into ideally good and bad persecutory figures is alluring because the illusory clarity it promises is much prized. This has become visible for example in the scandal about inaccurate descriptions of glacier melt. Splitting promotes persecution mania, and conspiracy theories can be very stable.

Based on Bion's perspective on group work, Keene points to some additional observations and experiences which I will relate here.

Capable and sophisticated leaderships, groups, and organisations unconsciously collaborate to produce a stable configuration, which Bion called "basic assumption activity". The basic unconscious premise is that the group should be emotionally absorbing, but nothing really novel should take place. Another basic assumption, according to Bion, is organised around the issue of dependence and can be seductive for both leader and followers. Here, all moral and practical responsibility is invested in the leader, who feels admired and powerful. In contrast, the followers feel like dependent children (ibid., p. 149)

Political parties in England, the author says, find it very difficult to break free of these assumptions and address the electorate. This is compounded by the media's need for dramatisation and for scapegoats.

CULTURE AND ENTITLEMENT

"The cultural expectations that surround us are the medium in which our individual super-egos swim and develop", Keene says (ibid., p. 151). This is a valuable insight.

Our culture is the ego relationship, in which the individual only makes a conscious use of his or her individual opportunities. This culture has now become the culture of the world. By the third decade of the century, Keene continues, CO_2 levels in the atmosphere may be reaching levels impossible to reverse because the actions needed to limit climate change have an unequal distribution of costs and benefits. While climate change affects all major economic systems and there is a general and well-defined threat, the effects of global warming are unevenly distributed. A consensus therefore continues to be unlikely.

Based on psychoanalytical categories and their links to our culture as well as his own experience, Keene states: "As a result of our successful mastery of so much of nature, we come to believe that life should be trouble-free, and we have poor means of integrating tragedy into our lives. We split tragedy off into characters in films and television dramas and into people 'not like us'" (ibid., p. 154).

SOME POLICY RECOMMENDATIONS

John Keene refers to recommendations for countering the sense of power-lessness that regularly affects members of the professions, company boars, and members of parliament. One suggestion is to establish a group of advisors similar to the one set up by John F. Kennedy during the Cuban crisis. At the time, Kennedy insisted that his advisors should regularly meet without him to avoid undue conscious and unconscious pressure on them to say what they thought he wanted to hear.

This is based on the idea that gaps between the interests of the people and the interests of the states should be filled in a meaningful way. If properly composed, such an adviser group would represent both the idealism of youth and an awareness of the mortality of the older generations. This idea evokes the "specialist work group" described by Freud and Bion (Bion, 1961).

Melanie Klein (1959) emphasised how much influence some people – even children – have on their environment through integrity, seriousness, and strength of character. As Keene says: "A reconsideration of what is needed for a good and sustainable life on the planet depends on social and national policies that foster such qualities and reinstate the values and practices that provide security for the development of loving relationships and creativity and respect for the planetary environment" (ibid., p. 157).

1.3.3 Next steps

Investigating climate change from a psychological and psychoanalytical point of view is a relatively new avenue of research. The London conference which was summarised in Sally Weintrobe's book provides an insight into different perspectives from which attitudes towards climate change can be analysed. This should help politicians, entrepreneurs, NGO, and scientists to understand that what they need to discuss is not only about global warming, environmental protection activities, and CO_2 pricing, but also about human beings.

It is human beings who act and react – often according to unconscious patterns – to climate change. And if the human factor is ignored in these debates, as it has been until now, many of the problems having to do with climate change will not be solved. Yet much remains to be done to understand the psycho-analytical aspects, and I do hope for further research in this field.

Notes

1 In this respect, the work of Leggewie and Welzer differs dramatically from Theodore Roszak's *Ökopsychologie* (1994). The latter looks at Sigmund Freud's psychoanalysis in detail. Yet it presents the most important results of Freud's research in a way that is not very illuminating.
2 I base this on experiences made during the many conversations I had with experts. The Fridays for Future movement and its claims are important, of course, but will not be discussed here.
3 Title translated into English by the author
4 Due to the COVID-19 pandemic, public debt is ballooning again, leaving the younger generation with an even heavier burden.
5 For this point, Weintrobe refers to Keene's analysis, which I will explain in Section 1.3.2.

Chapter 4

Other contemporary cultural phenomena and their connection to the unconscious

I Contemporary problems of leadership in social organisations

People working in social organisations (corporations, radio or television stations, banks, political parties, public administration, educational institutions, etc.) will – consciously or unconsciously – transfer certain patterns of emotional relationships to the organisation and their work colleagues. They can derive such patterns from their inner image of an idealised parental figure, especially if they have been working in the respective organisation for some time.[1] This idealised parental figure, combined with the ego-ideal of the employees, can have maternal traits.[2] With this transfer of emotional influence to the social organisation, the culture of the organisation tends to change.[3]

Google founder Larry Page has emphasised that employees feel part of the company and that the company is like a family to them. His family image has apparently been shaped by the mother, because Google offices look "like playgrounds and children's rooms with colourful swings, bean bags and air rolls" (DIE ZEIT, 03.04.2014). The article continues:

> Both principles [i.e. the so-called daddy principle as well as the so-called mummy principle] create an underage employee who remains in an infantile role and, like any spoiled child, develops unfulfillable expectations vis-à-vis his superiors and colleagues. As if the job was supposed to satisfy needs that people cannot satisfy in their private lives.

I will explain later why I find this interpretation too simple.

In large organisations, leadership can be provided by a direct superior. It is also possible for a team to take over the leadership. After all, the group of employees represents the valid norms and values, or more precisely, they can behave as if they did.

I will use two examples of guiding principles of organisational culture to explore the values and norms that are propagated as the first aspect of my investigation. Using the same empirical material, I will then focus on a second

DOI: 10.4324/9780429345449-4

aspect: Do these guidelines for organisational culture also provide indications of the disappearance of the traditional paternal authority? This disappearance, which many psychoanalytical authors have written about, should be detectable in the guidelines of an organisational culture.

I will then evaluate the results of a survey of leadership experts conducted in 2013: What challenges, according to the survey, will tomorrow's leaders have to face?

Experts from across the world took part in this survey, but their answers to these questions mainly document their bafflement. In my opinion, this reveals how little these experts, most of whom come from the business world, are aware of the particular narcissistic problems of our time.

Finally, I will discuss the model "Successful Management of Instability and Stability" developed by Peter Kruse (2004).

1.1 Aspects of the family pattern in two guidelines of organisational culture

As far as the following investigation is concerned, we cannot assume a re-actualisation of childhood relationship patterns as in the case of bullying. Guidelines for an organisational culture were not developed in any such process. Nevertheless, an unconscious meaning can be detected here, too. In this case, it will be about the first level of meaning that refers to the current psychological conflict situation of the people who are connected by a common organisational culture.

What is the nature of this new family pattern increasingly evident in the relationship of employees to their company and their colleagues, which is transforming and partly replacing the traditional pattern? In this respect, it is certainly possible to assume diverse and sometimes different emotional patterns. As far as the typical narcissistic problems of emotional development are concerned, I will refer here primarily to Kohut (1973).

Let me briefly outline the three basic narcissistic needs that Kohut distinguishes. All three needs can be satisfied in their own particular way by belonging to a social organisation:

- The need for reflection (which is initially satisfied by the glint in the mother's eye): This need can be satisfied primarily through performance appraisals by the direct supervisor, which mirror the professional self-respect of the employee. This helps employees to maintain their self-esteem with regard to their work performance.
- The need for idealisation (initially with regard to the parental figures): The respective social organisation or a direct superior can be the point of reference for this idealisation. The possible satisfaction of this narcissistic need is self-soothing and serves to productively handle aggressive and sexual emotions.

- The need to belonging and be equal: Here, the focus is on the working group, in which a sense of community can develop.

The aim of mobbing (in phases 2 and 3 of the process), according to my interpretation, is to completely deprive the victim of satisfaction through self-objects at the workplace, thereby pushing him or her out into the void. This is not contradicted by the fact that in our culture, full satisfaction of these narcissistic needs in social organisations seems to be rare. At least in the Western industrialised countries, a general dissatisfaction with work is clearly evident. In an international survey (2014) on the job satisfaction of employees in salaried employment, the industrialised countries (France, Spain, and Japan) rank at the bottom of the list, with Germany just below the international average.[4] The survey was conducted by the international personnel consultancy Kienbaum, which surveyed 7,400 employees in 20 countries.

There are various reasons for this dissatisfaction at work. From a depth-psychological point of view, it certainly plays a role whether the three different narcissistic needs can be satisfied at work.

Guidelines of corporate culture (as a specific case of an organisational culture) can give us an indication of the narcissistic needs that employees long to have satisfied. In this respect, the guidelines of corporate culture always correspond to wish lists of narcissistic needs in a social organisation that are not being well fulfilled.

To illustrate the theoretical background to my question, I would like to go back to Kohut's concept of self-objects.

According to his concept, an infant experiences its caregivers in such a way that they perform functions which awaken and positively influence the child's sense of self. Like the air we breathe, they are vital throughout our lives to bolster our self-confidence. According to Kohut, the needs for self-objective relationships are normal throughout life. At the time of publication in the 1970s, this was a revolutionary view within psychoanalysis because Kohut did not regard the psychological dependence of a person needing self-objective relationships as an adult as a disorder. Such self-object functions can also be performed by a company or social organisation.

In mobbing, according to my interpretation, it is the unconscious which eventually takes over control over the harassments. This is possible because the participants are fixated on the early narcissistic relationship problem with their primary reference person, that is it is an issue that they never got over, not even as adults. That which had to be warded off emotionally is now being re-actualised.

We cannot consider this as a given in the context of the guidelines of an organisational culture. After all, these guidelines did not come into existence the same way. We can, however, ask whether we can detect a contradictory mental structure. According to Kohut's findings, the emotional development of childhood narcissism culminates in the ego–ideal and in a self that vividly enjoys its creative power. He understands this to be the result of a "trans-forming internalisation" of narcissistic configurations. The crucial point is that in the results of this transformation, parts of the old, unlimited narcissism can also survive. These are the idealised parental imago and the grandiose self. This is exactly what I am assuming in the following: That a transformative inter-nalisation of the corresponding narcissistic configurations of early childhood is often difficult today. If that is the case, we should expect the psychological defence of repression through alterity and the not-knowing.

It is obvious that there will also be individual variations. They are a con-sequence of this transformation which – I believe – also belongs to the types of the psychic unconscious that I have listed above (cf. Chapter 1, Section 1).

In extreme cases, a company or social organisation functions as an external self-object and assumes all the functions that the subject could otherwise have developed for him- or herself, if a transforming internalisation of narcissistic configurations had occurred. These are mainly the functions of self-soothing and self-comfort. In extreme cases, however, the subject will be completely dependent on the respective company and permanent employment with it to maintain his or her self-esteem.

Organisational culture therefore represents a kind of hybrid formation. According to the common understanding, guidelines of an organisational culture are documents that reflect the sense of belonging together as a group. This is conveyed by the norms and values applying to a social organisation, of which one is proud. I share this view, but ask the question whether – and if so, how – parts of the narcissistic configurations of childhood have been preserved alongside this sense of belonging. As far as the group in question and its lea-dership is concerned, this part corresponds to the grandiose self; as far as the social organisation as a whole is concerned, it is contained in an ego–ideal. In this part, an idealised parental figure is preserved. According to Kohut, it can have predominantly paternal traits. But I think it is more plausible for it to show maternal traits.

The other aspect concerns the disappearance of paternal authority and possibly even the weakening of triangulation, that is the awareness of a third party. This is the psychological consequence of the fact that the traumatic shock caused by the primary caregiver tends to be too great in early childhood to allow the transforming internalisation to be completed. The close con-nection to the "narcissistic milieu" of the mother (Kohut) would then be preserved.

The two aspects of the family pattern mentioned here, which can take effect in a company, refer to the action imprint of the unconscious. As a result, the question arises how we can recognise this action imprint in different versions of a modern organisational culture. As far as the first level of meaning is concerned, which refers to the current psychological conflict situation of people who are connected by a common organisational culture, an answer should be possible. It will be much more difficult to investigate phenomena on the second level of meaning, that is to interpret peculiarities of the guidelines of organisational culture with regard to psychological problems of early childhood.

I would like to emphasise once again that in this context, I can only make trend statements. I am leaving out many other aspects of such a family pattern, which can unconsciously take effect in a company (more generally: In a social organisation).

Leadership based on the ego-ideal or the grandiose self

If this idealised parental figure actually continues to exist in an ego-ideal with maternal traits, we can speak of a maternalistic leadership in a social organisation. This is different from Freud's (1921c) explanation of the power of leaders over "great masses". Freud uses the example of army commanders and high dignitaries of the church who were put in the place of the ego-ideal by their followers, so that they could also identify with each other.

Under today's conditions, I consider it plausible that the ego-ideal, which has the traits of an idealised mother, is present in some organisations. It tends to outweigh the traditional paternalistic ego-ideal and quite possibly has taken its place. The idealised good mother is seen to be caring, protective, and a guarantor of life. These are all qualities that can be identified (unconsciously) with a social organisation.

It is an obvious next step to attribute the rigid application of political correctness to this maternalistic leadership organisation. What some critics of political correctness (P.C.) have pointed out – the presumptuousness of self-appointed guardians of virtue who judge cases of incorrectness with absolute certainty and considerable aggressiveness – can then be understood as a way of exercising power. However, a psychoanalytical interpretation should also include the possible unconscious motives which drive the political opponents of political correctness. Ariane Manske (2002) has analysed the discussion about P.C. in the United States, where this movement originally emerged. She convincingly demonstrated how conservatives are using this discussion to discredit the goals of protecting minorities and recognising differences.

Many of the functions that a company (more generally: A social organisation) can perform for its employees support the picture outlined above. The social organisation allows employees to earn a living, supports their medical care, organises training, ensures by means of the hierarchy that everyone knows exactly where they stand in their professional career, and relies on everyone to do their job as a contribution to the whole. Transferred to a social organisation, these qualities create a feeling of security, safety, and possibly pride through belonging to the company. Correspondingly, colleagues can be emotionally connected to each other as they all have a similar image of this ego-ideal and identify with each other through it.

The group standards and performance requirements at the workplace do not contradict this phantasm. On the contrary, they must be fulfilled if this psychological foundation of the group formation at work is to be realised.

It is also possible that leadership by a team, by a peer group[5], makes use of what Kohut calls the grandiose self of early childhood. It can be the hidden psychological part behind the proud and lofty feeling of belonging to group. It is based on feelings of efficiency, pride, and the emphasis on equality, which it can transform or otherwise connect to.

Finally, it is also possible that an ego-ideal is shaped by the metamorphosis of the traditional father image. As the group of "fathers" has (in a psychological sense) become increasingly implausible, society has transformed "fathers" into "experts", who do not betray any signs of their descent from the father image. Nevertheless, they can exhibit certain characteristics and functions that belong to the traditional image of the father – but in a specialised way. Dependent on the social group and strata, different characteristics will apply, for instance, for managers, sports stars, coaches, and so on. As a result, we can distinguish four different types of leadership in a social organisation:

- Paternalistic leadership (the traditional father image)
- Maternalistic leadership (the ego-ideal with maternal traits)
- By the peer group (the team as a grandiose self)
- By an expert (as a result of the metamorphosis of the traditional father image)

Let us take a closer look at two concrete examples. As my first example of a modern corporate culture, I will use the value matrix according to Josef Wieland (2004):

Performance values	Communication values
• Benefits	• Attention
• Competence	• Being part of it
• Readiness to perform	• Openness
• Flexibility	• Transparency
• Creativity	• Understanding
• Willingness to innovate	• Risk tolerance
	• Quality
Cooperation values	**Moral values**
• Loyalty	• Integrity
• Team spirit	• Fairness
• Ability to handle conflict	• Honesty
• Openness	• Contractual loyalty
• Communicative attitude	• Responsibility

The mission statement of the regional public broadcaster WDR can serve as the second concrete example:[6]

1 Mission and claim: Our programmes are for everyone – independent, distinctive, and valuable

2   Programme and audience: We broadcast to reach people
3   Quality and edge: Quality moves us forward
4   Creativity and change: We live by courageous ideas
5   Community and cooperation: WDR, that's all of us
6   Role model and leadership: Responsible leadership deserves trust
7   Motivation and performance: We want success
8   Communication and transparency: Everybody knows what is going on
9   Responsibility and profitability: Every cent is transparent
10 Flexibility and rules: We are a living company – rules support our goals

I will now examine the two guiding principles in the light of the two questions mentioned above:

1   Which values and norms are propagated by the respective organisation?
2   Do these guidelines give us an indication of the disappearance of the traditional paternal authority?

First of all, it should be noted that these two models of an organisational culture do not contain values which suggest that narcissistic needs are to be met here. Nor do they point to the existence of parts of an early childhood narcissistic configuration (in the sense of Kohut). "Care", "safety", and "security" do not appear as values at all; nor do "community spirit" or "pride".

"Performance" is the only such value that can be found in the guidelines: Under point 7 for the WDR, and under "readiness to perform" in the matrix of values. Satisfying the unspecified narcissistic needs of a particular organisational culture is apparently taken for granted to such an extent that it does not even seem necessary to name them. I suspect that they are beyond the reflection of those involved.

The tendency for the paternal principle of authority to disappear

Let us now look at the two examples of guidelines of an organisational culture from the second point of view. Here, I propose to examine the emotional pattern of the family which underlies the actions of people working in the organisation.

According to my interpretation, values that can be considered "modern", "contemporary", and so forth reflect the paternal principle of authority in the matrix of values. These include the values "creativity" and "willingness to innovate". From the point of view of ontogenetic development, these abilities are rooted in the early relationship with the mother. Winnicott (1973) has proposed a psychoanalytical explanation of their psychological origin in this respect.

However, we need to add an important caveat here. As "tradition" does not appear as a value in this matrix, the creation of something new for the sake of the new can also be understood as "creativity". Obviously, this matrix of values does not contain any connection to tradition. Yet one would need to address tradition in order to be able to determine the new as something different from it. This connection to tradition is replaced in both examples by a focus on the here and now. Linked to this, there is no longer any hint of the history that the corporate culture has gone through and which used to be repeatedly referred to in relevant works (cf. Schreyögg & Steinmann, 1990).

Similarly, the matrix of values lacks role models that can provide orientation, especially for young employees. The WDR mission statement appears to be different, but the question arises, however, whether "Role model and leadership" may actually refer to the type of leadership that I call leadership by a peer group. There, the person in the leadership position would be one among equals, albeit more prominent.

The cooperation values "team spirit", "openness", and "communication orientation" in the value matrix are also interesting. They emphasise how important the relationship with colleagues working together as equals has become. The type of leadership traditionally associated with the position of authority, which dictates action from the top-down through instructions and guidelines, receives no mention here. Neither does the complementary value of "willingness to follow".

However, in the case of the WDR guidelines, one question arises: How are decisions made about which television or radio contribution will be broadcast and which will not? With the disappearance of faith in the father, the Oedipal function of reference, which is so important, has apparently also disappeared. This concerns distinction, selection, and separation.

In case of conflict, this function would provide orientation by asking in whose name the decision about a programme should be taken. What do the WDR guidelines tell us about the criteria for this choice? Interestingly, the audience, that is the third party, whose reality is to be seen and taken into account, remains quite abstract. It is "the people" who are to be reached. This mission statement says nothing about their special interests, expectations, or the respective affiliation to age and educational groups, and so forth.

A pattern of perception of inside and outside seems to be effective here, because we learn a lot about the criteria that are supposed to exist on the inside as values, but we learn nothing concrete about the outside.

The internal values are named in the first four points: Programmes should be independent, distinctive, and valuable; people should be reached; quality and edge should be maintained (the latter probably refers to a comparison with the programmes of other broadcasters); and "courageous ideas" are in demand. Taken together, this is the trademark (or qualification profile) of a product that is offered on the market.

But how to decide what this market wants? The mission statement does not provide any information on this point. We can assume that the decision about what will be broadcast – and what will not – will be taken on a case-by-case basis by the group. Thus, these guidelines give us an indication that the (paternal) functions of distinguishing, selecting, and separating, which I see primarily in relation to conflict resolution, probably still apply in some way. But they no longer have a fixed, external point of reference in the sense of a higher instance to which they are directed.

The matrix of values does not refer to any individuality of employees which a social organisation might consider important to promote as a value. It appears that critical faculties are neither esteemed in the value matrix nor in the WDR mission statement. This would presuppose a position of the third party which would provide a perspective from outside the system. The traditional principle of authority, whose gradual replacement by the efficiency principle Mendel pointed out (cf. G. Mendel 1969), is thus not simply absent but gets systematically excluded from both the value matrix and the WDR mission statement. In both examples, the institutionalised infantilisation associated with the traditional principle of authority seems to have been replaced by an infantilisation of a different kind – namely, one which is specific to the early mother relationship. Tutelage has only found a new form here.

The question is whether this reflects a tendency of organisational culture in general, which would amount to a new form of the totalitarian. Using the WDR model as an example, we can – according to my interpretation – conclude that this image with its concentration on the inside, the exclusion of the capacity for criticism, and the disregard for tradition unconsciously suits the omnipotence phantasm of the new media.

Dangers of the maternal role model

A new form of totalitarianism is only one of the possible dangers that I associate with an organisational culture based on maternalistic leadership. The changes in the emotional basis of a social organisation have psychological and social consequences which the public is not yet aware of. The image of the strong, idealised mother is a model that can be reflected in the organisational culture.

A comparison with the paternalistic style of leadership shows the kind of power that the model of a mother wields. A paternalistic manager will directly confront the employee and state to which extent his or her work performance and/or social behaviour does not meet the standards of the company. The power that such a manager exercises is defined by the position that he or she occupies. It is through this position that he or she has assumed responsibilities, for example for ensuring that the work process runs productively.

However, the destructive conflict strategy of mobbing, which we examined earlier, avoids direct confrontation. And its aim is not to make the employee concerned see reason – it seeks to make him disappear, even if it means that person's social death. We have seen how mercilessly a group of employees can deal with the victim of their mobbing.

1.2 The leadership models of the global agenda (2012): Unacknowledged helplessness

Over a six-month period, a consultative assembly of experts discussed and developed new leadership models for business, universities, and NGOs and in sports. All the contributors are highly respected management experts, with a particular focus on human resources, psychology, and the leadership of large social organisations. They have both academic merits and practical experience in the management of organisations and the development of leadership training programs.

Their theses list manifold new challenges for leaders. Some are economic, ecological, demographic, or technological; others refer – mostly implicitly – to the prerequisites traditionally considered necessary for leadership. It is acknowledged (or assumed) that these are now absent.

In the following, I will show that the authors' concrete proposals on dealing productively with these new challenges are completely unrealistic. They document an unacknowledged helplessness.

Neither role model nor model of authority

Among the authors, especially Charlene Li (USA) sketches a picture of modern leadership which is no longer based on any personal or generally accepted role model. It cannot lay claim to a generally effective model of authority which would not only include social status (as the "superior") but also respect long-standing professional experience from which a manager can derive his or her authority. The author assumes (as do other contributors) that this source of authority has become obsolete as a result of the accelerated general change. Empirical knowledge is quickly considered outdated and thus proves to be inefficient.

The authors also explain what this means for the social relationship between the leaders and those who are being led: Leaders must now work to gather followers, and they must do this all the time.

> When CEO Marc Benioff gathers his top 300 leaders for their yearly strategy retreat, he also invites the top 25 Chatter users in the company (those with the most followers) to join as well. They even have a name – The Chatterati – and are given prime seats at the meeting. The Chatterati are individual contributors with no budget or people to manage. They are recognised as not only leaders but are also so crucial to the future success of Salesforce.com that they are invited to sit at the same table as the top official leaders of the organisation. When asked how much he valued the Chatterati – and how far he would expand their influence – he responded: "You can imagine the Chatterati creating as much value as an SVP in the organisation by sharing their institutional knowledge and expertise ... and

we should look at compensation structures with that in mind." For at least this chief executive officer, the definition of leadership boils down to what kind outcomes and values you can create because of your followership. (Li, 2012, pp. 48–49)

What is needed, therefore, is continuous work on a relationship that is aligned on the efficiency principle. Such a manager cannot have an emotional relationship with his employees since feelings are not functional. Yet working on the relationship with employees is functional: It serves to ensure that the employees follow the manager. Since this can no longer be achieved by status and personal professional experience – this is the implicit assumption – a leader needs to work on the relationship to his potential followers through his or her own efforts.

It is remarkable that none of the contributors mention the management task of "containment" (Bion, 1990). They appear to believe that there will no longer be any groups in a social organisation whose internal conflicts the leader may have to take on and resolve within himself.

In addition, there is the following contradiction: The leader must adapt to the wishes and personal expectations of his or her followers, which are, however, changeable. On the one hand, the leadership role becomes a mere function of the followers' wishes. On the other hand, as the employees also want to be led, they make themselves dependent on the leader. Is this a new kind of leadership: Leadership without leadership?

No more boundaries between public and private

Managers learn how to behave in a vulnerable and "human" manner vis-à-vis a media-driven public which subjects them to harsh attacks. An authenticity is suggested that is actually the dressing-up of personal feelings for public presentation.

Illouz (2009) has pointed out the contradictory identity of modern leaders: On the one hand, they must appear open and authentic to everyone, but on the other hand, they are unassailable because they do not commit themselves emotionally.

I take this important point about the lack of commitment of modern leaders mainly from the contribution of Max Levchin (Vice President, Engineering, Google, USA). He explains this point:

At their scariest, Twitter, Facebook and their international equivalents offer no more than a few moments between a single false communication uttered in the most private of settings and the public dissection and summary judgment that inevitably follows. At their best, a powerful single-sentence notion repeated by the few in the morning is driving a veritable crowd (constructive or otherwise) frenzy by evening. These extremes highlight the velocity of information dissemination and the level of public scrutiny a leader should expect as the boundary between their private and public personas fades away…. Social media offer leaders the chance to communicate from a platform where their constituents are effectively their peers. It is an opportunity to pull back the curtain, to connect with their audiences directly, and to be human, emotional, and vulnerable. It is a chance for leaders to earn the trust of their charges by being and communicating among them. (Levchin, 2012, pp. 12–13)

This point – the disappearance of the boundary between the private and public persona of a leader – runs like a red thread through many contributions to the new Global Agenda leadership model.

Even the personal development of the psyche must adapt to the demands of the new social context of leadership. Nowhere is it mentioned that the disappearance of the boundary between public and private implies that the differences in the social positions and functions will also disappear. In fact, both continue to exist both within the company and in relation to customers or clients. It also remains unclear how a new manager is supposed to acquire a confident demeanour in his or her appearances in the media.

If the demons that appear on the "inner journey" (see following discussion) are made public, the private is made public, and the boundary between the two is removed. The social trend towards transparency will then produce a CEO laid bare to the public's eye. The human element, which is already ignored for the sake of the efficiency principle, disappears completely in a company if its public communication also becomes subject to this principle. There is a tendency here to suggest that both for leadership under the power of the mother and for leadership of a peer group, there is no longer any room for individual subjectivity in social organisations.

The chimera of the authentic self and the lack of reference persons

Several contributions emphasise how important it is for the new leader to embark on the "inner journey". Especially Mario Alonso Puig (Harvard Medical School, USA) sings the praises of authenticity:

> We all are born with the possibility of becoming a source of inspiration and support for other people, but very few among us have the determination, persistence and patience which are needed to tap into our true inner resources and unfold our natural capacities. The inner journey of a leader is the process through which one discovers not who one is but who one could be.

> It is my experience that this journey starts with a new appreciation of the meaning of silence, because the only way to get in touch with our inner self is to get rid of the train of disturbing thoughts which break through

our consciousness without our permission. We also need to have the attitude of somebody who acknowledges that one does not know but is committed to explore and learn. Without that humility, some of the mysteries of our true nature will not be revealed to us.

… When we cross the threshold and leave our comfort zone, we need to have courage, confidence, and faith that sooner or later something extraordinary will show up. It is in our inner journey when we come across our own shadows, the parts of us that we do not want to acknowledge and that we project on other people. Many people live in the hallucination that they can truly lead other people without being able to lead themselves and this is pure fantasy. It is much easier to try to change other people and not be willing to change ourselves. This exercise of authenticity is very much needed if we truly want to inspire, touch, and move the brains and the souls of those around us. (Puig, 2012, pp. 35–36)

This "inner journey" presupposes that the true self already exists somewhere, and we just have to find it. Yet this true self, on which the new leadership model places so much hope in terms of personal power and clear orientation, is a chimera. Such a self is not simply there as something that is just waiting to be found. In the psychological development of subjects, it cannot take shape at all without the reference to others, to the respective reference persons.

It seems that the authors are drawing on a psychological pattern of conflict which used to occur in middle-class upbringings: There, the adolescent, because he or she is socially over-adapted, tried to meet the expectations of the parents. In doing so, the adolescent had to suppress or even repress his or her own feelings and desires. In a therapeutic perspective, it would undoubtedly be possible to address this traditional problem by creating an atmosphere in the therapeutic conversation that is conducive to the person's drives. However, the information available to us about the typical family conflict patterns of the present day leaves us in doubt that this true self can still be present.

The new leadership model of the inner journey is obviously unaware of the process dynamics and structural development of the self. It says that the new leader must create everything necessary from within himself. This includes resolving the contradiction between the reality of the ecosystem and the self-centredness of the ego-system. The question arises: How is a new leader supposed to manage this on his or her own? And how can he or she transform the "shadows", which are experienced as demons, in his or her self and thus gain new energy sources? Which reference person can help the leader to accomplish this miracle? In this model, the answer is: Nobody. It remains a mystery.

According to Winnicott (1973), highly specialised conditions are necessary for an individual to find him- or herself and come to exist as a single entity. These are essentially the conditions of creativity. It is somewhat doubtful that it is feasible to re-create them, especially for future business managers.

In this search for the true self, one particular issue remains entirely unclear: How can this search be successful if this generation of future managers suffers from a narcissistic problem which has already affected earlier generations in large parts of the Western world? I am referring to the unresolved traumatic experience of childhood. With many individual differences in intensity, it binds the person concerned to the two narcissistic configurations analysed by Kohut (1973): The archaic grandiose self, on the one hand, and the idealised parental imago, on the other. In the first case, according to Kohut, the child experiences a lack of empathy on the part of the caregiver. The greater this lack of empathy is, the more severe the damage will be to the self. This lack of empathy gives rise to this narcissistic configuration. However, it is difficult to discern a true self in this damage.

No assistance with the external journey

The idea that a manager can simply go beyond the boundaries of the system to see where it may be heading (as in Goleman's contribution) seems problematic. It does not take all the obstacles into account. Daniel Goleman (Co-Director, Consortium for Research on Emotional Intelligence in Organizations at Rutgers University, USA) explains his concept:

> We will need leaders with a dual capability of attention: alert to subtle, telling signals as well as a larger systems awareness. The steady signals of the environmental meltdown have been ignored by leaders who have failed to rise to that challenge, just as the early signals of market meltdowns in the mortgage bubble, and now in Greece and Italy, were discounted by leaders who failed us.... Tomorrow's leaders will need to go beyond the limits of the systems within which we operate today to see what those systems might become.... The Leader's Journey: What life experience might foster such emotional intelligence plus cognitive flexibility? I can think of at least two kinds. One is stepping outside one's comfortable life.... Living in a culture different from our own surfaces hidden norms and lets us see our own culture through the lens of other eyes. That's good practice for analysing any system. And living on the cheap strengthens our own adaptability and makes us more comfortable with the unknown and with risk. Another competence-builder might be a period of social service.... (Goleman, 2012, pp. 9ff.)

Then again, there is the enormous pressure to succeed that any system imposes on its managers. The functional differentiation in modern society also makes it increasingly difficult to relate social reality within one social system to the reality of other systems.

To live in a different culture that differs substantially from one's own so that "one's own culture can be seen through the lens of another's eyes" seems plausible at first glance. But here, too, managers need help to transform the inevitable culture shock (Flader & Comati, 2008) into a process of intercultural learning.

The lack of sociopolitical context

In most contributions to this model of new leadership, the social reality in which companies exist remains perfectly abstract. There is no reference to the existing internal contradictions of our economic system (cf. Schumpeter, 1950), no consideration of the enormous pressure to succeed under which managers operate, and no mention of politics at all. The new manager, robbed of his or her subjectivity, floats in empty space. With few exceptions, he or she lacks any concrete connection to social reality.

Most authors do not seem to realise the significance of their frequently correct diagnoses of our time. This is particularly true for the disappearance of the principle of tradition, which is taken for granted, and for the fact that cultural tradition has become largely irrelevant. The proposed measures for coping with the new challenges are somewhat superficial because they do not shed light on the problems they hint at.

However, they do agree on one thing: The new leader must master practically all the challenges listed here from within – each leader has his or her own power plant, with his or her own inner compass and self-drawn map, equipped with a sensorium for both environmental signals and social stimuli, with a converter that turns human doubts and insecurities into personal strengths, and a built-in social conscience that ensures that environmental damage is not forgotten. If you put the contributions together to form a picture of the new leader, a superhuman appears.

When some authors emphasise that the new generation of leaders will create their own reality in the future, then, in Mendel's perspective, this is based on an image of humanity that takes the complete separation from any cultural heritage for granted. No revolt against tradition is necessary.

In these contributions, modern management science celebrates the all-out victory of the efficiency principle – without, however, being able to answer the following question: How is the manager of tomorrow supposed to cope with all the social and psychological tasks that these management experts are burdening him or her with? And to what end?

2 A Modern model of successful management and its psychoanalytical interpretation

2.1 Successful management of stability and instability

The model of modern management in commercial enterprises developed by Peter Kruse (2004) is far more differentiated than the advice given by internationally active management experts in the "Global Agenda" survey. Kruse's complex model can also claim to be internationally oriented. At the same time, the author addresses the new management tasks in detail and comprehensively and explains in detail why they differ from the traditional tasks of management.

In accordance with Kruse's four theoretical perspectives, we can distinguish between four different aspects based on separate concepts of subject. I will show why this model is so interesting from the point of view of a psycho-analytical cultural criticism: It includes more or less hidden indications of the connection between the new management tasks and the widespread traumatic relationship experiences of childhood, about which clinical-therapeutic case reports provide information.

2.1.1 The four parts of a model of successful management

THE NEW CHALLENGES: THE ECONOMIC SUBJECT

Kruse assumes that the growing complexity and accelerating change in the market and in society are challenges to which the management of a company must react appropriately. Whether changes in the company meet with success depends above all on whether the management demonstrates a willingness to change, whether the employees have room for manoeuvre, how mistakes and conflicts are dealt with in the company, and whether information is shared. What is needed today is to create a culture of change.

Such change is not easy to bring about. People react to pressure to change by trying to improve performance within the framework of existing func-tionality. It is not feasible, either, to achieve significant change by establishing a standardised performance comparison, which is supposed to determine the direction of possible changes as accurately as possible. This will increase the effort, but the behaviour patterns that have proved successful will be main-tained. In fact, these are only attempts to design change processes in such a way that existing behaviour patterns are improved.

According to Kruse, a change in the overall pattern is necessary to achieve fundamental change in the company.

> For once it has been proven that a new pattern/technology also opens up new dimensions of performance, there is usually no stopping the free market. (ibid., p. 25)

From an economic perspective, Kruse gives a clear description of the new challenges that companies face. As the stabilising influence of tradition and habits is lost more and more, the better becomes the enemy of the good almost immediately.

Kruse points out that the information economy with all its possibilities represents a fundamental attack on older patterns of thought and action. Companies now focus less on production and more on product development, sales, trade, and services. On the Internet, being attractive for customers becomes the primary business objective. The value of a company on the Internet lies less in its turnover or direct profit than in the duration, number, and range of links to network users.

The increase in crosslink intensity can be seen in the context of two effects: On the one hand, complexity increases in both private and professional life, and on the other hand, the number of feedback effects in the system increases.

What is particularly interesting here is the change in the information behaviour of customers. According to Kruse, customer loyalty has mostly stopped being a reliable parameter. What matters is the attractiveness of the situation. The number of cross-sectoral deals is increasing (e.g. car manufacturers also successfully sell financial services). Everything is focused on the moment when the customer decides to buy. This has become the central new theatre of war.

The emerging network economy also creates new demands on the behaviour of managers, requiring them to rise to the next stage of professionalisation. According to Kruse, it is the human brain which offers the best answer to the complex new challenges. Brain research shows that the brain is a highly dynamic, self-organising network with a high density of connections between the individual nerve cells. This analogy brings us to the theory of dynamic systems.

SELF-ORGANISING SYSTEMS: THE SUBJECT AS A NATURAL PHENOMENON

Kruse adopts two categories from systems theory to classify systems, according to their complexity and stability. On this basis, there are four possible combinations for characterising systems: Systems can be simple and stable, simple and unstable, complex and stable, and complex and unstable. In each case, influence is exerted differently. For simple and stable systems, a system of giving directions is necessary. In contrast, complex and stable systems require a control system which minimises the deviation between target and actual values, namely through negative feedback. Control and directions are therefore linked to the stability of the system. This is different for simple and unstable systems: Here, the trial-and-error method is applied. "In simple, unstable situations, trial and error may well be a successful solution under certain circumstances", Kruse writes (ibid., p. 46).

The last combination is a system that is both complex *and* unstable, and this is where concepts of self-organisation become relevant. Kruse uses the image of "sailing to unknown shores" to illustrate the demands that managers face when fundamental changes in the company are considered necessary. According to Kruse, such sailing is about developing visions, trusting one's intuition, being highly aware of current circumstances, and being able to flexibly adapt to every small change.

People normally believe that behind every perceived order, there is an ordering instance. According to Kruse, the examples of spontaneous re-organisation that have appeared in biology, chemistry, and physics argue against this belief. Such sudden re-organisation arises from the inherent dynamics of systems. Nature has a system of complex order formation which is bound to the phases of instability of the system. Instability always also means a lack of predictability. If we look at the weather, for example, we do not know which tiny influences need to be measured and taken into account. The principle "small cause, big effect" applies.

Kruse emphasises that it may seem far-fetched to transfer principles from science and mathematics to management strategies, as this would be based on a metaphorical transfer. But such a transfer can be attractive and profitable because the theory of dynamic systems can function as a meta-theory. This is true even if areas such as business management are far from being scientifically exact. Nevertheless, the principles of the theory of dynamic systems, when used as a meta-theory, can also be applied to the interpretation, explanation, and design of management processes.

I would object, however, that meta-theory too easily becomes a theory of modern management, if the metaphorically understood transference is actually re-metaphorised. To put it simply: What is supposed to serve as a metaphor becomes a term that is used without reflection.

It is interesting to see how this approach can now be used to differentiate between different types of intelligence in a company. Companies have focused on team building at management level in recent years because the complexity and dynamics of the market situation mean, according to Kruse, that solutions can no longer be found by individuals. What is being developed here is a type of team intelligence. This next stage of development is characterised by organisational intelligence. It is more than the sum of the intelligence of individuals and is described by Kruse as "supersummative". The crucial point is that fundamental change does not come about because masterminds want a new solution. Rather, he says, fundamental change now comes about because those involved are prepared to accept instability.

While the management of stability can be metaphorically equated with sailing along known coasts, that of instability is a departure for unknown continents. This departure is becoming the norm as the dynamics of the markets accelerate. Columbus is used by Kruse as an example of the leadership demands made on managers in such a phase of instability. A captain will need to answer the question: If both the path and the goal are unclear, why should we, the crew, embark on this journey (a change in the company)?

Kruse points out that inspiring fascination is the best response to this question. The captain should exemplify a vision which is an imagination, not a destination. Then everyone builds up an emotional base which provides security under conditions of uncertainty.

To convincingly convey a shared vision is thus defined as a very personal leadership task. There must be willingness to bear the costs of a fundamental change in the company, but there must also be tolerance for instability. After all, in this phase of instability, a slump in performance is inevitable. However, the phase of instability should be kept as short as possible in a successful company because obviously money is only earned under stable management.

Kruse now distinguishes between various prototypical transitional situations, which require flexibility and adaptability:

- Introduction of new IT technologies and forms of organisation
- Profound change in the market situation
- Mergers and hostile takeovers
- Revolutionary product innovations
- Change in top management or a generation change in family businesses

Many change management models address these unstable transitions. According to Kruse, fundamental changes affecting the company should be tackled as early as possible. Five guiding questions should help companies assess the need for fundamental change.

1 Work organisation (for example, does the transition to automated production processes change traditional job descriptions?)
2 Market environment (for example, is there a new competitive situation?)
3 Company structure (for example, is there a merger?)
4 Product strategy (are there new markets or product lines?)
5 Change of leadership (a commonplace occurrence today, and always a strategic opportunity for reorganisation within the company)[7]

Kruse also distinguishes between management and leadership. If management is to be credible as a role model, then leadership is required. This means that managers need personal charisma to adequately perform the symbolic function of leadership. In this context, Kruse introduces the concept of iteration, which comes from fractal geometry: According to him, the "iteration of simple rules ... through its own dynamic leads to complex patterns of order" (ibid., p. 97). Furthermore, iteration creates a "supersummative" intelligence because it makes order tendencies visible. Kruse even goes so far as to assert that "iteration ... is the ideal way to use this inherent intelligence" (ibid., p. 100) of an "intelligence that is potentially greater than the sum of the individual intelligences" (ibid.).

RITUALS STABILISE CULTURAL PATTERNS: THE SOCIAL SUBJECT

In this context, Kruse refers to Berger and Luckmann and their famous book *The Social Construction of Reality: A Treatise in the Sociology of Knowledge* (1966). He takes the concept of "culture" from this sociology of interaction, with culture defined as the implicit rules that people follow in a social system. And indeed, this research approach, which is based on Alfred Schütz's phenomen-ological sociology, seems to open the door to a new understanding of cultural differences.[8]

> In a culture, the fundamentally new only has a chance to be realised when the hidden rules are also brought into the open, deliberately jarred, and replaced by different sets of rules. (Kruse, 2004, p. 108)

Even though the interaction sociology of Berger and Luckmann avoids the term "rules", it is plausible for the clash of different corporate cultures to lead to conflicts. After all, culture is, in Kruse's view, the sum of the self-evident. "If the rules, as they exist in the day-to-day business world, are in conflict with the reality we are striving for, change is rather unlikely" (ibid., p. 109).

At the end of this third part, Kruse's account takes an interesting turn in terms of quality. He points to the human being as the only measuring in-strument that can reliably detect traces and pattern formations in complex systems. This means that his perceptive faculty and intuition, specifically when exploring the views of employees and managers or those of competitors and customers, depends on nothing but him- or herself. At this point Kruse brings the fourth concept of the subject into play: The subject as an individual.

KELLY'S REPERTORY GRID METHOD: THE SUBJECT AS AN INDIVIDUAL

Kruse selected the Role-Construct Repertory Grid as an ideal measuring instrument for change processes and developed it on a mathematical basis to be suitable for group evaluations. This technique can be described as follows:

> The object of investigation of this method is theoretically determined as the so-called construct system – i.e. an individual network of dicho-tomous interpretations and assessments (constructs) based on similarity and contrast, with which an individual, according to Kelly, attempts to give meaning to his world. (Flader et al., 1993, p. 91)[9]

The self-conceptuality used by the persons investigated to give meaning to their personal world is at the centre of this investigative technique. While its linguistic dimension should be explored more closely, Kruse developed a computer-assisted interview technique based on this group evaluation, which was finalised as a "Nextexpertizer".

2.1.2 A psychoanalytical interpretation of Kruse's model

Let's take a closer look at Kruse's model. He distinguishes between four dif-ferent concepts of subject: The economic subject, the subject as a natural phenomenon, the social subject in the context of culture, and the subject as an individual. I will not go into the question of whether these four concepts of subject are theoretically compatible with each other. The practical significance of this model – in the sense of a basis for effective management consulting – is probably greater than its scientific consistency.

What seems more interesting to me is that, from a psychoanalytical perspective, this model eliminates the subjectivity of the participants from the outset. The concept of the personal construction of the world (based on data from the repertory grid technique) is also not explained in the context of the research discussion on psychosomatics. Nevertheless, this model, however covert, may be psychoanalytically interesting because it reacts to a psychological and communicative problem that is widespread today.

Let us start with the data collection technique of the Role-Construct Repertory Grid, which Kelly developed. It is no coincidence that this same data collection technique has also been used in psychosomatic medicine. In the initial psychoanalytical interview, the patient group in question can provide virtually no insight into their own emotional world. They have difficulty verbalising their feelings. This technique is used to gain access their world in a different way.

It seems that Kruse's model takes this peculiarity into account and turns it into a prerequisite: It is precisely the narcissistic problems, accompanied by a diffuse feeling of not being good enough, that elude verbalisation. And as already mentioned in connection with the Mobbing Report: Our culture has no code for the verbalisation of such feelings (cf. Chapter 2, Section 1).

This is bound to raise the question: Why should the repertory grid technology be suitable as "an ideal measuring instrument for change processes" (Kruse, 2004, p. 135) in companies? Isn't this suitability based on the fact that many employees in a company have difficulty verbalising both their narcissistic needs and injuries – that is the very same emotional processes with which people in a company react to change processes?

It is also interesting to note the importance of network intelligence in Kruse's model. After all, it is seen as "supersummative" intelligence, which is more than the sum of the individual intelligences. As such, it makes a closer examination of the details in a company unnecessary when a so-called transitional situation needs to be managed.

Here, we may have a new ego-ideal which is not based on a personal role model. This is different, then, from Freud's (1921) explanation of the psychological effect that the figure of a "great man" has on his followers. Network intelligence seems more likely to represent a psychological recourse to the idealised parent figure, which Kohut speaks of in his theory of narcissism. This interpretation also fits in with the fact that a senior executive, who wants to bring about fundamental change in the company without knowing exactly where it will lead to, has to address his own insecurity. The ego-ideal can serve this purpose very well because it is now embodied in the respective self-organising system: It represents what the leader is unable to do and must experience as his or her failure, namely to have the necessary overview and to know where things are going.

From this point of view, in addition to the four types of leadership distinguished above (cf. Chapter 2, Section 2.1.1), another type can be assumed:

- Leadership through network intelligence (as an idealised parental figure for coping with transitional situations in a company).

Finally, this model also seems to illustrate the replacement of the authority principle by the efficiency principle, which Mendel drew attention to as an explanation for the gradual weakening of paternal authority. Again, according to this concept, there is a tendency to replace personal experience, age, and personal status by a reference to immediate effectiveness.

Paternal authority is no longer mentioned in the modern Kruse model. Rather, creativity, tolerance of instability, and the living of visions are now required to enable the new. The necessary personal security under this condition of uncertainty is then achieved by believing in the complex dynamic system, which in itself contributes to the creation of new structures of order. It represents a kind of relief from personal responsibility in a company, achieved by the mystification of a company as a self-organising system.

3 Television programmes as a mirror of narcissistic problem situations

As the narcissistic development gets blocked ever more frequently, the damage to social interaction spreads. This seems to be accompanied by a fundamental change in the media. As early as the 1980s, Arno Gruen (1986) pointed to the entertainment industry which rarely tells complex stories today, preferring to provide short-term thrills to their audiences.

3.1 The psycho-service of television entertainment

In today's television programmes, we find a great variety of (mostly covert) offers to the viewers which create the illusion of helping them cope with narcissistic problems. The promise of freedom has been replaced by a service which temporarily increases self-esteem. For a short time, the widespread feeling of frustration, dejection, and smallness associated with low self-esteem is eliminated by a deliberate, illusionary increase in self-esteem. This is achieved through forms of narcissistic satisfaction. To this end, various templates are provided, which, despite their diversity, ultimately present an identical content: They all represent manifestations of superiority and perfection.

The relationship pattern of rejection and need has become the base for interpreting social interaction with regard to positions of power or powerlessness. This pattern now shapes many forms of action in the most diverse social areas. In all of these cases, emotional hardness and coldness are regarded as social values that give proof of superiority and normality.

One of the suggestive effects of the media can be explained by the fact that this relationship pattern is repeated many times in many variations. In all of them, the viewer is given the opportunity to identify with the position of superiority, which allow him or her to ward off existing feelings of self-deprecation and powerlessness.

I propose to look at three examples which illustrate how the media today continuously offer us such opportunities for identification. Example (a) is the sports spectator in front of television; example (b) is the narcissistic satisfaction obtained by watching political television discussions; and example (c) is an analysis of casting shows on television.

3.1.1 The sports spectator in front of television: Ruler over the arena

We find this offer in the language of sport or, more precisely, in the language of the commentators of competitive sports. Let us look at soccer matches, for example. When the commentators summarise the match, there is one device that they favour in particular: They grade the performance of individual players, team members or the whole team as if they were writing up job references.[10]

We can see this from the fact that commentators employ the language of job references. Good players are graded according to attributes such as their tackling skills, control over the ball, running ability, mastery of techniques, speed of approach, robustness, or initiative. With regard to the performance of a team, commentators make assessments regarding the field or game superiority, the use of goal-scoring opportunities, the pressure exerted on the opponent, the level of play, and similar.

For some time now, the performance evaluation of each individual player has been complemented by statistics giving the number of ball contacts in the game, the duels won, the shots on goal, and so forth.

Of course, one can say that performance evaluations of competitive and top athletes are part of the job of a good sports commentary. After all, the athletes are measured by their own standards, namely those of sporting performance. A spectator can get an "objective picture" of a match with the help of a commentary of this kind.

That is undoubtedly true. But this language of job references, for which qualification attributes and their individual fulfilment are essential, can also fulfil a function with regard to the narcissistic need of the spectator.

For a long time now, so-called leisure time has often been nothing more than an extension of the working world into the private sphere by more or less playful means. It is obvious that television viewers can recognise the working environment as society's backdrop for the social significance of competitive sport. They will then interpret sporting events based on the patterns of experience of the working environment with which they are familiar. And in this environment, the viewers are familiar with performance evaluations – namely those relating to their own work performance in the company where they are employed.

However, sports commentators who use the language of job references open up opportunities for viewers that these do not enjoy in their work environment. What they have to accept or even endure in everyday working life – that their work is the object of a performance assessment carried out by their superiors – they can now do to other under the guidance of the sports commentator. They can assess athletes whose sporting success or failure is reported to them. In this way, they can do in their imagination to others in their free time what is otherwise done to them (and often unpleasantly) in everyday professional life: They can impose high performance criteria on somebody and give the corresponding evaluations. This can come as a great relief if the required work discipline at work is stressful. And this is often enough the case (cf. Chapter 2, Section 1.4).

Here, the television viewers (or radio listeners) receive an offer of exchanging their position within the pattern of power and powerlessness. At the workplace, they are in a position of powerlessness. But as viewers, they can, either mentally or in their imagination, assume a position which they are denied in everyday life: The position of power. This position is characterised by the fact that the viewers, in identification with the sports commentator, strictly and merciless give the same kind of performance evaluation of the players that their boss gives them in the workplace. If the boss relentlessly enforces the observance of performance standards in the workplace – often based on equating an empathy disorder with strength – then the spectator, under the guidance of the sports commentator, can now evaluate the athletes just as relentlessly.

What is on offer here is a psychological relief and an upward revaluation of the self. But the commentator does not verbalise the narcissistic need of the spectator, whose satisfaction is at stake here. Nor does this verbalisation occur anywhere else in the multitude of offers of this kind provided by the mass media. They permanently offer a "psycho-service", which does not lead to an ending in satisfaction. The reason is that complete narcissistic satisfaction is not possible, because it can only carry the shortcoming at its root forward in a concealed way, without finding fulfilment. The psycho-service happens without addressing the precondition for it – the existing narcissistic need of the spectators. This needs explanation if we consider that nowadays, almost everything can be discussed in the media.

One reason for this is that this pattern of relationships is particularly deeply repressed due to the powerlessness it entails. Another reason is that, as already mentioned, the feeling of self-deprecation eludes verbal communication. In order to be able to communicate these feelings, we need to be able to trust the other person, because we allow him or her to participate in an inner process that is important for us. A particularly strong relationship of trust is necessary to verbalise feelings of self-deprecation, due to the fear of being rejected and even more devalued when one's powerlessness becomes visible.

In our culture, however, public appearances in the media in particular are dominated by holders of the position of grandioseness. According to the logic of the relationship pattern of rejection and need, the opposite position is banished to a non-public or even invisible place. That is the societal space created for the holders of this position – the failures, the people who are powerless.

If they are nevertheless given the chance to make a public appearance, it takes the shape of taking care of them in a quasi-professional form, that is from a position of superiority. But sports spectators would protest violently if they were told that somebody would like to address their self-esteem problems. The psycho-service only works if it is not discussed.

3.1.2 The narcissistic satisfaction in political television debates

It is now interesting to look at political discussions and talk shows – which are a daily fare of television broadcasting – to recognise the pattern in the positions of superiority and strength. These public discussions take place in such a way that the real issue is the holding of this position, no matter which political (or other) problem is being dealt with on the surface.

The aim of the contributions to the discussion is to score points in the competitive relationship of being superior to others. Non-knowledge, un-certainty, and so forth must be avoided at all costs as a sign of personal weakness.

This kind of public communication can be explained using traditional ca-tegories. It is then an expression of the political power struggle which, in a democracy, has to take place between the social groups competing in their interests and their political representatives. But this explanation does not meet the specificity of these public discussions. For it is striking that when the discussion focuses on weak members of society (such as children or the un-employed) or even on victims of war, none of the participants in the discussion ever say that they can identify with them and speak from their position.

Clearly, the position of weakness and powerlessness must be avoided at all costs. Paradoxically, it does not come up even when it is being discussed. The reason is that in the language of military strategy, technocracy, or bureaucracy, the very momentum has been erased without which the position of weakness cannot be mentally and emotionally adopted – there is no empathy.

Both the languages of bureaucracy and of military strategy are very well suited to maintaining the repression of the position of powerlessness as a psychological defence because they represent reality in an abstract way. Children, who need the love of their mother, are served through child care slots; civilian victims of war become collateral damage of air strikes.

3.1.3 An analysis of television casting shows

A now immensely popular genre in the entertainment industry are casting shows on television. In Germany, some of the most successful shows are *Germany Is Looking for the Superstar, The Voice of Germany,* or *Germany's Next Topmodel.* According to a study, 62 per cent of all male and 80 per cent of all female teenagers watch casting shows regularly (FAZ, 11 May 2013). Around half a million people in Germany have by now taken part in the selection process of a casting show. *Germany Is Looking for the Superstar* was awarded the German Television Prize as Best Entertainment Show in 2003 and 2006.

In the FAZ of 1 June 2013, Morten Freidel argued that active or passive participation in a casting show is not just about the dream of quick fame. The reason why so many young people recognise themselves in casting shows is because they are similar to other competitive situations. This is particularly true for work, but also for posting a particularly advantageous photo on an online dating platform. Still, casting shows are less about competition in the traditional sense than about evaluation. According to Freidel, we "have long since lived less in a competitive environment than in an evaluation society". On the one hand, evaluation is diffuse, because the clearly defined enemy image of the traditional competitive society no longer exists. On the other hand, this evaluation is more radical than traditional competition, because it applies to more or less everybody who is part of this anonymous process. This creates a compulsion to compare, but also an addiction.

However, the points that Freidel (2013) addresses – the dream of quick fame, the competitive situation, and the addiction to evaluation – have an inner connection that Freidel does not analyse. That is what I propose to do.

The participants in a show like *Germany Is Looking for the Superstar* are doing something specific to realise their dream of quick fame. Psychoanalytically speaking, they are realising their ego-ideal to be a star, and the audience recognises itself in this desire. After all, the participants do not choose the difficult path of a professional career but one that is mostly illusory, namely that of being discovered. Once discovered, they have already been turned into stars in show business. The participants firmly believe in this – a kind of magical thinking – although the biographies of stars could teach them differently.

If we were to look at the development process of an entertainment singer in real life, this process would lead to an end point where the person in question would have turned into a star. It is precisely this realistic end point that casting shows employ to directly reach the ego-ideals of young people. After all, these young people dream of reaching the end point by taking part in the competition while leaving out the beginning and the many intermediate steps that would be necessary in real life. It is this link to a realistic career path which, while remaining in the background, gives the whole programme a touch of reality.

It is nevertheless remarkable that the absence of a paternal authority seems natural. This absence indicates a legacy of the 1968 student protests; it is an important part of its "shadow". One of the functions of such a paternal authority would be to tell young people, who obviously do not have the necessary gifts for a show talent, that they lack talent. But in this programme, nobody thinks of explaining to the young people the difference between their wishful thinking of becoming a superstar and the actual work obligations and personal deprivations of a performer in show business.

One might object that the jurors in *Germany Is Looking for the Superstar* are like fathers who judge the talents of their children. The fact that they do this shows how much importance they accord to this evaluation. But because they have become "stars" themselves, they have move beyond any evaluation and can do whatever they want. Therefore, they are not in the position of a father who cannot act in such a fashion. The way in which the jurors evaluate the candidates has nothing in common with the love of a father who, in the interest of his own child, would advise him not to pursue the career of a singing star. Instead, the judgments are often merciless. It is not unusual for Dieter Bohlen to say from his position in the jury: "You don't sing, you squeal like a pig", "You sing like a chainsaw", and so forth.

These are attacks on the self-esteem of the candidate. In 2007, the Commission for the Protection of Minors in the Media initiated an investigation into this programme on the grounds of "possible socio-ethical disorientation" of viewers and actors. A mass medium was "demonstrating how people are mocked, belittled, and ridiculed. Antisocial behaviour is presented as normality. This can counteract values such as respect, compassion, and solidarity". Yet this attempt to move the show into the late-night programme unsuccessful.

What is it that actually transforms the jurors into the idols of young people? We should look at the idols of our time to discover to what extent they are indicators of the psychological deficiencies the persons affected suffered during childhood. Here, it is the lack of a positively experienced paternal figure. A child will hardly identify with a weak father as a role model.

The jurors then lend themselves to the role as idols, especially in the case of *Germany Is Looking for the Superstar*. They promise young people support on their way to stardom. This is an ideal state that some of the jurors themselves have already achieved.

What are young people looking for in these casting shows? In my opinion, these shows work like the stock market, except that it is not the values of shares that are determined here but the values of young people or, more precisely, their market value for the entertainment industry. In addition to the voice, the appearance and the body are also evaluated (separately for individual body parts). This is what counts as the performance of a star in show business.

Of course, it has always been important for young people to know what their peers think about them and how popular or respected they are among people of the same age and group. Here, too, one's "market value" has always played a major role – one's position on an (imaginary) popularity scale in comparison to others, or what the other sex liked about you, and so forth.

The participants of a casting, however, show go one step further: They are willing to promote themselves and to do so according to the evaluation criteria of the entertainment industry. For that, they must have internalised both the market mechanism and the evaluation criteria. The latter have become an integral part of their ego-ideal, even though it is mostly illusory to become a star in this way today. It is all the more surprising how many of these young people are willing to submit to the castings which are often humiliating. How strong must their narcissistic needs be to want to endure this treatment in front of a large television audience?

They do so also because by intuition, they correctly suspect that they are siding with a major power – the television industry and its entertainment function. I see the casting shows as a new wave of democratisation of forms of existence and decision-making that used to be reserved to the elites. First came the democratisation of hedonism that we have witnessed in party resorts like the "Ballermann" on Mallorca (a pleasure that used to be the privilege of a small group of playboys). Now, casting shows democratise the decisions about the taste of the masses, which has otherwise been limited to a small group of decision-makers in the television stations.

The reason is that now all viewers rate the respective performance of a candidate in the show. Not just some members of a group – no, all viewers who are willing to judge themselves as others do according to the criteria of the entertainment industry, which constantly says that it "only exists for the viewers". The casting shows, on the other hand, show that in fact, the viewers exist for the medium. The medium consumes its users. Thus, it manifests the character of something all-embracing and totalitarian.

Freidel sees a similarity between an evaluation in the casting shows and an evaluation in the world of work and in private life. But he does not analyse the deeper background. This compulsion to make comparisons is an aid to or-ientation in a social world which lacks role models which one could use to make realistic plans for career advancement. Instead, young people must compare themselves to each other according to the criteria that the en-tertainment industry has defined for them as attributes of stars or models. But this does raise the question of the power of the entertainment industry. Freidel completely ignores this issue.

The weakened father, as already mentioned, has long since stopped playing a role here. After all, it is parents and relatives who encourage their children to take part in these casting shows. Once the children have applied and have been accepted, their parents are presented by the programme as people who support their children and accompany them to the tests to be taken.

This contrasts sharply with the earlier competitive situation described by Freidel, in which two competitors could at least mentally duel each other at the workplace. Yet this may be the imaginative embellishment of the old generation conflict, in which the younger generation competed against the older in order to take its place in society.

As Mendel has shown, this generation conflict has not existed in the Western world since the student protests of 1968 at the latest (cf. G. Mendel, 1969).

4 An action-oriented analysis of films by A. Hitchcock and S. King

In this chapter, we will be examining two films by Alfred Hitchcock and the film adaptation of a book by Stephen King. In my interpretation, a relationship problem in the psychological sense (Hitchcock) and a relationship problem in the clinical sense of a narcissistic personality disorder (King) covertly determine the course of events so that they can be interpreted as a subtext of the film. I will first discuss the various psychoanalytical methods of film analysis as explained by Mechthild Zeul (2007).

Zeul believes that psychoanalytic film interpretations that focus on the content of the film make the specifics of the film disappear. Like me, she criticises the unfortunate tendency of such film interpretations to simply extend the therapeutic perspective to society or, in this case, to film.

> The idea of understanding a film through psychoanalytical theory is based on the mistaken assumption that it is a patient whose images can be translated into words, i.e. whose primary process associations can be transferred into secondary process understanding.... An interpretation of the medium using Oedipal conflict constellations with their regressive movements and various self-pathologies deprives the films of their concrete aesthetic expressiveness. It turns them into vignettes of psychoanalytic treatment of the sick. (ibid., p. 988)

Psychoanalytic film interpretations should not simply rely on Freud's various theoretical models. First, we should ask how much such models need to evolve to be suitable for investigations outside the clinical context. Freud's dream theory, for example, is problematic from a psychoanalytical point of view and urgently needs to be revised.[11] Finally, we need to investigate Freud's discovery that not only dreams but neurotic symptoms and mistakes, too, have an unconscious meaning. This meaning is not always unconscious because it has been repressed. It can also be unconscious because the reactualisation of an earlier conflict dynamic in social interaction creates a double structure. By the same process that the subject intends to carry out as interactant, he or she also addresses the unresolved mental conflict that was reactivated by the context. This simultaneity of the non-simultaneous produced in action cannot be recognised by the subject in question in his or her actions.

I have explained this idea in the introduction and the chapter on mobbing, and I am now examining three selected films – two by Alfred Hitchcock and one by Stephen King – to see what we can learn from them in terms of these two unconscious layers of meaning:

1   The unconscious meaning of the plot (in the sense of a framework for action) in the context of a currently existing mental conflict between the protagonists.
2   The unconscious significance of the same plot in the context of a psychological conflict in early childhood that has been re-actualised.

This distinction is important because the search for clues to the nature of the underlying psychological conflict is quite different on the two levels of meaning. On the level of the current psychological conflict situation, we must look for indications of this conflict in the actions of the protagonists. The second level of meaning concerns typical mental conflict situations of a whole era or generation. There, we need to look for indications which are mostly contained in the clinical-therapeutic case reports of the time. Only when both levels of meaning are examined separately can we determine more precisely how they are ultimately connected.

A film can represent a connection that a psychoanalyst in a therapeutic context can only recognise to a very limited extent, namely the connection between the development of the plot and the individual psychological development of the main character which takes place as the plot develops.

It is precisely this connection that can be shown very clearly in some of Hitchcock's films, possibly because he intuitively staged them. Another special feature of his films is that only the main character recognises a common thread that remains obscure to all the other characters in the film. The viewer alone shares the insight of the main character.

The psychoanalytical point here is that the protagonist remains alone with his insight because it is his subjective truth that has brought him to this insight. His subjective truth agrees with the objective facts. Here, Hitchcock follows a premise of psychoanalytic therapy according to which an adult's subjective truth can be stronger than the objective truth to which all others adhere.

4.1 Hitchcock's Rear Window (1954)

I interpret the famous Hitchcock film *Rear Window* as an example of an un-resolved psychological conflict in the relationship of a couple which de-termines the course of events. My first question, therefore, is how we can analyse the course of action depicted in the film according to the first level of meaning. In other words: How does an already existing mental conflict get addressed by means of the ongoing interaction?

The plot starts out very simply: Jeff, the main character portrayed by James Stewart, has broken his leg. Confined to a wheelchair, he is interested in the events taking place in the courtyard, which he observes closely through his binoculars. At the beginning of the film, his fiancée (Grace Kelly) urges him to finally marry her. He refuses, using superficial arguments such as the dangerous nature of his profession.

In my interpretation of his emotional relationship, Jeff has an unresolved ambivalent conflict with his fiancée. Where this aggression comes from, why he loves his fiancée on the one hand and hates her on the other, the analysis initially leaves open. One of the constituents of the conflict is that Jeff's aggressiveness towards his fiancée is hidden from himself because it contradicts his own moral claims.

This aggression is then addressed in the further course of the action, and in such a way that both constituents of the conflict – defending against his own aggressiveness, and partially satisfying it – can be interpreted as two sides of an act signature. This is the motive behind Jeff's great curiosity about what the neighbour is doing and his detective-like observation of the man.

Through the action-related handling of this conflict, the double structure of the unconscious meaning takes shape. On the one hand, a social event takes place in the film that is familiar from detective stories: The protagonist assumes the position of a self-appointed detective on the trail of a crime. In Jeff's imagination, the neighbour acts out the aggressiveness that Jeff unconsciously feels towards his fiancée. This creates a covert possibility for Jeff to satisfy his own aggressiveness by pursuing his neighbour as a surrogate. In that sense, he gets into (an albeit unconscious) complicity with the neighbour.

The other side of the event has to do with the neighbour's defensive function. After all, it is he, not Jeff, who is the subject of the aggressive act on his wife.

This double structure can be expressed in the following way: While Jeff is the detective and the neighbour the criminal, both are also accomplices (Table 4.1).

One could argue that this double structure cannot exist here because Jeff is confined to a wheelchair. His actions are limited to his intensive observation of the neighbourhood through binoculars.

This objection corresponds to a widespread interpretation of this film, according to which it is an illustration of Hitchcock's theory of film. According to this interpretation, Jeff, who is sitting in his wheelchair, is the typical cinema spectator.

Table 4.1 Jeff's detective work as an imprint of the unconscious in the process

Defending against one's own aggression	Satisfying one's own aggression
"It's not me who commits the deed, it's the neighbour".	An unconscious participation as accomplice to the crime.
Conclusion of the detective work: The search for the perpetrator is complete.	The neighbour's wife was murdered by him.
The neighbour did it.	Jeff's aggressive wish unconsciously came true.

Out of a fear of failure, he does not find his way into real life and projects all his repressed wishes and impulses onto the film. Therefore, the director can limit himself to mere allusions because the viewer, for his part, completes everything necessary through his or her own imagination. This interpretation concentrates solely on the mental part of the plot – Jeff's activity as a detective and its conclusion – and takes out the immoral, "evil" motives.

Yet this interpretation ignores the fact that Jeff cannot deal with the un-resolved conflict structure through his own actions, but only in the mental dimension of detective-like observation. For example, he hears his neighbour having a loud domestic quarrel with his wife. Then he sees shadows appearing, and suddenly the quarrelling parties fall silent, which immediately makes Jeff suspect that the neighbour has murdered his wife. A feverish search for evidence is launched, for example, for body parts buried in the yard. So this is very much a development of detective activities – but they essentially take place in the mental dimension of perception: Taking notice of suspicious clues, substantiating the suspicion, and finally the certainty of a murder, the interest in evidence for the crime, and so forth.

How is this conflict resolved in the film? The satisfaction that comes with complicity is abruptly ended by the escalation of the detective story. For what was initially just Jeff's subjective truth – the fantasy that the neighbour had killed his wife – turns into an objective truth when the neighbour appears in person at Jeff's house to eliminate a witness to his crime.

Can the current ambivalence conflict also be resolved once this detective story has reached its solution, so that the path to Lisa (Grace Kelly) is clear? In my interpretation, Jeff's defence against his own aggression towards his fiancée remains precarious even after the perpetrator has been caught. After all, Jeff did indeed, unconsciously and with great relish, take part as an accomplice in the murder committed by his neighbour. To atone for the guilt he thereby incurred, he has to fall from the window and break his leg a second time.

The meaning of the leg fracture

This second layer of meaning in the film is hinted at by an interpretation presented by Heinrich Racker (1978):

> The protagonist Jeff ... has regressed to the level of a voyeur to escape his fear of castration. From this regressive position, he observed the various couples in the back of the house from his window. In all of this, the murder story [represents] the "sadistic primal scene". (Zeul, 2007, p. 989)

I follow this interpretation insofar as I also assume that a broken leg can make a man feel insecure about his manhood. It is possible, too, that this insecurity stems from an anxiety preserved in the repressed, a sentiment which Freud called the fear of castration. But we must understand this term as a metaphor and not as a concept, because a little boy cannot know what an adult man knows: That castration is done by destroying the gonads.

I have shown elsewhere (Flader, 2000) that a metaphor such as the fear of castration functions as a bridge from the adult world to the children's world. When the adult man is confronted with a familiar and very frightening intervention, it can give him the approximate idea of a shock he experienced as a child – a shock that can be interpreted as being afraid of an intervention into his own developing male integrity. Since this childhood shock has long since been repressed, there is no other way than to touch upon the anxiety that men have in the adult world.

One important question has not really been answered by Racker and the other scholars who have interpreted this film: How do you explain the fact that Jeff, after a fierce fight with the neighbour who visited him, falls from the window and breaks his other leg? Racker overlooks the double structure of Jeff's detective activities. Instead, he assumes that in the end, the fight with the neighbour, who represents the murderous father, resolved the Oedipus conflict: "This courage to fight is the necessary prerequisite for becoming a man and getting married" (quoted in ibid., p. 999).

Here, too, Racker in his interpretation is too quick to focus on a specific conflict constellation of childhood. He neglects the layer of meaning of Jeff's current relationship conflict, which I have analysed.

Does it really make sense, as Racker suggests, to take the "sadistic primal scene of childhood" as the motive for the alleged observation of the various couples at the rear of the house?[12] This may be a possible unconscious motive, but it would be very helpful to have a reference to relevant clinical-therapeutic case reports of the time that could support this interpretation. Before I return to this point, one more remark about the allegedly sadistic primal scene:

I do not follow Racker's interpretation. If there had actually been an Oedipus conflict that Jeff had to resolve, the second leg fracture would have to be interpreted accordingly. Jeff would then, for example, accept to submit to paternal law with the second fracture. In that interpretation, however, Hitchcock would have used the wrestling match between Jeff and his neighbour to symbolise the castration fantasy of a son. This son wants to overpower his father and rob him of what he, the son, fantasises about as a privilege of his father's power.

I think another interpretation is more plausible. It is based on indications taken from clinical-therapeutic work which concern the role of the father for the US middle class. Geoffrey Gorer (1948) – on whom Mitscherlich (1963) relies – has examined the "contempt for the father" in US civilisation in more detail. I follow his clues and read the second leg fracture in a very different way: It is not the symbolic submission to the law of the father, for the latter would probably have been experienced as too weak in Hitchcock's time.

I see the second leg fracture as the symbolic punishment that is imposed by a dominant mother. From her point of view, the protagonist has been so brave and manly in his wrestling match with his neighbour that his masculinity is becoming a little too much. Since she is the boss in the family, Jeff accepts her punishment. He is now the good boy who, with his mother's blessing, is free to marry Lisa.

If we assume that the family dynamics consist of a weak father and a dominant mother, then Jeff has a particular issue: In his neighbour, he seeks an answer to his own question of how to deal with his aggressive feelings towards his lover (i.e. from childhood: The mother). I understand Jeff's ambivalent conflict with his fiancée to be the result of a shift in this conflict, which in Jeff's life story was originally connected to his dominant mother. That is probably where his unconscious anger towards his fiancée originates – an anger that Jeff's conscience must psychologically ward off. Jeff is disappointed by the weak father, who was unable to give a satisfactory answer. Here, we have another motive for Jeff to wish that the neighbour would prove to be a strong man. Ultimately, this means that there is a fantasy of matricide in Jeff's unconscious mind.

We can then combine the results of the analysis on the first level of meaning with the interpretation on the second level of meaning. The connection could be the following: The broken leg may have made Jeff feel insecure about his own manhood. This is an insecurity that can easily turn to anger if, as I assume, Jeff has carried over a certain hypersensitivity from his problematic relationship with his dominant mother. Jeff has shifted his ambivalence towards his own mother onto his fiancée and now (unconsciously) associates the restoration of his manhood with the murder of his wife (the mother). He can then unconsciously experience with pleasure the act that the neighbour commits on his behalf.

The punishment for this unconscious enjoyment takes a shape that was already imbued with symbolic value: The fracture of the leg. But now, this fracture is no longer associated with a threat to Jeff's manhood, because unconsciously, this manhood was sufficiently served: His wife was killed by the neighbour in a process of substitution. The neighbour's manhood (unconsciously) triumphed – and so did Jeff's. Therefore, Jeff can gladly accept the punishment of a second broken leg.

What is interesting here is how Jeff's ambivalent conflict, which existed at the beginning, could be resolved. How could the symptom that I see represented in his detective work disappear? According to my thesis, Hitchcock considers, however covertly, that it was not the help of a psychotherapist which enabled Jeff to resolve his unconscious emotional conflict. Rather, it was the intensification of this conflict by means of the detective work that led to its resolution. What also played a role was that Jeff was able to live out his – more or less hidden – impulses with the help of his neighbour.

The role of the audience

From my perspective, it makes no sense to discuss the validity of different interpretations and the nature of the earlier conflict structures of childhood without referring to the audience. It is the viewers who, in such a film, project their own experiences onto the images they see. When confronted with the unconscious conflict dynamics presented in each case, they themselves decide what their subjective truth is. A good film, like any good work of art, is open to all kinds of interpretations. It thus establishes a connection to the extra-filmic expectations of the viewer, to his or her interests and unconscious experiences of conflict.

According to the two levels of unconscious significance, we can assume two different scopes of application of the psychological mechanisms and structures. On the first level of unconscious meaning, these can be assumed to be more universal (such as the defence mechanisms of projection and repression and the forms of interpersonal defence), while on the second level, psychological conflicts from early childhood that have been experienced in a generation-specific way become relevant.

In my analysis, a film must be a reflection of the viewer's existing conflict dynamics. If this is not the case, the film is simply incomprehensible. Accordingly, my interpretation of the second fracture is just one of several. But it touches on the kind of family conflict structure that Gorer considered characteristic of his time, which was shaped by a dominant mother and a weak father.

The concept of the psychological defence by repression is particularly important here.[13] In my opinion, we can work with the concept of alterity, that is the complete otherness of what has been repressed. This alterity is caused by the negation of what one is not oneself and by the ignorance of those affected which results from this negation.

The application of this concept requires a coherent self of the person concerned to be present in the process of psychological development. For this form of defence can only negate something that is part of the subject, a wish, characteristic, desire, and so forth. This means that the repressed remains part of the subject, which may eventually make it is possible to accept it as belonging to it. In the film by Stephen King that I chose we will not find this kind of a defence concept for lack of a coherent self.

In Hitchcock's *Rear Window*, however, this characteristic of the defence against repression is made very clear: The photo reporter's continuous attention and exaggerated awareness of the house across the courtyard contribute to the fact that he quickly interprets the perceived events as the preparation and execution of a murder. I see this as the documentation of a subjective truth of a protagonist. It is this subjective truth which, at the end of the film, leads him to uncover an objective fact. On the one hand, the father position for Jeff is occupied by a weak figure. On the other hand, however, it is strong enough for him to find a way out, both from his voyeurism and the ambivalent conflict with his fiancée, which he plays out in an unconsciously fantasised complicity with his neighbour.

4.2 Hitchcock's The Birds (1963)

Another example is Hitchcock's film *The Birds*. Here, we have another conflictual relationship structure between the main protagonists on the first layer of

unconscious meanings, which is shown from the point of view of one parti-
cipant. Hitchcock externalises this conflict and turns it into the plot of the film.

The visit of a good-looking, blonde woman to the place where the protagonist Mitch lives with his mother triggers an unprecedented aggressive
behaviour of birds towards people. Several people are actually killed by birds.
Interestingly, the first attack on the woman takes place on the mainland even
before she takes the boat across the bay to where Mitch lives with his mother.

The film shows two developments in parallel: One addresses the growing
affection of the two young people and the mother's distant attitude towards
the blonde woman. The other shows how Mitch, faced with a growing
number of highly aggressive birds and the rising number of their victims, finally leaves the house that has been besieged by the birds together with his
mother and his lover and thus saves everybody.

Unlike Mathias Hirsch (2006), I do not believe that there is any guilt involved
on Mitch's side which can be traced back to the Oedipus conflict of childhood,
that is to the fantasy of patricide. Hirsch's interpretations of the details are only
plausible if the reader can recognise his own childhood conflicts in them.

How can one decide whether these unconscious layers of meaning do not
simply originate with the interpreter's imagination? He or she might share
such layers with others, if they had similar experiences of conflict in their
childhood. To be able to take that decision, one would need to follow the
path I have sketched out in this book for my own investigations:
Psychoanalytic therapies should be understood as seismographs of cultural
upheavals in society. Therefore, in any interpretation, clinical-therapeutic case
reports should be included with regard to the typical conflict situations of
childhood they depict. In any case, why should the Oedipus conflict of
childhood – as Hirsch assumes – continue to be produced when the father was
already in a weak position in Hitchcock's time?

The two strands of development mentioned earlier – Mitch's personal relationships with the blonde woman and the mother on the one hand, and the
increasingly aggressive birds on the other – at first do not seem to be connected in the film. However, I interpret the unusually aggressive behaviour of
the birds as the mother's aggressive rage which has turned outwards. She is
reacting to the young woman, whom Mitch increasingly likes and whom she
considers an intruder. Her fear of losing her son is combined with anger at this
woman, who she wishes would disappear.

The meaning of avian aggression

The mother's no towards the blonde woman corresponds exactly to the phantasm
of the bird of prey, with which this no is expressed in the first year of life.[14]

On the second level of meaning, the aggressive birds embody a pre-linguistic
form of aggressive intervention by the mother. This originates with the mother's
former relationship (symbiosis) with the child. This representation of the no of

the mother as a bird of prey, is probably part of the collective unconscious in Western culture. In his film, Hitchcock turns the pre-linguistic notion of the mother's no outwards, duplicates it, and transforms the idea into imagery. This means that a relationship element (from Mitch's relationship with his mother) and an interaction element (from the plot) are joined in this film. For Mitch still has to deal with his mother's rejection. He must not only withstand the constant attacks of the birds, but ultimately also resolve the threat from the birds by his own efforts.

For a child, the idea of a bird of prey representing the mother's no is not already linguistically symbolised. But in Hitchcock's film, the birds very concretely represent certain aspects of the child's world of experiences. In the child's early relationship, the mother is experienced as a self-object. The child is affected by her no when it wants to take its first steps.

We can distinguish the following aspects which make the structural analogy of mother and birds, which we are unconsciously aware of, plausible:

a   The small child does not understand the reasons for the mother's no
b   The mother's aggression is experienced as tremendous. The small child has no possibility to elude the no; rather, it is an either/or situation
c   The mother's no is an existential threat to the child; the child is threatened with the loss of love and thus with falling into nothingness

These three aspects are also present in Hitchcock's The Birds.

a   None of the people in the film understand what is going on with the birds
b   The birds do not allow for negotiations or compromises
c   Finally, they are not only an existential threat, they actually fatally injure people in their attacks

In his film, Hitchcock publicly staged the power of the mother in the first year of life, while making the power of the actual mother disappear. This can be described as a transformation of the phantasm.

However, this connection only emerges from Mitch's perspective. His affection for the blonde woman triggers this maternal reaction, which at the same time unconsciously makes him fear the mother's reaction. But in the film, the birds are a more general symbol of the son's unconscious fear that the mother will react highly aggressively to his leaving with a lover. This unconscious conflict dynamic of infancy will also be unconsciously present in all those who are actually affected by the consequences – including the viewers, who presumably identify with Mitch.

Mitch finds the solution to this conflict at the end of the film. He overcomes his fear of his mother, that is he is unhindered as he leaves the house together with his mother and the now distraught blonde woman. He bravely passes a huge gathering of birds gathered in front of the house. They no longer attack

Mitch and his companions because he has been able to overcome his fear. According to this interpretation, the continued presence of the birds is a mere staffage at the end of the film. What was at first a concretion of aspects of the experience has now turned into a backdrop, because the birds no longer symbolise the small child's original fear of the mother's no. In terms of developmental history, Mitch has broken the bonds of symbiosis with the mother. Her no is no longer a threat to him. The mother probably helped him to do so, because at the end of the film, her initial no has been muted.

We also find references to the second layer of meaning – the typical family conflict constellation of this time – in this film. Interestingly, no father figure appears at all. The only power that Mitch and his blonde fiancée must deal with is, in my opinion, the mother's power. This seems to correspond to the family situation in the United States characteristic of Hitchcock's times, in which a dominant mother marginalised the weak father.

Nevertheless, as far as the courage of the main character is concerned, there is also an influence from the father's side in this film: How else could one explain the fact that Mitch gains the strength and nerve to escape the many birds waiting around him at the end of the film, together with his distraught fiancé and the mother? The father is not present here as a character, but he is implicitly assumed to be one of the main characters, providing strength.

In both films by Alfred Hitchcock, we can identify a particular conflictual relationship structure which determines the course of events until the story reaches a positive end. In both cases, we are dealing with cases of repression. However, we would not expect this kind of a defensive measure to appear in cases of narcissistic problems going back to very early childhood. The coherent self that the application of this measure requires is not present there. Instead of the defensive measure of repression, the defensive measure of splitting is used. In the case of a splitting of negative self-parts and negative parts of the reference person, this defence has its origins in serious deficiencies in infancy. In contrast to the defensive measure of repression, what is being defended against is no longer perceived as something that is part of the subject.

This mode of action of splitting and some other characteristics of this narcissistic problem – the so-called crystal ball fantasy and the complete lack of empathy – are best described through the psychoanalytic-therapeutic perspective by Otto F. Kernberg (1978). I will illustrate this with a film by Stephen King, because his films are shaped by the peculiarities of this problem. It follows, however, that we can no longer apply the concept of act signatures of the unconscious there.

4.3 King's The Langoliers (1995)

After landing, a group of air passengers finds itself in a deserted airport building. The passengers realise that they are the only survivors of a flight on which everybody who was not asleep disappeared. Yet the survivors are emotionally uninvolved in this mysterious event. What happened to those who are missing is of no interest to them. What they do notice is that at the airport all the food and drink appear artificial and tasteless.

A little blind girl soon attracts the other passengers' attention because she is the first to become aware of the approach of an invisible evil power, the so-called langoliers.

Without anybody else noticing, yet another passenger, a perfectly dressed businessman, is haunted by a vision of his dead father. In this vision, the businessman sees his father appealing to his conscience; he, in turn, is willing to bow to his father's will. The father reminds him that lazy and indolent people are beset by langoliers as a punishment. Following this vision, the businessman threatens his fellow passengers and seriously injures the little girl by stabbing her with a knife, as if he was possessed by the evil langoliers.

In a new scene, the businessman sees himself standing in front of his superiors, who ask him about his work and discover that he has failed. In the meantime, his fellow passengers are hearing terrifying noises made by the approaching langoliers and decide to try to escape in one of the planes ready for take-off. By now, the langoliers have become visible: They have the shape of spherical monsters with a huge shark's mouth. With their teeth, they break up the airfield and destroy the airport building. The surviving passengers – without the businessman and the blind girl who has died from the injuries she received from the businessman – manage to escape by plane. From the windows, the passengers see the destroyed airport against a background of nothing. In a sharp contrast to these terrible experiences, two pairs of lovers have found each other among the passengers; they represent the possibility of a wonderful counter-world to the horror.

The plan of the rescued passengers is to fly back to the crack in time that they believe they passed through on their original flight, which put them into a kind of in-between space.

On the return flight, the rift in time once again becomes visible in the sky as the same huge, colourful and complex structure that the blind girl had described on the outward flight. Even before she had ever seen this phenomenon through the eyes of the businessman possessed by evil, she had exclaimed "wonderful".

In order to return to real time, all passengers on board must go back to sleep – with the exception of the one person who sacrifices himself and stays awake to steer the plane. The new airport where they finally land initially seems as deserted as the one destroyed by the langoliers. But soon, the passengers realise that the everyday life of an airport is going on around them. They are safe.

Narcissistic problems originating in infancy

In my interpretation, this is an example of the "glass ball fantasy". One of the meanings of this fantasy is that the people affected keep themselves "under a glass top" in order to control their relationships with others and escape having to react to the expectations or wishes of others. In the film, this becomes apparent in the behaviour of the air passengers, who find themselves in an air hall as the only survivors. There, they are surrounded by plastic objects (cf. Volkan & Ast, 1994).

What is striking about this behaviour is a trait which is also characteristic of narcissistic problems that originate in infancy: The complete lack of empathy towards those who appear to have fallen victim to a catastrophe. What happened to them does not interest the survivors in the least.

It is also remarkable how this film presents another characteristic (in the sense of an early blocking of narcissistic development): The use of the defensive measure of splitting in connection with the insecure, unstable relationship with the early mother. I will briefly explain this point.

There are two powers facing each other in this film, the so-called time rift, which is portrayed as the cradle of creation, and the manifestations of evil, the langoliers. Both powers are portrayed in such a way that they remain outside language, communication, and social reality. In this respect, the concepts of a time jump and an in-between time chosen in the film are quite appropriate, as ordering time is an important part of social reality. We can relate these two strictly opposed forces in the context of the subject's developmental history to the very early phase of childhood development, in which there is neither a coherent self nor a stable relationship to the other. At this stage, even language does not yet have its function of structuring reality.

Against this background, the psychological defence measure aimed at the psychological elimination of evil cannot be that of repression. Repression as a defence measure presupposes – as already explained – that the child has already mastered the structuring process of speaking and acting. What is being repressed must be removed from this process – that is as something "that I do not want", "that I am not", "that I do not think", and so on. The use of this defensive measure is supported by the child identifying itself with the negative behaviour of its reference person. For example, the photo reporter in the film *Rear Window* could quite accurately verbalise what he had repressed: "I would like best to kill my fiancée."

In contrast, the langoliers should not be interpreted as something that has been repressed. Instead, we should assume that we are witnessing the defensive measure of splitting – either the splitting of the evil self or the splitting of the evil object. This is backed up by the outward appearance of the langoliers who embody, above all, the threat of being horribly destroyed. An appropriate verbalisation would be extremely difficult here. Such fear and horror can occur in the very early psychological development of the infant under the conditions of serious narcissistic problems. The langoliers embody the immense anger towards the primary caregiver that the child feels when the latter does not accept important aspects of independence of its developing self.

When such a split happens and evil erupts, it destroys all social reality. This is the reason why my approach to deciphering the act signature of the unconscious does not work. This eruption does not take place – as the film by Stephen King shows very clearly – during a process of social action. We can therefore no longer speak of an imprint of the unconscious here. What in clinical perspective is called a "severe narcissistic personality disorder" cannot be the object of my approach.

Hitchcock versus King

What is revealing here is the difference to the two films by Hitchcock, which I have interpreted earlier, *Rear Window* and *The Birds*. In both films, the plot is unconsciously determined by a pre-existing psychological relationship problem of the main protagonist. In *Rear Window*, it is the sexual and aggressive insecurity of the main character, who, due to his broken leg, unconsciously sees his own masculinity threatened.

In *The Birds*, it is the hero's unconscious fear of his mother's aggression, who in turn is afraid of losing her beloved son to another woman. In both films, the development of the storyline is accompanied by a further development of the psychological conflict situation of the actors. We do not find anything comparable in the film by Stephen King. In this sense, there is no story that is created by linking the psychological development of a subject with the development of actions.

The only thing that evolves in this film by Stephen King is the situation of the surviving passengers in relation to the evil power. While they are caught in the intermediate zone between past and future, they are close to this power, which is threatening to swallow them up. Their salvation is very simple; it consists of being able to return to the safety of time in social reality by means of the cradle of creation. The power of the langoliers has not diminished as a result, it continues to exist. It is only kept away from the remaining passengers thanks to the cradle of creation.

It is interesting to see how this film depicts the counter world to the one of evil power. Apart from the cradle of creation, emotions and the desire for life and love are crucial there. Both are characteristic of the kind of narcissistic problem that we have assumed here: Life and one's longing for love are indeed experienced as being under threat. This is caused by the very early traumatising experience of not having one's wishes and ideas respected.

The figure of the businessman who is tormented by the fear of not meeting the expectations of his father and his business partners does not seem to fit in with this pattern of interpretation. In fact, from a therapeutic perspective, Stephen King has probably combined two different types of psychological problems here: The traditionally neurotic problem and the problem of severe narcissistic personality disorder (in the clinical sense). On the one hand, the businessman has, quite traditionally, a feeling of failure vis-à-vis his authoritarian caregiver; at the same time, he is afraid that he will not meet performance expectations in his profession. On the other hand, however, he is experiencing what his father always warned him about: An evil power that besets lazy and indulgent people. This is exactly what happens to him when he, possessed by the evil, threatens his fellow passengers and, in the case of the blind girl and another passenger, even kills them. However, this should not be understood as killing a particular person, but as a general act of destruction.

This combination of a neurotic and a massive narcissistic disorder corresponds to clinical findings. The reason is that forms of narcissistic disorders do not simply replace neurotic disorders in therapeutic treatment; instead, they mask them. As we can see from clinical case reports, successful therapeutic treatment makes it possible to address the neurotic problems once the massive narcissistic disorder has been treated (cf. Volkan/Ast, 1994).

Let us summarise: Both Hitchcock films confirm the interpretation suggested by the psychoanalytical perspective with regard to the social weakening of the paternal authority (cf. G. Mendel 1969; P. Legendre 1988). We can also say that the two films document in their own way the social consequences that can result from the psychological problems of a dominant mother and a weak father.

The film by Stephen King marks a sharp contrast. Here, the existence of a massive narcissistic problem is taken for granted. My approach to investigation reaches its limits: We can no longer recognise an imprint of an act of the unconscious since social reality has been completely destroyed by the collapse of the split-off negative self-parts. The clinical category of severe narcissistic personality disorder (borderline and psychosis) tries to do justice to this mental problem. For the subject of my research, however, this problem can only be of marginal importance.

5 Vegetarians and vegans: The link between psychology and political effectiveness

Vegans and vegetarians have my sympathy. By refraining from eating meat (and fish), they express an empathy with nature which I share. In former times, farm animals were often part of the family, had a name, and sometimes were protected even when they got old.

Industrialised breeding, in contrast, degrades farm animals to mere suppliers of meat. With factory farming, animals are denatured, and so are humans. With the current food industry, we are all losing an essential part of ourselves: Respect for living creatures. This is in line with other processes that threaten other natural foundations of our existence: The progressive loss of species, climate change, and much more.

If vegans and vegetarians aim to stop this negative development by political means, an important question arises: In order to influence politics, what do they need to understand about the connection between psychological (mostly unconscious) processes and political effectiveness? I will describe this link in individual aspects in the hope that this will help the necessary political action against factory farming and killing.

In a first step, I will concentrate on some of the psychological aspects that are related to the decision of vegans and vegetarians to stop consuming meat. It is important to be aware of these aspects because they can make a political intervention into social reality more difficult, although such intervention is certainly desirable. To put it bluntly, these psychological aspects may be among the unrecognised problems of some vegans and vegetarians.

With regard to the psychological aspects, I distinguish what is subjectively and psychologically possible from what exists in the individual case. Anxieties, desires, illusions, feelings of guilt, different kinds of desire, and so forth are subjectively possible. They always relate to something specific. Whether these subjective processes and situations are also present in each individual case is a different question. One's own experience of analysis as well as one's knowledge of the relevant methods and their theoretical context are the elements that enable access to the psychological. We gain access to the individual through one-on-one therapy, interviews, coaching, group discussions, and the like.

In the following I will limit myself to what I consider subjectively possible with regard to vegetarians and vegans. What will remain open is how common each of these psychological aspects really are among vegans and vegetarians.

In a second step, I will be looking at the new understanding of politics that is expressed here, which is particularly relevant to the younger generation. According to this understanding, we can contribute to a better world as consumers through conscious purchasing decisions. By avoiding, for example, the products of textile companies which manufacture in low-cost countries, consumers protest the working conditions and starvation wages of the workers exploited by those companies. Vegetarians and vegans usually also want to make a political statement. But which other political steps can they take, and which psychological hurdles may be blocking their way?

In my view, we need to consider both the psychological and the political aspects that lead vegetarians and vegans to their choice and the desirable political consequences that follow from that decision. If we leave out the psychological aspects, our political concept may be shaped by goals and paths that are neither realistic nor effective, whereas a mere focus on the psychological aspects runs the risk of being politically ineffective.[15]

5.1 Possible psychological aspects

Many vegans and vegetarians agree that the way meat is produced today by industrialised farming amounts to a form of violence. Melanie Joy writes that "the extensive violence around which meat consumption [carnism] is organised today is so great that most people are not willing to see it. If they did, they would be seriously disturbed" (Joy, 2010, p. 33, D.F.).

Let's look at this point a little more closely. What does it meant that "most people are not willing to see this"? A brief cultural-historical outline may be helpful.

How cultural progress can turn into a hidden social contradiction

The development towards factory farming and slaughtering began in the Middle Ages with the invention of the kitchen for the nobility. Animals were now slaughtered and gutted in the kitchen, and this was, too, where meat was cut up and prepared. This led to the first spatial separation of meat preparation and meat consumption. In the dining room, the nobility could now eat meat without being disturbed by the sight of the bloody preparation.

According to the cultural sociologist and historian Norbert Elias, this was indeed an important step in the development of our civilisation. From that time, on it was considered unrefined and uncivilised to practice the bloody process of evisceration and preparation of meat and its consumption in the same place (cf. Elias, 1976, Vol. I, p. 162).

With the rise of the middle classes in the 18th and 19th centuries, the cultural history of the kitchen entered the next phase. Now, even the preparation of food in the kitchen became civilised. This happened (and still happens) in what one might call the "genteel kitchen", which has nothing in common with the kitchen of the Middle Ages and the bloody business which took place there. The aggressive act of slaughtering now became even further removed from the place where meat was consumed. From this time, slaughtering took place mainly in the slaughterhouse.

Today, this tradition of separating the slaughtering and preparation of meat spatially from the consumption has reached an almost perverse climax. As civilised beings, we actually should no longer be disgusted with the blood that is being shed, but with the automated, instant killing of the largest possible number of animals that must exist under sometimes horrible conditions before they are killed.

The invention of the kitchen, which was analysed by Elias in terms of a cultural advance, has changed over time into a social contradiction due to factory farming. I refer to the contradiction that a civilised society meets its needs of animal meat in a truly barbaric and violent way.

It is no coincidence that large factory farms are now located far outside the cities and are therefore hidden from the eyes of consumers. This is exactly what meat consumers want: To eat without being bothered. And this is what they have wanted for a long time. The meat lobby and large industrialised meat production companies know that meat consumers do not want to be disturbed during their meals by the perception of a meat production that is repulsive and disgusting. Actually, meat eaters do not want to be reminded of this even when they are not eating.

The modern kitchen, just like the meat industry, saves meat eaters from feeling guilt or shame for supporting this barbarism. Meat eaters do not see the path that factory-produced meat has taken until it is nicely packaged and offered for sale in the store, from where it ends up on their plate. Consumers usually do not want to know what barbaric path a piece of meat has taken until it has reached the shop.

Nevertheless, solving a societal contradiction by looking away is a very one-sided solution. While the consumers are spared the feelings of guilt or shame, which would otherwise probably arise, the animals' lot is not improved. This widespread attitude of turning a blind eye has become part of normality. It contributes significantly to the fact that the societal contradiction remains hidden.

Turning a blind eye seems so normal because it is facilitated by the meat industry: Most of its large facilities for breeding and killing animals operate out of the public eye. Television crews usually only get access to the model farms. This observation is confirmed by the television documentary *Unser täglich Tier* (Our daily animal) (2014), to which I will come back later.

Vegetarians and vegans deal with this social contradiction quite differently from meat-eaters. They, too, do not want to feel guilt or shame when they eat, but instead of looking the other way, they take the side of the animals that are being tortured. For them, industrialised meat production is an unbearable form of violence in which they do not want to take part. This is why they renounce meat.

This brings me to a potential subjective problem. On the one hand, their decision not to consume meat is more radical than the attitude of the meat eaters, because it is set against what is considered normal and appears to open up a way to actually solve the societal contradiction one day.

On the other hand, however, radical solutions can always be associated with psychological aspects that make it difficult, if not impossible, to translate them into politically successful action. I will discuss this in more detail here:

The problem with moral superiority

One Vegan woman described the reason for her decision to stop eating animal products with the following words: "I want to lead a life that is free of violence". This is a sentiment which is frequently expressed. But it can be interpreted very differently.

One possibility is to see it as a reference to one of the Christian commandments, namely "Thou shalt not kill". Of course, many people are aware of the fact that in real life, it is impossible to always respect every one of the Christian commandments. Therefore, one must necessarily sin. The Christian prohibition of killing, for example, has always had two exceptions: Killing in war and the killing of animals. Nevertheless, these commandments can have a positive cultural meaning if we behave more humanely because we strive to observe them.

It is also possible, however, that some vegetarians and vegans interpret the decision to live a life without violence in such a way that the renunciation of meat consumption is equivalent to the renunciation of any violence. In extreme cases, this non-violence also entails the absence of any kind of aggression.

In my opinion, that would be an illusion. One would be following an ego-ideal which – as numerous examples from our cultural history show – is quite unrealistic. Aggression is an integral part of human behaviour.

The renunciation of meat is no protection against one's own aggressive potential. It is highly likely that completely independently of food, one's aggressiveness will find a different object that is suitable. In other words, vegetarians and vegans must also cope with their own aggressiveness.

If violence is equated with being evil, then the renunciation of violence is an attempt to keep one's ego free of all evil. But then the fact that death is part of life is also being denied. What can actually be an issue of keeping humans alive is reinterpreted as a question of morality.

Many vegans and vegetarians appear to be feeling morally superior to meat eaters. This feeling can be based on insights into the world-wide food industry that rely on scientific research. T. Colin Campbell and Thomas M. Campbell (2011) have vividly documented the connection between (wrong) nutrition and disease. They also describe an everyday reality in the United States, where government, science, and industry all contribute to the disease-causing status so that a minority can enrich itself.

This is an insight which will make it easier to distinguish between what is deception and what is reality in the food industry; which of the supposedly tasty foods are in fact unhealthy and sold only for the profit they promise, and so forth. All of this can lead to a feeling of superiority which also has moral aspects.

The feeling of being morally superior to meat consumers may also be based on a certain egocentricity. Vegetarians and vegans feel morally superior because they consider their own behaviour to be the yardstick of proper consumption. They mainly think of themselves and not so much of those people who cannot afford a balanced meatless nutrition. Meat is highly subsidised (see following discussion), especially when consumed as fast food, so it is often less expensive than vegetarian and vegan cuisine.

But perhaps they are right, when they consider their eating habits to be the yardstick of proper nutrition? Aren't vegans and vegetarians the spearhead of a movement that can resolve the societal contradiction mentioned earlier?

In my opinion, the social reality is much more complex. What is at issue here is to turn an individual decision into a socially accepted norm. And this requires political action.

5.2 Proposals for a political concept

To be able to show how a psychological problem can make targeted political intervention more difficult, I would first like to discuss in more detail the new understanding of politics that we encounter today, especially among the younger generation.

5.2.1 Consumer choice as a part of politics

Young consumers in particular assume that conscious decisions for or against a certain product can have a political impact and promote a better world. Renouncing cheap textiles produced under miserable conditions becomes a political statement, as does the decision to do without fish and meat products in order to stop supporting factory farming and killing.

It is understandable that young people turn to taking deliberate decisions about their personal consumption in order to improve social reality. Today, many do not see how else they can intervene in the highly complex system of politics. The new way of consuming more deliberately appears to be the last remaining instrument for getting politically involved. But how realistic is this approach of exerting political influence through deliberate consumption decisions?

Most older people have not been able – or have not wanted to – exert much influence on politics. For the older generation, politics was essentially about a theatre performance where politicians act on stage and responsible citizens sit in the auditorium. Every four years, the citizens clap and cheer after voting for those actors whose performance on stage they considered the most convincing.

Even for the older generation, the personal element of politics has always been important. With the modern media, it has become even more prominent, especially personal appearances in public. In addition, however, the younger generation now brings the consumer component of politics into play.

Max Weber famously described politics as "the slow and difficult drilling of holes into hard boards while employing passion and a sense of proportion" (Weber, 1987 [1919], p. 67). In this process, consumers now have a real chance of influencing the producers because the policy of consumer choice is based on the market mechanism of supply and demand. It is only because the demand for meat (and fish) is so enormous that the current system of the meat and fish industry can continue to exist. In the long run, it could be shaken up if more and more people renounced meat and fish produced in factory farming.

Therefore, deliberate consumption as a political decision can, under certain circumstances, be quite successful. But people who believe they are role models that others should follow – that's a more questionable way of turning a personal decision into a socially effective measure. It would be better to take the next step in terms of politics: Vegetarians and vegans could over time transform their individual decision into a norm required by society through changes of the law. They should intervene in the highly complex system of politics by involving the legislators.

But how can this be done without getting trapped by a psychological problem situation which can endanger the political impact? Weak arguments and irrational statements, for instance, can easily undermine even an important cause in the public's eye.

5.2.2 Psychological problem situation and political action

Here, too, act signatures of the unconscious may become visible. A person's unresolved psychological problems, which shape the structural elements of action, can determine that person's actions in the political dimension.

I will now use four examples to show how the mental preconditions of political action – for example, concepts of the situation, images of one's self and the others, plans of action – can be impaired by the presumed psychological problems.

a   A person believes that his or her behaviour as a consumer somehow does damage to the meat or food industry. In fact, this hope is illusory. The basic problem of how to move from an individual consumption decision to a socially effective attitude has not yet been solved.

b   The feeling of moral superiority that some vegans and vegetarians have can make it difficult for them to analyse the structural power represented by the food industry as a whole. The food industry is all about profit in a highly competitive environment. Under those circumstances, somebody's feeling of superiority remains a purely private matter which has no significance for this power. And as a private matter, it is also insignificant in terms of changing conditions.

c   The food industry, especially the industry responsible for meat exports, will not voluntarily forego any of its power or profit. It will have to be forced to do so – yet this is precisely what peace-loving vegetarians and vegans may find difficult. Dividing the world into a pattern of peacefulness on the one side and violence on the other does not correspond to political reality. For example, a lobbyist for the meat industry does not have to be a person who is prone to violence.

d   If the self-image is such that the self needs to be kept free from all evil, then all-or nothing situations easily arise. Vegans and vegetarians who feel this way find it difficult to push for small steps. Yet only a policy of incremental improvements is realistic, as we will see at the conclusion of this chapter.

5.2.3 A step-by-step approach

Nick Cooney (2011) has compiled psychological studies on how people can be influenced in their everyday behaviour. For his studies, he predominantly follows the approach of behavioural social psychology. While this is quite different from my own research approach, I consider one of the findings obtained to be plausible, namely the recommendation to proceed in small steps. This is the only way that the existing self-image of people can be changed.

The first step can be to insist on compliance with existing laws. Thomas Schröder, president of the German association for animal protection, points out that Germany has strict animal protection laws which forbid unnecessary cruelty to animals. Yet the authorities do not monitor compliance. According to Schröder, parliament is at fault because it failed to specify standards for the practical implementation of the law. The importance of such standards becomes clear by the fact that chickens may still be fattened to the extent that they almost become unable to walk. The methods of cramming pigs together and fattening them up is also entirely contrary to proper animal husbandry.

The next step could be to motivate people to eat a little less meat. A reduction in meat consumption seems more realistic than to insist that nobody should eat any meat at all. Economically speaking, the amount of meat produced in factory farming has tripled in some cases while the price of meat has fallen. This is a consequence of the high subsidies for this industry which, for instance, the Heinrich Böll Foundation described in 2013 (Benning, 2013, pp. 16–17.).

Intervening by law to reduce these subsidies is difficult because indirect subsidies play the main role. Uncovering them is no easy task, but it can be done. That would allow parliament to adopt a law to ensure that those subsidies are reduced, which will result in an increase the price of meat. Less meat originating from factory farming will be consumed, and the consumption of meat will decrease overall.

These would be two first steps to stop factory farming through legislation.

The (covert) contradiction that a civilised (Western) society consumes meat produced in a barbaric way cannot be completely resolved in the long run. The social power of the meat lobby, its close links to politics, and the fact that it is normal for meat consumer to turn a blind eye are serious obstacles. Even so, exposing this contradiction, reflecting on possible psychological problems, and pursuing the legal option just mentioned are important steps to try and regain a part of nature to which we also belong. If we do not get engaged, it will soon be lost to us.

6 A brief summary

We have now examined a wide array of examples of social interaction to understand how the unconscious shapes social behaviour. In each case, I have focused on showing what becomes visible and understandable once you take the influence of the unconscious into account.

There is a reason why I chose these particular examples: They represent phenomena that are both topical and symptomatic today. Mobbing is a problem which does not only affect employees in companies and institutions but also children at school. We can only find solutions if we look at the underlying causes, and not just at the description of symptoms.

There is a worldwide debate on climate change which is sometimes conducted very aggressively, not only among scientists and climate sceptics, but also among the general public. This is not surprising as these are survival issues that trigger fear and resistance among many people around the world.

The question of how a company can be managed in such a way that it is not only successful but also conducts its business responsibly is also highly topical. Managers undergo countless consultations and coaching sessions to learn how to address their increasingly difficult tasks. Yet they are faced with emotional conflicts that make it difficult for them to exert authority in a positive way.

Modern media and films reflect what people are interested in, but they are also indicators of unresolved inner conflicts. Finally, even the meaningful impulse to forego eating meat and stop the unspeakable treatment of animals in the meat industry can become so ideologised that political implementation becomes difficult. Here, too, we see the unconscious at work.

Of course, there is any number of other social phenomena which we could include in our examination, such as how to deal with the pandemic, with xenophobia, the massive rise of right-wing populist movements, or the increasing frequency of terrible terrorist acts. I can only hope that my (admittedly somewhat arbitrary) selection will encourage others to follow my line of investigation and shed more light on the unconscious patterns underlying those phenomena.

Notes

1 In Kohut's psychology of the self, this inner image corresponds to the narcissistic configuration of the idealised parental imago, of which the maternal side is emphasised here.

2 The analysis of mobbing in the previous chapter is compatible with this thesis.

3 This change is also documented in sociological literature. For example, the patriarch as a traditional type of entrepreneur has been disappearing for some time (Illouz, 2009). The new organisational structure of a flat hierarchy has replaced the traditionally strong hierarchy that used to be the norm (see Sennett, 1998).

4 See Frankfurter Allgemeine Zeitung, 26 March 2014.

5 Jürgen Grieser (1998) gives an interesting overview of the peer group discussion (see p. 174ff.).

6 Written communication from an employee of WDR in an e-mail dated 18.01.2014. Guido Baumhauer, Director of Distribution and Technology at Deutsche Welle, told me that while WDR has a director-general, my interpretations seem to indicate that one would be right to speak of a "pseudo-consensual culture".

7 According to Kruse, every year, "hundreds of thousands of changes take place in the top management in Germany alone" (ibid., p. 79).

8 Unfortunately, the corresponding essay by Schütz (1964), in which he reflected on his own experiences as an immigrant in the United States, has not yet given rise to further work.

9 In a study I conducted at the psychosomatic department of a hospital in Berlin, this repertory grid method was used by the doctors working there (see Flader & Bartholomew & Bublitz, 1993.).

10 On language and the hidden communication conflicts from job references, see Presch (1985).

11 Oral communication from Grodzicki. Similarly, as Gemma Jappe (1971) has shown, the distinction between primary and secondary process is nothing more than the transposition of a neurological model originally developed by Freud to the psychological.

12 Mertens (2005, pp. 228–229), too, proposes to start from a "culpably experienced voyeuristic view of the primal scene". He also interprets Jeff's second leg fracture as a punishment but sees his guilt in his "imaginary participation in the primal scene experience".

13 Why the spatial metaphor of repression can be misleading, I have explained in an earlier publication (Flader, 2000).

14 Žižek (2001) also pointed to this meaning of the birds.

15 Some of my theses I explained on 27 February 2015, in an interview for the radio programme *Das Kulturgespräch* in Baden-Baden.

Chapter 5

Psychoanalysis in the perception of modern science

I Psychoanalysis from the perspective of the social sciences

It is hardly surprising that all the examples presented in this book are about people: Both actively, in their role of taking action, and passively, as recipients and consumers. Some people exercise power and responsibility in society; others feel powerless and forced to accept circumstances or facts without being able to influence them. But irrespective of role and social status, a great many of them face a problem that affects all strata of society: A lack of self-esteem.

This is a phenomenon which is so pervasive that it amounts to a modern symptom. It does not matter whether someone is rich, powerful, and influential, whether he or she is accepted at the heart of society and fulfils a role in the family or other social constellations, or whether he or she is a person living on the fringes of society: They can all share the fundamental feeling of not being "just right".

In part, this goes back to our achievement-oriented society, in which perfection, performance, success, and profit are highly prized. Another reason, as I have shown and continue to show, are the family constellations which shape us.

Clinical reports from psychotherapists of various disciplines leave no room for doubt. Most patients today suffer from a lack of self-esteem. If we assume that outside of therapy, this psychological problem also occurs frequently, an interesting question arises: What conclusions can we draw from the clinical-therapeutic reports about non-clinical patterns of thought and behaviour that are related to the same psychological problem? Can we recognise patterns that supersede the individual because they have something to do with our Western culture?

This, of course, was the question I asked at the very beginning of my investigation. To conclude this book, I will now discuss three papers which also offer an answer to this question but take different paths, both from one another and from the interpretation I have presented here. I believe it useful to analyse those differences.

DOI: 10.4324/9780429345449-5

1.1 The psychoanalytical interpretations in the social sciences

In 1995, Reiche (1995) discussed "applications of psychoanalysis to other sciences" in a knowledgeable and differentiated manner which I find highly informative. Reiche points out that all these applications always ended in a "functionalist reduction".[1]

Yet Reiche bases his analysis on a tacit assumption which I consider problematic. He believes that psychoanalytical statements about social reality must always be bound to the specific form of the theory which Freud developed and bequeathed us. This form includes both the model of the psychic apparatus and Freud's scientific ways of thinking, which are rooted in his training in the natural sciences and in certain theoretical models of the 19th century. This connection is often referred to (and rightly so!), especially in scientific theoretical discussions (see Lichtman, 1990). One example of this is Freud's tendency towards dualism, as, for instance, in the dualism of inside and outside emphasised by Reiche, which he considers fundamental. Others are the mechanistic conception of psychological processes, the almost complete exclusion of the dimension of social action as a result of a "peep box psychology" (as Michael Balint aptly called Freud's basic theoretical approach), and many more.

Apparently, Reiche believes that psychoanalysis can only contribute to the investigation of social phenomena under a very specific condition – the condition of orthodoxy. And it is precisely this condition which is bound to bring research to a dead end. In fact, we need to continue developing the fundamental theory of psychoanalysis to be able to see where it can gain us a better understanding of the social context.

As a science, psychoanalysis is still young, even though more than a hundred years have passed since the publication of the *Interpretation of Dreams*. The term "young science" does not mean that the explanatory potential of Freudian theoretical models has been exhausted. From a hermeneutic point of view, such exhaustion will never be complete because each generation continues to reinterpret these models according to its own interests and problems. What is meant by young science instead is that the entire theoretical construction is not yet consistent and that the metaphorical content of basic concepts has only partially been considered. Above all, metapsychology lacks important theories that are needed for a psychoanalytic explanation and which Freud did not develop: A profound theory of meaning; a psychoanalytic theory of action; a theory of the relationship between psychic energy and psychic structure, to name those that are perhaps the most important.

A different path than the one Reiche has in mind may be more promising: By further developing one's own theoretical foundations, the explanatory potential that the respective science holds can be better exploited. This is what happened after Freud's death. Narcissism research, for example, took up and expanded Freud's thoughts on narcissism after his death (cf. Kohut, 1973).

The continued development of psychoanalysis is based on changing attitudes towards tradition. Each generation can only assimilate Freud's discoveries by interpreting them against the backdrop of its own experiences. The theoretical foundations of these discoveries, if we take them seriously, set us a task: We must continue work on them to secure the foundations of the theoretical models. The neighbouring disciplines of psychoanalysis can contribute important suggestions to help us in our task, provided that the concepts developed in other disciplines can be used productively without losing proven psychoanalytic insights. These neighbouring disciplines can benefit in turn by adapting insights of psychoanalysis to their theoretical models.

In a young science such as psychoanalysis, this form of interdisciplinary cooperation presupposes a healthy stubbornness and a certain scepticism towards attempts to finding something that is specific to psychoanalysis in neighbouring disciplines. Reiche, however, seems to be making such an attempt when he agrees with Jürgen Habermas' view of how psychoanalytic methods and results can be used. Habermas believes they can serve as an auxiliary method for analysing social processes in cases where "systemically induced lifeworld pathologies" occur (Habermas, 1981, p. 565; Reiche, 1995, p. 252).

Habermas and the lifeworld approach

Already in his earlier works, Habermas (1981) referred to the sociological concept of the "Lebenswelt" (universe of living) when he tried to do theoretical justice to the experiential world of everyday life. This is a concept which Alfred Schütz developed in his phenomenological sociology. But it is based on a notion of the subject which is not compatible with that of psychoanalysis. The subject of the lifeworld – as Schütz and others see it – is conceived as an entirely rational being since it produces social contexts of meaning exclusively in a cognitive way. This is done by using typification schemes and relevance criteria or by constructing the other as an alter ego and so on (cf. Berger & Luckmann, 1977). Even the process of developing emotional relationships with another person, which is elementary for psychoanalysis, has no place in this lifeworld of cognitive sociology, let alone what we assume to be true about the unconscious.

The task assigned to psychoanalysis here – to assist in the investigation of lifeworld pathologies – seems to be a defensive strategy against psychoanalysis, which is widespread in science today. The psychoanalytic explanatory potential is marginalised by limiting its competence to pathological special cases and recognising its validity only there.

In my opinion, a similar form of hostility is documented in the explanation that Habermas uses to connect crisis-like changes in family life worlds with, among other things, the "diminishing importance of the Oedipal problem".

He refers to the change in the typical symptoms of the time that were observed by psychoanalytically trained doctors and gives the following explanation:

> These confirm that the current significant changes are beyond a socio-psychological explanation based on the Oedipal problem and the internalisation of social repression masked by parental authority. Explanations are more effective which are based on the premise that communication structures unleashed in the family represent socialisation conditions that are both *demanding* and *vulnerable*. A potential for irritation arises. (Habermas, 1981, p. 569)

The subject we are talking about here is an evolving social subject. It is – as I pointed out earlier – by definition a bearer of competences (interaction competence, language competence, competence of moral awareness, etc.). It becomes part of society when it has acquired these competences.

A therapeutic-clinical observation – the decreasing importance of the Oedipal problem – is interpreted theoretically by Habermas in terms of its consequence: The unleashing of communication structures. These consequences are then evaluated according to whether they are conducive to socialisation or make it more difficult. The Oedipal problem is understood not psychoanalytically at all but rather in terms of its possible resolution, the internalisation of parental authority.

We arrive at a different perspective of research when we do not examine society but its cultural phenomena, bearing in mind that the latter are already embedded in psychoanalysis, albeit in a mostly hidden fashion.

Every patient in psychoanalytic therapy represents a part of social reality – the social reality in which he lives, about which he reports, and which has shaped him to a certain extent. Moreover, we can assume that the activity of the psychoanalyst is by no means, as Reiche claims, primarily to "translate external reality into internal reality" (Reiche, 1995, p. 230). Rather, the analyst works together with the patient on the emotional relationship pattern which the patient brings to him and which he takes up in a controlled manner. If that is so, the question of the correct application of psychoanalysis to society is misplaced. The therapeutic material and the analysis of the case based on this material already contain indications of a psychoanalytic cultural diagnosis, albeit condensed and structurally abridged. This applies above all to clinical information, psychological conflict constellations, and their history of development in childhood. The extent to which these can be regarded as typical – for a social group or a generation – must then be clarified more precisely.

From this perspective, psychoanalytic therapy is a seismograph of current cultural upheavals in our society. However, we must also learn to read this seismograph. In Chapter 1, I have shown how productive the concept of the act signature of the unconscious is. The concrete implementation in selected social fields, together with the appropriate analytical concepts, was the purpose of my investigations in Chapter 2.

1.2 A modern social critique from a psychoanalytical perspective (Ch. Lasch)

Christopher Lasch's study is in the tradition of a socio-critical psychoanalysis, which combines a critique of capitalism with reports about the mental suffering and unresolved mental conflicts that arise under the working conditions produced by capitalism. In contrast to the work of Twenge/Campbell (cf. Section 2), Lasch sees the urgent need for more theoretical work on the concept of narcissism. To do this, he draws on the work of psychoanalytical narcissism research, especially that of Kernberg (1978). According to Lasch, this narcissism research, especially its concept of the narcissistic personality disorder, provides us "with a way of understanding the psychological impact of recent social changes" (ibid., p. 64). In other words, the therapeutic-clinical data are used to draw an accurate portrait of the narcissistically disturbed personality of our days.

Lasch accepts Kernberg's clinical observation that the narcissistic patient divides society into two groups, "the rich, great, and famous on the one hand and the common herd on the other" (ibid., pp. 103–104). The narcissist strives to belong to the first group and is afraid of being discovered to be merely mediocre. I find the extension of therapeutic symptom descriptions to society somewhat problematic. But Lasch arrives at the conclusion that we live in a narcissistic society.

Some of the observations and interpretations, however, which Lasch makes about recent cultural history and current social reality, continue to be interesting in their socio-critical claim. This is particularly true for his remarks about the United States, which are often based on relevant commentators, contemporary critics, and sociologists. For example, his depiction of the decay and devaluation of sport is still relevant today, and not just to the United States. Especially Lasch's analysis of modern competitive sport, in which certain conventions and rules that would be essential to a game are no longer observed, is very revealing. Lasch shows that modern competitive sport no longer has anything to do with playing. Instead, it destroys the spell that would have been created by a game (ibid., p. 134).

Lasch also very vividly describes the widespread phenomenon of parents who do not know how to bring up their children. He describes how the ideal of perfect parenthood has devastating consequences for the upbringing of children:

> The invasion of the family by industry, the mass media, and the agencies of socialized parenthood has subtly altered the quality of the parent-child connection. It has created an ideal of perfect parenthood while destroying

parents' confidence in their ability to perform the most elementary functions of childrearing. (ibid., p. 202)

If we disregard these problematic generalisations, Lasch's descriptions from the 1970s bear an astonishing similarity to the clinical-therapeutic findings made by the child therapist Bergmann (2006) about "the drama of the modern child". In contrast to Twenge and Campbell, Lasch illustrates how difficult it is today to ensure the continuity of generations within the family, on which every culture is based:

> Instead of guiding the children, the older generation now struggles to 'keep up with the kids,' to master their incomprehensible jargon, and even to imitate their dress and manners in the hope of preserving a youthful appearance and outlook. (ibid., p. 202)

Yet Lasch's suggestion that it is possible to draw a direct line from the diagnoses of narcissism research to the cultural phenomena of our time often appears to fall somewhat short.

For example, he claims that there is an affinity between the theatre of the absurd and borderline disorders which are the clinical manifestation of a narcissistic personality disorder. Such an affinity may be true in the case of individual theatregoers. But Lasch's diagnosis says nothing at all about the aesthetic quality and truthfulness of Beckett's plays, which show the decay of the social model of the individual down to language. Lasch's tendency towards generalisation reinforces his thesis that we live in an age of narcissism. He says, for example: "The prevalent mode of interaction today is antagonistic co-operation" (ibid., p. 143). "Society", from this perspective, easily becomes a threatening overall subject that appears to embody the narcissistic disorder suffered by the patients, which was studied by Kohut and others. This view of society is determined by Lasch's theoretical approach. He explains his perspective in the epilogue of his book:

> My underlying assumptions were drawn from a tradition of studies, carried out for the most part by cultural anthropologists, sociologists, and psychoanalysts, that concerned themselves with the effect of culture on personality. Scholars in this tradition argued that every culture works out distinctive patterns of childrearing and socialization, which have the effect of producing a distinctive personality type suited to the requirement of that culture. (ibid., p. 282)

As an example of this connection, it is worth looking at Lasch's criticism of the American education system:

> Contrary to the pronouncements of most educational theorists and their allies in the social sciences, advanced industrial society no longer rests on a

> population primed for achievement. It requires instead a stupefied
> population, resigned to work that is trivial and shoddily performed,
> predisposed to seek its satisfaction in the time set aside for leisure.
> (ibid., p. 153)

The perspective presented by Lasch is that of people holding power in the
United States. The new managerial elite, according to Lasch, is a new ruling
class of administrators, bureaucrats, technicians, and experts who are responsible for "paternalism without father".

> The difference between the new managerial elite and the old propertied
> elite defines the difference between a bourgeois culture that now survives
> only on the margins of industrial society and the new therapeutic culture
> of narcissism. (ibid., p. 260)

Lasch continues his description:

> As the new elite discards the outlook of the old bourgeoisie, it identifies
> itself not with the work ethic and the responsibilities of wealth but with an
> ethic of leisure, hedonism, and self-fulfilment. (ibid., p. 263)

With the help of psychology and small group research, methods for "human
leadership" have gained influence in modern companies, Lasch explains.
Under the guise of participation, managers are in fact sticking to hierarchical
forms of organisation. The modern manager no longer bosses his subordinates
around; he has discovered more subtle means of keeping them in check.

> Even though his underlings often realize that they have been "conned,
> pushed around, and manipulated," they find it hard to resist such easy-going
> oppression. The diffusion of responsibility in large organizations, moreover,
> enables the modern manager to delegate discipline to others, to blame
> unpopular decisions on the company in general, and thus to preserve his
> standing as a friendly adviser to those beneath him. (ibid., p. 220)

To sum up his investigations, Lasch combines social criticism and the clinical-
therapeutic findings of a narcissistic disorder in the following way:

> In a society without authority, the lower orders no longer experience
> oppression as guilt. Instead, they internalise a grandiose idea of the
> opportunities open to all, together with an inflated opinion of their own
> capacities. (ibid., pp. 220–221)

I consider both of Lasch's premises to be problematic. A given culture can only
have such a one-sided effect on the educational practices of parents and thus

on the psyche of the growing child if the requirements of the respective culture not only are generally accepted but also remain constant. This assumption may apply to so-called traditional societies – this is what Erikson (1968) assumed in his study on "Childhood and Society". But it does not plausibly apply to modern society. Here, an interaction of culture and individual as well as collective psychological dispositions is to be assumed.

The second assumption – that a certain type of personality is produced in each case – follows the clinical approach of a psychological diagnosis. This approach is based on personality types or personality disorders which are useful in the clinical day-to-day business of therapeutic treatment of patients. But it is detrimental to the theoretical analysis of the connection between mental conflict structures and the cultural phenomena on which those conflict structures can have an impact.

At the conclusion of his research, Lasch explains this aspect:

> Our society is narcissistic, then, in a double sense [sic]. People with narcissistic personalities, although not necessarily more numerous than before, play a conspicuous role in contemporary life, often rising to positions of eminence.... Modern capitalist society not only elevates narcissists to prominence, it elicits and reinforces narcissistic traits in everyone. It does this in many ways: By displaying narcissism so prominently and in such attractive forms; by undermining parental authority and thus making it hard for children to grow up; but above all by creating so many varieties of bureaucratic dependence. This dependence, increasingly widespread in a society that is not only paternalistic but maternalistic as well, makes it increasingly difficult for people to lay to rest the terrors of infancy or to enjoy the consolations of adulthood. (ibid., pp. 274–275)

It is above all the socially organised dependency of individuals, in the professional field as well as in private life, which Lasch sees as the societal precondition of a narcissistic disorder.

> In its pathological form, narcissism originates as a defence against the feeling of helpless dependency in early life, which it tries to counter with 'blind optimism' and grandiose illusions of personal self-sufficiency. Since modern society prolongs the experience of dependence into adult life, it encourages milder forms of narcissism in people who might otherwise come to terms with the inescapable limits on their personal freedom and power – limits inherent in the human condition – by developing competence as workers and parents. But at the same time that our society makes it more and more difficult to find satisfaction in love and work, it surrounds the individual with manufactured fantasies of total gratification. (ibid., pp. 273–274)

Lasch's essay, which appears to be a diagnosis of the present day and focuses on the social phenomena of modern narcissism, has only seemingly found a workable approach to these and other burning questions of our time.

The author mostly sticks to an essayistic depiction of conspicuous social behaviour, which only rarely refers to the emotional conflict structure existing in the unconscious of the persons concerned. Even though Lasch takes a closer look at the clinical literature of psychoanalysis, his investigation of cultural phenomena in politics, advertising, family upbringing, and the relationships of men and women rarely goes beyond a superficial representation. For his "diagnosis of our time", he mostly contents himself with terms and concepts taken from the editorials of an enlightened press and relevant cultural-critical works from sociology and philosophy.

1.3 Psychoanalysis from the perspective of cultural sociology (E. Illouz)

In *Saving the Modern Soul. Therapy, Emotions and the Culture of Self-Help* (2008), Eva Illouz gives a cultural-sociological explanation of the extraordinary success of psychoanalysis in the United States and its consequences for Western culture as a whole. Illouz believes that it is one of the main tasks of cultural sociology to answer the question of how and where texts influence actions. Texts are defined not only as systems of expert knowledge but also as systems of popular knowledge, provided that the latter are sufficiently detailed and disseminated by the mass media.

The self in the approach of a sociology of culture

In accordance with Durkheim's sociology, the self is understood "as an inextricable ensemble of cognition and emotion" (ibid., p. 38). With this understanding of the self, it becomes clear why texts can feed into actions through cognition and emotion. According to Illouz, texts in the form of films, psychic guides, and so on influence us not only as hermeneutical tools that help us (in the sense of American pragmatism) to understand the world and solve everyday problems of action. Texts are also cultural tools which help to tap into, evoke, and channel complex emotional structures.

Psychological texts feed into actions, for example, if novels or guidebooks offer scenarios through which actors can cognitively rehearse their emotional experience and reflect on how others act and express themselves emotionally. In this way, they arrange their own feelings and those of others, subtly establish rules for dealing with feelings, and bring forth a vocabulary and method of self-observation (ibid., p. 39). On this theoretical basis, Illouz then devotes herself in more detail to the question of how the remarkable success of psychoanalysis in the United States can be explained and what extraordinary contribution Freud made to culture – a contribution which continues to be present in various forms today.

Illouz' core thesis is that the boundary between specialised psychological knowledge – including Freudian thought – and the so-called popular psychology is permeable. This is because both the language of professional psychology and its popular version focus on the self, using similar metaphors and narratives.

According to Illouz, the various cultural fields of professional and popular psychology are united by a common emotional style. This emotional style is established when a new idea of interpersonal relationships is developed. Freud's ideas have done just that in the United States.

Before I go into this in more detail, I would like to briefly mention one more of Illouz' main points. She emphasises that as a result of this new emotional style, therapeutic discourse has become omnipresent in professional articles, talk shows, self-help guides, and television programmes. Therapeutic is defined by her as "the quantity of claims made by accredited psychologists and the quantity of texts in which psychologists and/or therapy play a role" (ibid., p. 33).

Freud's thinking, according to Illouz, made it possible to reformulate the relationship of the self to the other. She sees this as Freud's greatest influence on culture because he effectively created a new way of envisaging one's own family past and imagining a liberation from that past.

I will briefly examine these interesting theses of Illouz for their validity. First of all, it should be noted that the self is apparently understood here as an instance of individual experience; occasionally the term is also equated with identity. Illouz' concentration on this self is very well suited to the family structure and individual disposition existing in the American middle class in the first half of the 19th century, which she presents in detail.

It is remarkable that with Illouz' cultural-sociological approach, we can no longer systematically distinguish between the part of Freud's widespread thoughts that is popular-scientific and the scientifically revolutionary part, which is independent of the former. In order to show how Freudian thought has carved out new conceptions of the self from its themes, metaphors, norms, values, and ideals, she concentrates on the *Lectures on Introduction to Psychoanalysis* and the five lectures Freud gave at Clarke University in 1916/1917. With these, she aims to show how "psychoanalytic imagination" could produce a new emotional style.

As an example, she cites the famous study on the *Psychopathology of Everyday Life*. According to Illouz, Freud gave an unprecedented glow to banal everyday life by indicating that in fact everyday life is the relevant theatre in which the self is built and destroyed.

Yet Illouz, as a consequence of her view that the boundary between expert psychological knowledge and popular psychology is permeable, misses an important fact: Many of the metaphors that Freud used in his theoretical writings are merely attempts to capture a new discovery in linguistic imagery. This function of metaphors is characteristic of the early days of a new science which will bring a new paradigm into the world – which is precisely what happened in the case of Freud. It is a mission for academics to take the metaphors that contain Freud's theories and explain their explosive force for science. However, this explosive force makes it very unlikely that some of these discoveries will find their way into everyday life in popular scientific form.

The main theoretical objection to Illouz' interpretation concerns her concept of self. The research paradigm of psychoanalysis does not focus on the self as an instance and crystallisation point of individual experience but on the unconscious. Against this background, the unconscious meaning that Freud revealed in the slips of the tongue in everyday life and in neurotic symptoms is by no means a set of meanings with which our everyday life is charged (ibid., p. 84). Rather, they are very specific forms of meaning which Freud discovered but was unable to conceptualise in a sufficiently scientific manner (Flader, 1995).

The success of Freudian theory in the United States

Illouz rightly points to the tremendous success of psychoanalysis in the United States, which cannot be explained without the help of medicine. In the United States, psychoanalysis could rely on the powerful medical profession and became "medicalised". Illouz rightly sees this as a significant difference to Europe and especially Germany, where psychoanalysis had to start from scratch after the Second World War. However, Illouz leaves out an important consequence of this medicalisation of psychoanalysis in the United States: The Freudian concept of illness was subordinated to the concept of illness in medicine, although Freud's discoveries actually contradict this.

This can be easily shown using the example of the term "symptom". In medicine, it is used to indicate the presence of an organic dysfunction. By attempting to uncover the unconscious meaning of a neurotic symptom, Freud changed the medical concept of the symptom into a metaphor (cf. the famous XVIIth lecture "The Meaning of Symptoms" from the *Lectures on Introduction to Psychoanalysis*). With this discovery, symptoms mainly became important as conveying an unconscious meaning. In contrast, their nature as a disorder, while still being taken into account, became secondary. According to my suggestion, we can analyse both the mini-neurotic symptom of the slip of the tongue and actual (neurotic) symptoms as phenomena which occur because an unresolved mental conflict is being addressed (cf. Flader, 1995).

Illouz gives another reason for Freud's enormous success in the United States. Following John Demos, she points out that the American family structure in the second half of the 19th century was particularly well suited to the inclusion of psychoanalysis. According to Demos, the American family was characterised by a clear dividing line between parents and children. Also, there was a specialisation in gender roles, that is the couple was separated from the rest of the family as a functional unit, and women were seen as mothers in their psychological function. In addition, middle-class families in the United States placed their hope for improving their social standing in their sons, which in turn led to a competitive relationship between sons and fathers. The traditional Oedipus story fitted perfectly into this "hothouse family". Since Freud understood the Oedipus complex as a universal conflict structure, the American family was generalised to be a model of the family in general. The increasing differences between the sexes thus became something that could be considered quite natural.

Here, however, the question arises how a family structure of a completely different kind in another culture – for example, France in the 20th century – could also be considered appropriate for the Oedipus story and how, for example, Pierre Legendre (1998) also developed the idea of universalism in the Oedipus story.

Illouz believes that Freud made another outstanding contribution to culture through his narratives on the constitution of the self. Following the thinking of Suzanne Kirscher, she sees these stories as harmonising with an ancient narrative of Western culture, the salvation story of the Bible. Illouz also sees the corresponding primitive narrative patterns in the developmental history of the self, which psychoanalysis narrates. These patterns include, for example, the protagonists God, humanity, soul, and an eschatological goal.

I want to leave it open whether this interpretation actually provides a basis for the reception of Freudian theory by the United States middle class and its puritanical beliefs. What is certain, however, is that from a scientific point of view, no psychoanalytical theory of development exists. A developmental psychological history of the self can probably only be found in Freud's writings under the aforementioned theoretical preconditions of a sociology of culture.

Illouz rightly points out that Freud blurred the line between the pathological and the normal, that for him the difference between so-called normality and neurosis was only gradual. Illouz interprets this important aspect in terms of a power strategy: With this core thesis of Freud's, normality became an unassailable cultural category that has no referent and no clear signifier. At the very moment when health and normality became goals in the narratives about the constitution of the self, these goals could no longer be assigned a clear content. This means, however, according to Illouz, that any action and any desire can then point to a problematic and neurotic psyche. In this way, psychoanalysis would have created a "hermeneutics of suspicion" in everyday life.

> The Freudian concepts of 'resistance' and 'denial', which were to gain enormous popularity with the popularisation of psychoanalysis, helped to produce a new narrative of the self, in which the narrative core of identity

was defined precisely by what people do not think, what they do not talk about, and what they do not do. (ibid., p. 86)

According to Illouz, the fact that Freud made everyday life the object of a "hermeneutics of suspicion" was closely related to his tripartite system of the psyche, that is the instance model of ego, id, and super-ego.

> For Freud, the repression of sexual desires could destroy the ego's ability to assert its authority. The healing consisted of tracing the hidden sources of conflict, and in so doing, of finding the conditions under which the ego could regain its power. From a cultural perspective, this search for 'unconscious' sources of conflict was extremely productive as anything and everything could become meaningful. (ibid., p. 85)

The first question here is why this ego or self is not understood as the same element that Freud described elsewhere as the servant of three masters to emphasise its weakness and vulnerability. If we examine the attempt at self-analysis as the hidden thread in the cultural-sociological reconstruction, Illouz' concentration on this self becomes understandable. For then it becomes plausible how psychoanalytical interpretations can have devastating consequences. Illouz dramatically emphasises this in connection with the structuring and restructuring of the self. One should not impose a psychoanalytical interpretation on the behaviour of another person outside therapy and the relationship of trust between the analysand and the analyst. This is an abuse – not to say a perversion – of interpretation as a means of revealing a hitherto unrecognised connection in that person's behaviour.

Applied outside the therapeutic situation, this means of interpretation may be a weapon. If we regard the American middle class as the theatre of a permanent competition, it makes sense that the processes of wild and injurious interpretation described by Illouz are applied to behaviour. Illouz thus describes the possible abuse of a means of psychological help in therapy, the application of which to everyday life should only be warned against.

In any case, I believe that the focus on this self excludes from the object of psychoanalytical research its very essence: The patterns of emotional relationships in which the child's self develops. This development never happens on its own and in isolation from the object of the relationship. Only in this emotional relationship do the characteristics and conflict structures that are relevant to psychoanalysis appear. We find none of them in the cultural-sociological reconstruction.

The social power of the psychologising therapy discourse

What Illouz has seen very clearly is the great social power of the psychologising therapy discourse. It appears in many different forms and has long since found its way into other areas of society, such as business, politics, and education, alongside the entertainment industry. Illouz does not clarify the psychological dynamics of this discourse. Nor does she analyse the unresolved current mental conflict, which must be dealt with again and again but can never be resolved. This conflict opposes the need to heal the mental suffering which affects many people today – a type of narcissistic problem – and the defence against these very anxieties which arise precisely because in the pursuit of this healing, there are mental abysses which the person concerned feels unable to cope with. Illouz' implicit desire for control of psychological processes, which may also be characteristic of the American middle class, plays a major role here, because maintaining this control is jeopardised if the narcissistic problem really is actualised.

What can a cultural-sociological interpretation tell us that is truly relevant to a better understanding of psychoanalysis? An interpretation that Illouz makes of a sentence by Freud, which is part of the fifth and last lecture of his stay in the United States, is revealing: "The energetic and successful person is the one who succeeds in turning his wishful fantasies into reality through work" (quoted in Illouz, 2009, p. 87). Illouz' interpretation does not take note of the theoretical context of this statement. In fact, to clarify this context, we must remember that in the *Lectures*, Freud analyses the process of symptom formation in connection with the fantasies produced by a neurotic sufferer. Here, Freud points out that these fantasies possess psychic reality. They are important because, according to his theory, the libido has attached itself to the fantasies and therefore turns away from the possibility of real satisfaction in the outside world (Freud, ibid., p. 364).

Freud's speech about the energetic and successful man thus describes him as different from the neurotic. His wishful fantasies can become real through work and do not require childlike fantasies which can only serve as a substitute for satisfaction.

Quite possibly, Illouz accurately reflects the specific American interpretation of this sentence – namely, that "the Freudian search for the lost self could discreetly ally itself with the striving for social success" (ibid., p. 87) and that "emotional health could be found in social success" (ibid.). She then reconstructs this connection between the ideal of success and emotional health as the starting point of a cultural development in the United States. By reconstructing this development from its endpoint, she finds that the therapeutic discourse that was marketed by the cultural industries in the United States has become omnipotent. She uses this discourse as a powerful narrative framework in which these cultural industries could operate.

Freud's repeatedly noted reticence to formulate an ideal of health is completely neglected by Illouz. She focuses exclusively on the American reception and marketing of Freud's ideas. However, a comparison with the reception history of psychoanalysis in another culture – such as the European – would have been helpful and probably necessary in terms of a sociology of culture.

How else can one determine what is and what is not specific to a particular culture in a history of reception? But Illouz does not draw any such comparison. Should we understand this to mean that the reception of psychoanalysis in the United States is believed to be universally valid? In that case, any comparison with other cultures would indeed be superfluous.

Illouz shows in great detail how each of the three most important cultural industries in the United States – self-help books, cinema, and advertising – have used psychoanalysis in their own way. She expresses her basic insight, which is the theoretical credo of her investigations, with the following words: "Culture influences action by shaping the self, the technology, and the world views from which people derive their life strategies" (ibid., p. 104).

How concepts of this sociology of culture block access to Freud's discoveries

What can be learned from this basic insight in terms of Freud's theoretical efforts and ingenious observations? Does this theoretical premise provide us with access to the discoveries of the unconscious, which Freud, as he entered uncharted territory, often could only grasp metaphorically, support by analogy, and thus conceptualise quite imperfectly in scientific terms?

We have already seen that it remains unclear how the self or identity – which "is a thoroughly institutionalised form" (ibid., p. 271) – relates as a sociological concept to the model of psychological instances. With this model, Freud tried to do justice to the "inner conflict of modern man" (Freud). To understand this inner conflict in terms of a psychological conflict, Illouz would have to examine the structure of psychological conflicts as a sui generis reality more closely. Yet she fails to do this.

We do not find any contribution to specifying Freud's metaphors which are constitutive of his theory – for example repression, symptoms, and transference. Nor has Illouz been able to develop the still-missing psychoanalytical theory of development in any way. Not even Freud himself had any adequate concept of development.

Illouz simply claims that the narrative of therapeutic self-help, which she reconstructed in the American reception, is not a distortion of psychoanalysis, but was part of it from the very beginning. In doing so, she cites Margaret Mahler as proof – "indeed one of the early leading representatives of psychoanalysis in America" (ibid., pp. 297–280). In this quote, Mahler points out that crises are inevitable for the psychological development of every child, especially in the process of separation and individuation.

From this simple finding, Illouz derives a strategy for psychoanalysis: She sees it as constructing an ideal of mental health for all children that they can never achieve, so that they become dependent on the help of psychoanalysis.

We do not learn anything enlightening about Freud's writings criticising the culture of his day, in which he referred to religion, society in general, and art. It is revealing how Illouz, although she repeatedly speaks of emotions, uses her social-cognitive research approach to keep anything psychological at bay. She certainly does not engage in any psychoanalytical interpretation of our current cultural phenomena.

If, however, she did decide to pursue such an interpretation, she would need to change her attitude towards her object of research. She would have to employ not just the subject-subject pattern of non-rationalist theories, but also use and methodically reflect her own individual subjectivity. Starting out from the rather trivial observation that our experiences are always shaped by our culture and that cultural production is based on a cognitive foundation (narrative structures, typification schemes, language patterns, etc.), she misses the revolutionary nature of Freud's concept of experience. Freud had discovered that the traditional pattern of experience, according to which a subject gains experiences, is no longer valid in the contexts in which Freud discovered the workings of the unconscious. In those cases, bodily processes that have been stored in memory determine the actions of a subject, and in such a way that the subject is unable to reflect them. If these forces had to be repressed in early childhood, they could not reach the point of development in their psychogenesis to become experiences shaped by language and culture.

Illouz' socio-cognitive approach to research does not cover Freud's discoveries in this field: The child's way of thinking and experiencing that has been preserved in the adult's memory; the sophistication of desire in personal relationships; the many ways in which the unconscious meaning of neurotic symptoms can manifest in everyday life. In his *Lectures*, Freud characterised neurosis as a prison which the person concerned has built for him- or herself and which henceforth holds that person captive.

What remains completely incomprehensible is Illouz' belief that a self can free itself from its family history (cf., ibid., p. 181). Does she really assume that it is possible to leave the "mother soil" of one's spiritual development completely and establish one's identity in a new place? If this thought had indeed played a role in the American reception of psychoanalysis, then it would be appropriate to interpret this very phenomenon psychoanalytically. After all, the fantasy of being able to free oneself from one's own family background is very similar to a neurotic symptom. The prison metaphor that Freud introduced in this context is shifted from one's own neurosis to the family, where a self-high-handed, overpowering self is realised in the form of a self-chosen, new constitution.

It is interesting in this context that Illouz also discovers other cultural productions which we can analyse, in her language, as part of the "symptom repertoire" of our contemporary culture.

Here, too, Illouz assumes that this programme is already laid out in Freudian thought itself. She points out that psychologists in the United States have defined a new category of people based on the ideals of self-fulfilment: Those who fall short of these ideals are now considered to be sick.

> Putting self-fulfilment at the centre of models of the self had the consequence that most lives were suddenly 'not self-fulfilled'. This basic idea formed the core of the uncanny public success of psychology. (ibid., p. 270f.)

According to Illouz, psychologists have expanded their scope enormously by defining good health and self-fulfilment as synonyms. What is refreshing, however, is that Illouz' critical view includes the marketing efforts of the pharmaceutical industry. She also links the diagnostic instruments to their marketing strategy.

> The attempt to codify and classify pathologies with great care has led to a rather broad and vague concept of mental disorder. It now included behavioural traits or personality traits that are simply outside what psychologists considered 'average'. (ibid., p. 278)

She rightly points out that the *DSM III manual* – the third edition of the *Diagnostic and Statistical Manual of Mental Disorders* which was published by the American Psychiatric Association in 1980 – never gives a precise definition of what exactly makes the respective behaviour a mental disorder.

It seems plausible to me that we are seeing an attempt at self-therapy at work here that has been widely copied. At its core, we find an unresolved psychological conflict of autonomy, which may have been typical of the members of the 1968 protest movement. The way it is being dealt with has the same structural characteristics that we see in the unconscious meaning of an attempt to address conflict in psychoanalysis: An existing desire (here: The desire for autonomy) is satisfied in such a way that the desire can be warded off at the same time.

Illouz' reconstruction of the reception history of psychoanalysis offers numerous interesting references to the concepts and strategies of psychologists who went into business, health care, education, and other social fields to conquer a market for themselves. Illouz presented this in her book *Cold intimacies: The making of Emotional Capitalism* (2007).

What is irritating is that Illouz repeatedly refers to basic structures of psychoanalytic therapy without being able to rely on empirical studies, which she uses extensively as evidence in other contexts. For example, she describes the therapeutic narrative or therapeutic discourse as an extraordinarily influential cultural construction. Yet it does not really become clear on what information basis she equates the psychoanalytic discourse with a therapeutic narrative, and how she has identified the inner structure of this discourse.[2]

To conclude, I would like to go into more detail about a paper which takes a very different path from the one I have proposed. In my opinion, the authors are misguided in believing that they have developed a test capable of identifying people suffering from narcissistic problems.

2 The psychology of narcissistic epidemics (J. Twenge and W. Campbell)

The authors of this popular publication in the United States, *The Narcissism Epidemic*, combine two different concepts of narcissism, a naturalistic concept (Twenge & Campbell, 2010, p. 260), according to which a narcissist is infected by a something like virus, much like an epidemic; and a mentalistic concept, according to which narcissistic values and ideals are part of a person's beliefs.

Unlike Lasch, they do not base their diagnosis on psychoanalytic–clinical concepts of pathological narcissism but rather use a test to determine whether the characteristics of a narcissistic personality can be identified. This survey instrument is designed to recognise specific beliefs and convictions of the test person that are considered narcissistic or non-narcissistic. If the former occur more frequently, this is taken as an indicator of a "narcissistic personality".

The test consists of 40 narcissistic findings, supplemented by non-narcissistic findings. Examples of narcissistic findings include "If I ruled the world, it would be a better place". Or: "I like being the centre of attention". Or: "I like to show off my body". Or: "I think I'm a very special person".

The non-narcissistic equivalents would be: "The thought of running the world scares me to death". Or: "I prefer to blend in with the crowd". Or: "I don't particularly like to brag about my body". Or: "I'm neither better nor worse than most people".

The authors stress the difference between the characteristics of narcissism that can be detected with this method of investigation and the diagnosis of a narcissistic personality disorder commonly used in psychiatry. While the latter, according to a statistical study, is supposed to characterise about one in 16 Americans, the authors emphasise that "normal narcissism" as defined in their concept is much more common and therefore potentially much more destructive (ibid., p. 26).

What is striking about this survey instrument for identifying a narcissist is that it assumes that the relevant narcissistic personality traits are so easily identified through the corresponding findings. Obviously, the authors assume that an individual's consciousness is the decisive factor in determining which characteristics are relevant to his or her personality structure. They waste no thought on the discovery by various 20th century sciences that our consciousness is an unreliable and often deceptive mirror of inner processes. Nor do they pursue the question of whether cultural values and ideals are in fact – as they assume – reflected by the person concerned.

This test is also intended to clear up a confusion that they believe common among certain psychotherapists, namely, that extroverted narcissist suffers from low self-esteem and a deep lack of self-confidence. The test described shows the opposite, namely that adults who score high on the measurement scale also score high on the scale measuring self-confidence. The authors obviously share the high appreciation accorded to measuring methods in science. "We want to see numbers that prove it", they say in their book (ibid., p. 66). As a consequence, the authors orientate themselves towards a branch of psychology which considers itself as a natural science and therefore favours methods that are commonly used in traditional physics.

But since neither social values nor subjective meanings can be counted, the question remains open as to what this test actually determines. I will go into this in more detail later. What I want to say here is that the investigations of Twenge and Campbell that are based on this test and their two concepts of narcissism remain strangely superficial with regard to the psyche. They do not delve deeper, despite the fact that in the appendix to their book, they explicitly refer to a model which assumes a mutual constitution of culture and psyche (ibid., p. 305).

In this context, culture is understood as a system of society based on a foundation of ideas and values, including the morality and social role of individuals. The core ideas of a culture are particularly important for understanding narcissism. In the United States, they have developed into the narcissistic value of feeling good about oneself. The authors call this value the importance of self-admiration.

The authors distinguish five key causes of narcissism in US culture: The focus on self-admiration ("I am something very special!"), child-centred parenting ("You are unique"), celebrity glorification, together with media encouragement ("I also want to be unique"), attention-seeking promoted on the internet ("I have my own homepage and a thousand friends on Facebook") and easy credit ("I buy what I like, even if I can't afford it") (ibid., p. 268).

The socio-psychological process of conveying the core ideas of a culture is – according to the authors – carried out through the education system, the educational practices of parents, the media, and the legal system. Twenge and Campbell believe that if these authorities do not fundamentally change, the "virus" of narcissism will infect even more people.

The symptoms of this virus include a personal craving for recognition and a new sense vanity (e.g. in the continuing cult of youth; in the appreciation of personal appearance and physical attractiveness; in the popularisation of cosmetic surgery); an unbridled materialism (in buying and using products that affirm social status and one's own importance, but also in the desire of the social middle class to achieve the living standards of the rich, favoured by easily obtainable loans and by role models in TV series); the cult of celebrity (in the early drilling of children to become stars; in the unbridled desire for attention from others); a sense of entitlement (in the belief that one is entitled to receive more than others); an anti-social behaviour (the "The winner takes all" mentality favours deception as a widely accepted means of personal enrichment, ibid., pp. 206f.); and problems in personal relationships (in shying away from commitment, in the instrumentalisation of personal relationships for the purpose of feeling great; in changing sexual partners frequently and quickly).

Spreading the narcissistic virus

I will use the example of parental upbringing to illustrate how the authors imagine that parents convey narcissistic values. The authors refer to two studies in which American parents were asked to choose among five possible answers to describe what their child should learn for life. The results show that since 1958, the support for learning obedience has steadily declined. In 2004, the last year of the survey, a record low was reached. What has remained constant, however, is that all American parents believe that the most important goal of learning for their children is to think of themselves (cf. ibid., p. 75f.).

The authors conclude that there must have been a historical change in parents' educational practices. These have turned away from social rules and the setting of boundaries and moved towards a willingness to treat the child as a prince or princess who gets everything he or she wants (cf. ibid., p. 80).

The educational practices of the parents who "produce" a narcissistic child consist mainly of a permanent confirmation of how great the child is. When asked about the reasons for their educational behaviour, these parents respond that if the child thinks it is special, it will succeed later in life.

The authors summarise their examples of parental educational practices as follows: Parents are overindulgent; they constantly praise the child and put it in charge of the family. One or two generations earlier, the roles of parents and children were defined completely differently. Then, the parents were in charge, and the child was supposed to obey. The authors assume, of course, that the values and social roles of earlier times were on all accounts better than the narcissistic tendency of our time, which they believe will end in an epidemic.

In a historical comparison, the authors use the "good old" values of the nation as a yardstick for their negative judgement about the present. For example, they describe work morale under the sign of narcissism with the following words: "In general, Americans have lost the idea that there is value in an honest day's work for an honest day's pay, even if the work is not fulfilling" (ibid., p. 242).

Twenge and Campbell go back as far as the founding of the US Constitution to say that it propagated individual freedom from tyranny and the fundamental equality of all citizens as social values but not narcissism.

In their outline of the historical changes in US culture, Twenge and Campbell identify the 1960s as the time when "the American flag of self-admiration" began to unfurl (ibid., p. 60f.). Stimulated by offers from the mass media, certain political movements, and psychological publications, the 1970s then propagated, with a further narcissistic thrust, the values of self-exploration and self-expression. By the 1980s, an extroverted, shell-shocked, materialistic form of narcissism had firmly established itself in the United States.

As a yardstick for identifying narcissism as a destructive behaviour, the authors use a simple cost-benefit calculation: The concept of the time-delay trap (ibid., p. 55). This means that narcissism, similar to other forms of destructive behaviour, brings short-term benefits but long-term costs.

Based on those values and the two concepts of narcissism, the authors suggest courses of treatment after each chapter in which they give examples of the symptoms of the narcissistic epidemic. For example, they suggest that parents should limit their child's narcissistic impulses by saying no and meaning it. "Don't give your child too much power"; "Carefully consider the messages you are sending to your children about competition and winning"; "Think twice before you buy your kid something that announces how great he is" (ibid., pp. 87–89). Also, parents should not, for example, give their child T-shirts printed with logos like "Princess" or such (ibid., p. 76).

Educational advice to parents here consists mainly of communication instructions and rules of conduct. The child's individual psyche is perceived as a mental apparatus that receives certain messages and actions and translates them into experiences for itself. If, for example, Americans are encouraged by their parents to make their own choices at an early age, they will also experience themselves as independent individuals and learn to express their individuality.

To curb unbridled materialism, it is recommended to change the corresponding social norms. This means above all to feel ashamed, as one did in the past, of incurring unreasonably high debts (ibid., p. 177). The (alleged) decline of general work morale, according to the authors, can be dealt with by re-establishing the values of modesty and work discipline.

Blind to the inner life of the psyche

Twenge and Campbell believe that the narcissistic epidemic has extremely serious consequences for American society. Many people are caught dreaming in a fantasy world instead of dealing with reality. In addition, narcissism has undermined interpersonal relationships, since it leads to the destruction of trust and an increase in aspiration and selfishness (ibid., p. 222). The term "narcissistic epidemic" is taken literally in the sense of the naturalistic concept. As in an epidemic, there is a host (a person or a group that has a virus); there are transmission routes of the virus (in this context mainly the entertainment industry), and there are individuals or social groups that are not yet infected.

As one of the many proposed cures for this epidemic, the authors seriously discuss the possibility of holding those identified as narcissistic in quarantine. Especially from a German perspective, this proposal has a fatal historical connotation of selection and ghettoisation.

In the end, however, the authors distance themselves from this proposal, among other reasons because they see it as impossible to escape from the social forces that promote narcissistic values, such as the mass media and the consumer society (ibid., p. 282). Instead, they propose a large-scale, targeted change in narcissistic values to be achieved by propagating "better" values. For example, the belief that modesty is a characteristic only of great figures like

Gandhi or Mother Theresa should be questioned. Another value that can curb narcissism is compassion for oneself. It is a reaction to the discrepancy which often occurs between what you are and what you want to be.

At no point in their detailed documentation of narcissistic behaviour today do the authors attempt to understand what may be going on in the narcissist. What happens with a person who believes he or she is above the law and therefore does not shy away from defrauding a company? Or who is unwilling to commit to personal relationships and instead instrumentalises them for his own purposes of self-affirmation? We also learn nothing about how the cultural meaning of sexuality has changed and how we can try to relate this change to a change within the family constellation of relationships. At no point do the authors refer to the inner psychological life of an individual and the collective unconscious of a culture.

Many of the examples can be found not just in the United States but in Western European countries, too. Twenge and Campbell, for example, emphasise something essential with regard to modern educational practices: Many children today are involved in decisions that affect the household. The authors even report cases where children advise their parents on the decision to buy a new car (ibid., p. 82). Yet the authors do not address the inner psychological world of the people involved. Nor do they ask what this redefinition of social roles means for the psychodynamics of positions in the family. As a result, they have to stick to what the parents tell them – or to what children/young people in turn reveal about their parents – when attempting to explain.

Twenge and Campbell, in the narrow perspective of their scientifically oriented psychology, do not give us deeper insights into the psychological background. Their many examples are descriptive variations of the same repeatedly applied strategy: The narcissist uses the means of xyz to make him- or herself and others believe that he or she is cool, great, and special.

It is not only from a European point of view that the strategies they propose for changing values in the United States seem strangely naïve. These strategies turn the relationship between social values and social practice upside down. The values that people base their lives on are not seen to have their roots in the social practice which produced those values in the first place; instead, it is the values that should determine social practice.

The authors' nostalgic cultural idealism considers the various symptoms of narcissism to be nothing but the aberrations of people who have strayed far from the good old values of culture, but who can be put back on the right track by targeted propagation of these same old values. In doing so, they play down the cultural upheavals that accompany the increase in narcissistic problems. The break with regard to parental educational practices, social role patterns of men and women, and general values has long been observed in Western countries. In their optimism about being able to shape national culture, the authors overlook the fact that this break cannot be reversed.

If social values are anchored in a social practice that has psycho-pathological traits, then these values will also have a psycho-pathological background. But we will not find this background with the help of a test that checks for beliefs.

This connection is not understood by the authors. In order to at least begin to explore it, they would have to examine forms of this social practice, which they do not do. Instead, they collect convictions, beliefs, and observations that they can associate with narcissism.

The authors' view that it is easy to reflect about social values (as the basis of a culture) is contradicted by the results of intercultural communication research (cf. Flader & Comati, 2008). Any cultural system – national, organisational, or otherwise – that includes social values is represented in a collective knowledge which is predominantly implicit. In other words, it is part of the knowledge base of the self-evident and is usually not reflected at all.

A valuable lesson, nevertheless

Although the investigations of Twenge and Campbell are disappointing in some respects, they allow us to gain a valuable insight: In our approach and theoretical assumptions, we can be very easily affected by the psychological characteristics of our object of investigation without even realising it. Twenge and Campbell (involuntarily) serve as an example.

Let us consider their concept of narcissism as well as their use of the survey tool to identify narcissists and their proposed strategies of propagating better values. In my interpretation, all these attempts contain the exact same narcissistic virus which the authors want to fight. Indeed, we may find in this approach characteristics and fantasies that can be interpreted as the expression of a narcissistic problem of the people involved. I will briefly explain.

By carrying out the test described earlier, the authors create a controlled distance between the subject under investigation and his or her object, which can thereby be kept at bay. The distinction between narcissists and non-narcissists, which is the purpose of the test, ensures that the investigator can under no circumstances be considered to be one of the narcissists. This methodically prevents the research subject from turning his or her object into a co-subject. Otherwise, this might happen because the research subject experiences feelings that are very similar to the ones he or she assumes that the object has. It is these feelings that he or she includes – in a more or less controlled manner – in the interpretation of the object.

From this point of view, *The Narcissism Epidemic* documents a strong limitation of empathy, because at no point is an attempt made to find access to the inner life of the psyche, that is to the individual and collective subjectivity, of those affected. This is supported by the idea that the psyche can be reduced to a series of beliefs and behaviours. This idea makes it understandable how the authors can assume that people can be easily manipulated by representatives or agents of certain institutions.

From a high vantage point, society is viewed as a collection of individuals who may or may not be infected by the narcissistic virus. A deluded belief in feasibility – the idea that cultural development can be controlled – is documented in the strategies proposed to contain the epidemic.

Who is the social subject making proposals that seem so unreal? They are justified by the authors' nostalgic longing for the "good old" values of American history. But can Twenge and Campbell be certain that everybody else finds these values desirable, too? With their one-sided focus on an epidemic, the authors overlook the fact that positive qualities may well be associated with the "new" narcissistic values, for example, an increase in individual creativity and flexibility. Indeed, they are highly in demand as professional qualifications in the new professional fields of the creative industries (advertising, new information technologies, management consulting, etc.).

Here, the authors combine the grandiose fantasy of being able to recommend the right remedies for a sick culture with the egocentric certainty of taking their personal preferences and considering them to be valid for everybody.

Finally, the authors express their hope that they will be able to experience the retreat of narcissism and the rebirth of America (ibid., p. 303). At least in their imagination, they play a role in bringing about a grandiose cultural change which would likely not be happening without their own achievements as cultural diagnosticians and cultural therapists. The readers who have followed them to this point can share in this fantasy. Thus, the authors unwittingly continue, by means of their investigation, the very phenomenon that their investigation was intended to define and contain: The narcissistic problem.

I have chosen to explain this aspect in detail because the investigations of these two authors provide us with a great example of how easily an investigation of narcissistic problems can be guided by psychological defence. What makes it so difficult to investigate such problems? I would like to emphasise two points:

First of all, they go deep "under your skin" because their psychological background reaches far into childhood. To understand specific injuries and traumas, an investigator must be able to engage with them.

Moreover, narcissistic problems by their nature evade communication. It requires a lot of trust to communicate one's own feelings of being small and "somehow not right" to another person. This difficulty is exacerbated by our Western cultural demand for professional motivation and individual perfection. This demand undermines the solidarity without which we can neither see the other person as a co-subject with whom we share our own suffering nor communicate this to him or her.

The test used by the two authors is based on the various aspects of the meaning of the word "narcissistic". It includes the informant's positive or negative evaluation of what is understood to be narcissistic in everyday life.

Strictly speaking, the test measures only the colloquial aspects of the word's meaning, namely the subjects' self-assessments of their willingness to fit in with society, which is considered positive. If this self-assessment surpasses a certain level of insignificance, it will be interpreted as a narcissistic belief or conviction. Test subjects, if they do not consider themselves to be narcissistic, will not choose the statement "I think I am a special person". Instead, they will opt for the alternative "I am no better or worse than most people".

The narcissism researcher Heinz Kohut (1973, p. 13) has pointed out that narcissism as an object of research "includes half the contents of the human psyche - while the other half ... represents the objects". It is remarkable in this context that in everyday life, the meaning of narcissism is often confused. When "narcissistic" is used to describe a person, it often has a negative connotation. It usually refers to a form of narcissistic problem but ignores narcissistic needs or a narcissism that has not been blocked in its development. My research also aims to help resolve this confusion of meaning.

To this end, I wanted to give this critical overview of the theoretical approaches which explain narcissism as a basic cause of social phenomena. As with all theories, it is important to appreciate the explanations they provide. At the same time, scientists and academics need to continue developing and improving theories.

Where narcissism is concerned, this is by no means a theoretical exercise but a mission of enormous importance to our society. Family constellations and our focus on performance and achievement give rise to many individual, social, and political conflicts which can be explained by narcissistic causes. Yet we cannot make the mistake of confusing or mixing the therapeutic viewpoint with a psychoanalytical investigation of the collective. This is why, in this book, I opted for a double perspective: On the one hand, I have looked at individual suffering and its life-historical causes; on the other hand, I have examined collective conflicts, but with the awareness that every human being is part of society and every society consists of individual human beings.

Notes

1 As theoretical examples of such applications, Reiche lists the Freudo-Marxist discourse (Fromm et al.); the structural-functional theory of Parsons; the theory of communicative action of Habermas; and the ego-psychology of Hartmann (the latter as an application of psychoanalysis by academic psychology).
2 My own investigations which I have presented in detail elsewhere (cf. Flader et al., 1982).

Conclusion

In my preface, I ironically asked why we should make such a huge effort to explore how the unconscious is shaping social action. I hope that this book has shown why it is worthwhile. I would like to encourage my readers to look at the unconscious sources of problems that occur in their daily life. I also want to show that investigating the unconscious can help us to address conflicts of great relevance to our society. I have presented some examples in this book: Problems caused by mobbing, by the lack of leadership in companies, by massive communication conflicts in the climate debate, and so forth.

This perspective on social reality is my attempt to do justice to an ambition I believe is important for science as a whole: To contribute to addressing, investigating, and explaining the most urgent problems. As scientists, we need to pursue this path to get to the bottom of things, to pay attention to suffering and destruction, search for causes, and propose solutions. For me, this ambition is linked to the roles ascribed to scientists today and the expectations placed on them.

The role of the scientist

It is a remarkable contradiction that, on the one hand, society today holds scientists in high esteem and sometimes even glorifies them as heralds and prophets. On the other hand, they are frequently accused of speaking in such an abstract and aloof manner that they have become incomprehensible.

What is reflected in this contradiction is two different things: There is the expectation that scientists – in contrast to politicians – should actually be able to solve and explain problems. But at the same time, people feel annoyed and humiliated that they do not understand science. This explains the public's critical attitude vis-à-vis science, which is reflected in sentences like "I don't get it anyway".

Such contradictory expectations breed conflicts, as the debates about the COVID-19 pandemic and climate change clearly show. I believe it is all the more important for scientists to be aware of these problems and act in

DOI: 10.4324/9780429345449-102

accordance with the philosopher Georg Henrik von Wright, whom I mentioned earlier: It is all about explaining and understanding. Whoever explains well will be understood. And to explain well, you have to understand something well.

This truth applies not only to the relationships between scientists and laymen but also to the relationships among scientists. This becomes evident when scientists from different disciplines work together, for example in climate impact research. Physicists use different concepts and methods than sociologists, who in turn have different concepts and methods from geologists and geophysicists. The latter have no clue, for example, what the psychoanalytically influenced concept of the unconscious is supposed to mean. There are numerous examples for such communication problems. We scientists face an enormous task not only to do justice to the need to explain and understand but also to engage with people from outside our own science.

Even apart from the obvious problems of concepts and methods, we can expect both conscious and unconscious obstacles. There will always be resistance to engaging with a different perspective and to recognising that one's own discipline is often not sufficient to find explanations for the phenomena of our time.

The link between theory and practice

I often come across people who tell me, in a mix of modesty and arrogance, that they are "only" practitioners. They usually add that problems can only be solved by practical means. This statement is true, but it is also false, quite simply because such assertions usually fail to clarify the meaning of "practice". Any kind of action? Do anything at all? Simply move the table from right to left when it is in the way?

Every action is preceded by a knowledge of things. And every knowledge is preceded by experience through action and speech, not only in everyday life, but also in science. Knowledge and reflection are reflected in the formation of theories, the practice of research, and the view of social reality, for example in social and intellectual sciences.

I respond to such criticism of everything that is theoretical with the following argument: Without good theory, there can be no good practice, and without practice, there can be no good theory. If we know nothing and do not think – and think ahead – we cannot take practical action. This applies to even the simplest action.

As for science, my understanding is that it exists to be a part of society and deal with reality, whatever that means in a specific situation, and not to be self-referential. Sociologists such as Karl Mannheim, who methodically developed the interplay between theory and empiricism, have taken this ambition very seriously. Climate researchers, who work on an interdisciplinary basis and use their knowledge to act in a politically responsible manner and exert influence as advisers, also share in this ambition.

Of course, we run into additional problems here. On the one hand, there is the internal scientific debate on the role of scientists. Do they have a duty to interfere politically? Should they even be allowed to interfere politically? My answer is that scientists should communicate their research results and make recommendations about the conclusions to be drawn from them. On what knowledge can society and politics possibly base decisions, if not on science?

On the other hand, the public as well as politicians generally expect scientists to give consistent and irrevocably correct statements. If this is not the case, then it is not real science (this has become an issue in the debate on global warming as well as for experts on the pandemic). One possible response to such overblown expectations is to say that science is not a supplier of ideology but a form of discourse in which one moves towards truth without being able to propagate definitive truths. It would be an important task for democratic societies to teach and to learn to cope with contradictions and different statements of scientists. People need to understand that research and science take place as part of a process and cannot offer absolute answers.

The logical conclusion is that in schools and universities, teaching to think is at least as important as communicating facts and data. This is a goal I have always pursued in my teaching as well as in publications such as this one.

With this book, I wish to contribute to encouraging thinking. There are some important theories which have emerged from practice-oriented research in social sciences and humanities. I hope I have been able to arouse some curiosity about the insights they offer which can help us to better understand and overcome the crises of our time.

Bibliography

Aigner, J.C. (2001). *Der ferne Vater. Zur Psychoanalyse von Vatererfahrung, männlicher Entwicklung und negativem Ödipuskomplex*. Gießen: Psychosozial-Verlag.

Amendt, G. (1990). *Das Leben unerwünschter Kinder*. Bremen: Univ.

Arentewicz, G. (2009). Worum es geht. Wie wird aus alltäglichem Streit, ungelösten Konflikten und Konkurrenz Mobbing? In G. Arentewicz, Fleissner, A. & Struck, D. (Editors), *Mobbing. Psychoterror am Arbeitsplatz, in der Schule und im Internet. Tipps und Hilfsangebote* (pp. 11–33). Hamburg: Ellert & Richter.

Arentewicz, G., Fleissner, A. & Struck, D. (2009). *Mobbing. Psychoterror am Arbeitsplatz, in der Schule und im Internet. Tipps und Hilfsangebote*. Hamburg: Ellert & Richter.

Arieti, S. (1955). *Interpretation of Schizophrenia*. New York: Basic Books.

Assmann, A. (2010). Hilflose Despoten. In D. Thomä (Editor), *Vaterlosigkeit. Geschichte und Gegenwart einer fixen Idee* (pp. 198–214). Frankfurt a.M.: Suhrkamp Verlag.

Bachofen, J.J. (1978). *Das Mutterrecht. Eine Untersuchung über die Gynaikokratie der alten Welt nach ihrer religiösen und rechtlichen Natur* (2. edition). Frankfurt a.M: Suhrkamp Verlag.

Balint, M. (1966). *Die Urform der Liebe und die Technik der Psychoanalyse*. Bern: Huber.

Bassyouni, Chr. (1981). Über die Bedeutung der Vaterfigur für den Entstehungsmodus einer Symptom- oder Charakterneurose mit der geschlechtsspezifischen Unterschiedlichkeit in der Verhaltensbewertung des Vaters. *PsA – Info*, 16, pp. 1–18.

Bassyouni, Chr. (1990). *Macht oder Mündigkeit. Über den Zwang zum Gehorsam und die Sehnsucht nach Autonomie*. Frankfurt a.M.: Verlag für Akademische Schriften.

Bassyouni, Chr. (1997). *Die sadomasochistische Schaukel. Narzisstische Abwehr von Nähe als chronischer Autonomiekonflikt*. Unpublished manuscript of a lecture given at the conference "Trauma and Conflict" in Fulda.

Beck, U. (1994). Jenseits von Stand und Klasse?. In U. Beck & E. Beck-Gernsheim (Hrsg.), *Riskante Freiheiten* (pp. 43–60). Frankfurt a.M.: Suhrkamp Verlag.

Beck, U. & Beck-Gernsheim, E. (Hrsg.). (1994). *Riskante Freiheiten. Individualisierung in modernen Gesellschaften*. Frankfurt a.M.: Suhrkamp Verlag.

Benjamin, J. (1993). *Phantasie und Geschlecht*. Basel: Stroemfeld.

Benning, R. (2013). Stille Subventionen, verdeckte Kosten, offene Rechnungen. In Fleischatlas 2013. Daten und Fakten über Tiere als Nahrungsmittel. https://www.boell.de/sites/default/files/assets/boell.de/images/download_de/oekologie/fleischatlas2013_s1617_WEB.pdf?dimension1=division_oen (pp. 16–17).

Berger, P.L. & Luckmann, Th. (1977). *Die gesellschaftliche Konstruktion der Wirklichkeit*. Frankfurt a.M.: S. Fischer Verlag.

Bergmann, W. (2003). *Digitalkids. Kindheit in der Medienmaschine.* München: Beustverlag.
Bergmann, W. (2006). *Das Drama des modernen Kindes. Hyperaktivität, Magersucht, Selbstverletzung.* Weinheim/Basel: Beltz.
Bion, W.R. (1961). Experiences in Groups. London: Tavistock.
Bion, W. (1990). *Lernen durch Erfahrung.* Frankfurt a.M.: Suhrkamp Verlag.
Black, M. (1979). More about Metaphor. In A. Ortony (Hrsg.), *Metaphor and Thought* (pp. 19–43). Cambridge: Cambridge Univ. Press.
Blomert, R. (2003). *Die Habgierigen.* München: Antje Kunstmann Verlag.
Bode, S. (2004). *Die vergessene Generation. Die Kriegskinder brechen ihr Schweigen.* Stuttgart: Klett-Cotta.
Bude, H. (2010). Die Metamorphosen des Ödipus im Generationenverhältnis. In D. Thomä (Hrsg.), *Vaterlosigkeit. Geschichte und Gegenwart einer fixen Idee* (pp. 269–279). Berlin: Suhrkamp Verlag.
Busch, H.-J. (2001a). *Subjektivität in der spätmodernen Gesellschaft.* Weilerswist: Velbrück Wissenschaft.
Busch, H.-J. (2001b). Die Anwendung der psychoanalytischen Methode in der Sozialforschung, Teil II. *Psychoanalyse – Texte zur Sozialforschung, 5*(8), pp. 203–232.
Busch, H.-J., Leuzinger-Bohleber, M. & Prokop, U. (Editors). (2003). *Sprache, Sinn und Unbewusstes. Zum 80. Geburtstag von Alfred Lorenzer.* Tübingen: Edition diskord.
Butler, J. (1991). *Das Unbehagen der Geschlechter.* Frankfurt a.M.: Suhrkamp Verlag.
Campbell, T.C. & Campbell, T.M. (2011). *China Study. Die wissenschaftliche Begründung für eine vegane Ernährungsweise* (2. edition). Bad Kötzing: Verlag Systematische Medizin AG.
Camus, J. le (2001). *Väter. Die Bedeutung des Vaters für die psychische Entwicklung des Kindes.* Weinheim/Basel: Beltz.
Cooney, N. (2011). *Change of Heart. What Psychology Can Teach Us About Spreading Social Change.* New York: Lantern Books.
Davidson, D. (1979). Paradoxes of Irrationality. In R. Wollheim (Editor), *Philosophical Essays on Freud* (S. 289–305). Cambridge: Cambridge Univ. Press.
Devereux, G. (1973). *Angst und Methode in den Verhaltenswissenschaften.* München: Hanser.
Ecarius, J. (2002). *Familienerziehung im historischen Wandel. Ein Forschungsbericht.* Leverkusen: Leske & Budrich.
Ehrenberg, A. (2004). *Das erschöpfte Selbst. Depression und Gesellschaft in der Gegenwart.* Frankfurt a.M.: Suhrkamp Verlag.
Ehlich, K., Rehbein, J., & (1979). Sprachliche Handlungsmuster. In Soeffner, H.-G. (Ed.) Interpretative Verfahren in den Sozial- und Textwissenschaften, 243–274. Stuttgart: Metzler.
Elias, N. (1976). *Über den Prozeß der Zivilisation. Soziogenetische und psychogenetische Untersuchungen.* Frankfurt a.M.: Suhrkamp Verlag.
Erikson, E.H. (1968 [1950]). *Kindheit und Gesellschaft.* Stuttgart: Ernst Klett Verlag.
Festinger, L. (1964). *Conflict, decision, and dissonance.* Stanford, Calif.: Stanford Univ. Press.
Flader, D. (1995). *Psychoanalyse im Fokus von Handeln und Sprache.* Frankfurt a.M.: Suhrkamp Verlag.
Flader, D. (2000). Metaphern in Freuds Theorien. *Psyche, 54*(4), pp. 354–389.
Flader, D. (2002a). Psyche und Macht – ein Buch-Essay. *Psyche, 56*(11), pp. 1157–1169.
Flader, D. (2002b). Der Witz als sozialer Vorgang und als Ausdruck von Subjektivität. *Psyche, 56*(3), pp. 275–302.

Flader, D. (2003). Wie konzeptualisieren wir angemessen Freuds Entdeckung des unbewussten Sinns von Fehlleistungen? In G. Poscheschnik, R. Ernst & Klagenfurter Psychoanalytische Mittwoch-Gesellschaft (Hrsg.), *Psychoanalyse im Spannungsfeld von Humanwissenschaft, Therapie und Kulturtheorie* (pp. 333–348). Frankfurt a.M.: Brandes & Apsel.

Flader, D. (2004). Das traumatisierte Kind, narzisstische Beziehungsmuster und kulturelle Erschütterungen. *Dynamische Psychiatrie, 204/205*, pp. 34–68.

Flader, D., Bartholomew, U. & Bublitz, U. (1993). Patienten-Idiolekte – Eine Untersuchung sprachlicher Daten, die mit dem Role-Repertory-Grid gewonnen werden. In P. Löning & J. Rehbein (Hrsg.), *Arzt-Patienten-Kommunikation. Analysen zu interdisziplinären Problemen des medizinischen Diskurses* (pp. 91–113), Berlin/New York: Walter de Gruyter.

Flader, D. & Comati, S. (2008). *Kulturschock. Zur Methodologie einer Untersuchung interkultureller Handlungskonflikte westlicher Manager in Mittel-Ost-Europa – am Beispiel Polens.* Wiesbaden: VS.

Flader, D., & Grodzicki, W.-D. (1982). Hypothesen zur Wirkungsweise der psychoanalytischen Grundregel. In Dies & Schröter, K. (Hrsg) (1982). Psychoanalyse als Gespräch (pp. 41–95). Frankfurt a.M: Suhrkamp Verlag.

Freidel, M. (2013). Vergleiche dich! Erkenne, dass du nichts bist. In *FAZ*, 01.06.2013.

Freimüller, T. (2008). »Selbstvergewisserung in therapeutischer Absicht« – Alexander Mitscherlich und die »vaterlose Gesellschaft« nach 1945. In J. Brunner (Hrsg.), *Mütterliche Macht und väterliche Autorität. Elternbilder im deutschen Diskurs* (pp. 182–196). Göttingen: Wallstein.

Freud, S. (1901). *Zur Psychopathologie des Alltagslebens. GW IV.*

Freud, S. (1905). *Der Witz und seine Beziehung zum Unbewußten.* Ibid., Stud. Ausg. IV. (pp. 9–220).

Freud, S. (1907). Zwangshandlungen und Religionsübungen. Ibid., *Stud. Ausg. VII* (pp. 11–22).

Freud, S. (1908). Die »kulturelle« Sexualmoral und die moderne Nervosität. Ibid., *Stud. Ausg. IX* (pp. 9–32). Frankfurt a.M.: S. Fischer Verlag.

Freud, S. (1909). Analyse der Phobie eines fünfjährigen Knaben. Ibid., *Stud. Ausg. VIII* (pp. 9–124). Frankfurt a.M.: S. Fischer Verlag.

Freud, S. (1912–1913). Totem und Tabu. Ibid., *Stud. Ausg. IX* (pp. 287–444). Frankfurt a.M.: S. Fischer Verlag.

Freud, S. (1915). Das Unbewußte. Ibid., *Stud. Ausg. III* (pp. 119–174).

Freud, S. (1916–1917). Vorlesungen zur Einführung in die Psychoanalyse. Ibid., *GW XI.*

Freud, S. (1920). Jenseits des Lustprinzips. Ibid., Stud. Ausg. III (pp. 213–272).

Freud, S. (1921). Massenpsychologie und Ich-Analyse. Ibid., *GW XIII* (pp. 71–161).

Freud, S. (1924). Kurzer Abriß der Psychoanalyse. Ibid., *GW XIII* (pp. 405–427).

Freud, S. (1926). Die Frage der Laienanalyse. Unterredungen mit einem Unparteiischen. Ibid., *GW XIV* (pp. 207–284).

Freud, S. (1927). Die Zukunft einer Illusion. Ibid., *GW XIV* (pp. 325–380).

Freud, S. (1930). Das Unbehagen in der Kultur. Ibid., *GW XIV* (pp. 419–505).

Freud, S. (1939 [1934–1938]. Der Mann Moses und die monotheistische Religion. Ibid., *GW XVI* (pp. 103–246).

Friesen, A.v. (2006). *Schuld sind immer die anderen! Die Nachwehen des Feminismus: Frustrierte Frauen und schweigende Männer.* Hamburg: Ellert & Richter.

Gadamer, H.-G. (1960). *Wahrheit und Methode.* Tübingen: J.C.B. Mohr (Paul Siebeck).

Giddens, A. (1997 [1984]). *Die Konstitution der Gesellschaft*. Frankfurt a.M./New York: Campus.

Glasl, F. (1992). *Konfliktmanagement. Ein Handbuch für Führungskräfte und Berater* (3. Aufl.). Bern/Stuttgart: Paul Haupt, Freies Geistesleben.

Grieser, J. (1998). *Der phantasierte Vater. Zur Entstehung und Funktion des Vaterbildes beim Sohn*. Tübingen: edition diskord.

Goffman, E. (1972). *Asyle. Über die soziale Situation psychiatrischer Patienten und anderer Insassen*. Frankfurt a.M.: Suhrkamp Verlag.

Goleman, D. (1997). *Emotionale Intelligenz*. München: Econ.

Goleman, D. (2012). Resource Scarcity. Accelerations of World Changes. In *Global Agenda Coucil on New Models of Leadership*. Available online: http://reports.weforum.org/global-agenda-council-on-new-models-of-leadership.

Gorer, G. (1948). *The American People. A Study in National Character*. New York: Norton.

Gruen, A. (2002 [1986]). *Der Verrat am Selbst. Die Angst vor Autonomie bei Mann und Frau* (15. Edition). München: DTV.

Grünbaum, A. (1985). *The Foundations of Psychoanalysis. A Philosophical Critique*. Berkeley, London: Univ. of California Press.

Habermas, J. (1968). *Erkenntnis und Interesse*. Frankfurt a.M.: Suhrkamp Verlag.

Habermas, J. (1981). *Theorie des kommunikativen Handelns*. Frankfurt a.M.: Suhrkamp Verlag.

Hegener, W. (2001). *Wege aus der vaterlosen Psychoanalyse. Vier Abhandlungen über Freuds ›Mann Moses‹*. Tübingen: edition diskord.

Hennecke, H.J. (2003). *Die dritte Republik. Aufbruch und Ernüchterung*. Berlin: Propyläen.

Hirsch, M. (2006). »Die Vögel« von Alfred Hitchcock. *Freie Assoziation, 9*(2), pp. 89–95.

Huber, B. (1993). *Mobbing. Psychoterror am Arbeitsplatz*. Niederhausen/Ts.: Falken.

Illouz, E. (2009). *Die Errettung der modernen Seele*. Frankfurt a.M.: Suhrkamp Verlag.

Illouz, E. (2007). *Gefühle in Zeiten des Kapitalismus*. Frankfurt a.M.: Suhrkamp Verlag.

Jauer, M. (2012). Christian Wulff. Was es heißt, ein Mann zu sein. *FAZ*, 16.09.2012.

Jappe, G. (1971). *Über Wort und Sprache in der Psychoanalyse*. Frankfurt a.M.: S. Fischer Verlag.

Joy, M. (2010). *Why We Love Dogs, Eat Pigs, and Wear Cows. An Introduction to Carnism*. San Francisco, Calif.: Conari Press.

Kaus, R.J. & Heinrichs, J. (1991). Reflexionsbedarf beim Wissenschaftstheoretiker A. Grünbaum. *Jahrbuch der Psychoanalyse, 27*, pp. 114–145.

Kandel, E. (2006). *Psychiatrie, Psychoanalyse und die neue Biologie des Geistes*. Frankfurt a.M.: Suhrkamp Verlag.

Kaufmann, V. (2010). The Dreamers oder: Vaterlos Kulturen und Traditionsbruch im Mai 68. In D. Thomä (Hrsg.), *Vaterlosigkeit. Geschichte und Gegenwart einer fixen Idee* (pp. 215–231). Berlin: Suhrkamp Verlag.

Keene, J. (2013). *Unconscious obstacles to caring for the planet*. In S. Weintrobe (edt), *Engaging with Climate Change* (pp. 144–159). Sussex: Routledge.

Kelly, G. (1955). *The Psychology of Personal Constructs*. New York: Norton.

Kernberg, O. (1978). *Borderline-Störungen und pathologischer Narzißmus*. Frankfurt a.M.: Suhrkamp Verlag.

Klein, M. (1940). Mourning and its relation to manic-depressive states. In *International Journal of Psychoanalysis, 14*, 125–153.

Klein, M. (1959). Our adult world and its roots in infancy. In *The Writings of Melanie Klein, Vol. 3*, 247–263. London: Hogarth.

Knop, O. (2015). Wer zweimal lügt, dem glaubt man nicht. *FAZ*, 19.01.2015.

Kohut, H. (1973). *Narzißmus*. Frankfurt a.M.: Suhrkamp Verlag.

Kohut, H. (1981). *Die Heilung des Selbst*. Frankfurt a.M.: Suhrkamp Verlag.

Kolodej, Chr. (2005). *Mobbing. Psychoterror am Arbeitsplatz und seine Bewältigung*. Wien: Facultas.

Kraft, A. (2008). Über Väter und Großväter – Die Lehre der Ambivalenztoleranz in der deutschen ›Generationenliteratur‹ nach 1945. In J. Brunner (Hrsg.), *Mütterliche Macht und väterliche Autorität. Elternbilder im deutschen Diskurs* (pp. 165–181). Göttingen: Wallstein.

Kreckel, M. (1997). *Macht der Väter – Krankheit der Söhne*. Frankfurt a.M.: S. Fischer Verlag.

Kristeva, J. (1978). *Die Revolution der poetischen Sprache*. Frankfurt a.M.: Suhrkamp Verlag.

Kruse, P. (2004). *Next practice – Erfolgreiches Management von Instabilität. Veränderung durch Vernetzung*. Offenbach: GABAL.

Kuhn, S.Th. (1973). *Die Struktur wissenschaftlicher Revolutionen*. Frankfurt a.M.: Suhrkamp Verlag.

Lacan, J. (1973). *Schriften I. Olten*. Freiburg/Br.: Walter-Verlag.

Lacan, J. (1975). *Schriften II. Olten*. Freiburg/Br.: Walter-Verlag.

Lampl-de-Groot, J. (1962). Ego-Ideal and Super-Ego. *Psychoanalytic Studies of the Child, 17*, pp. 94–106.

Lang, H. (1986). *Die Sprache und das Unbewußte. Jacques Lacans Grundlegung der Psychoanalyse*. Frankfurt a.M.: Suhrkamp Verlag.

Laplanche, J. & Pontalis, J.-B. (1973). *Das Vokabular der Psychoanalyse (Vol. 1 &. 2)*. Frankfurt a.M.: Suhrkamp Verlag.

Lasch, C. (1979). *The Culture of Narcissism*. New York: W.W. Norton & Company.

Levchin, M. (2012). The New Transparency. Social Media and the New Connectivity. In *Global Agenda Coucil on New Models of Leadership*. Avalaible online: http://reports.weforum.org/global-agenda-council-on-new-models-of-leadership

Legendre, P. (1998). *Das Verbrechen des Gefreiten Lortie*. Freiburg/Br.: Rombach.

Leggewie, C. & Welzer, H. (2009). *Das Ende der Welt, wie wir sie kannten*. Frankfurt a.M.: S. Fischer Verlag.

Leuninger H. (1993). *Reden ist Schweigen, Silber ist Gold*. Zürich: Ammann.

Lévi-Strauss, C. (1960). *Traurige Tropen*. Köln et al.: Kiepenheuer & Witsch.

Leymann, H. (2009 [1993]). *Mobbing. Psychoterror am Arbeitsplatz und wie man sich dagegen wehren kann*(14. edition). Reinbek/H.: Rohwohlt.

Li, C. (2012). Social. The Power Of Followership. In *Global Agenda Coucil on New Models of Leadership*. Available online: http://reports.weforum.org/global-agenda-council-on-new-models-of-leadership

Lichtman, R. (1990). *Die Produktion des Unbewußten. Die Integration der Psychoanalyse in die marxistische Theorie*. Hamburg/Berlin: Argument.

Loquai, H. (2000). *Der Kosovo-Konflikt*. Baden-Baden: Nomos.

Lorenzer, A. (1972). *Zur Begründung einer materialistischen Sozialisationstheorie*. Frankfurt a.M.: Suhrkamp Verlag.

Maaz, H.-J. (2012). *Die narzisstische Gesellschaft. Ein Psychogramm*. München: Beck.

Mahler, M.S. (1972). *Symbiose und Individuation. Psychosen im frühen Kindesalter* (Band 1). Stuttgart: Klett.

Maercker, A. & Rosner R. (Hrsg.). (2006). *Psychotherapie der posttraumatischen Belastungsstörungen. Krankheitsmodelle und Therapiepraxis – störungsspezifisch und schulenübergreifend*. Stuttgart: Georg-Thieme.

Manske, A. (2002). *Political Correctness und Normalität. Die amerikanische PC-Kontroverse im kulturgeschichtlichen Kontext.* Heidelberg: Synchron.

Mendel, G. (1972 [1969]). *Die Generationskrise. Eine sozio-psychoanalytische Studie* [French original: *La Crise de générations: étude sociopsychanalytique.* Paris: Editions Payot & Rivages]. Frankfurt a.M.: Suhrkamp Verlag.

Mentzos, S. (1988). *Interpersonale und institutionalisierte Abwehr.* Frankfurt a.M.: Suhrkamp Verlag.

Mertens, W. (2005 [1981]). *Psychoanalyse. Grundlagen, Behandlungstechnik und Angewandte Psychoanalyse*(6. edition). Stuttgart: Kohlhammer.

Mertens, W. & Lang, H.-J. (1991). *Die Seele im Unternehmen. Psychoanalytische Aspekte von Führung und Organisation im Unternehmen.* Berlin et al.: Springer-Verlag.

Meschkutat, B., Stackelbeck, M. & Langenhoff, G. (1993). *Strategien gegen sexuelle Belästigung am Arbeitsplatz. Konzeption – Materialien – Handlungshilfen.* Köln: Bund-Verlag.

Meschkutat, B., Stackelbeck, M. & Langenhoff, G. (2002). *Der Mobbing-Report. Eine Repräsentativstudie für die Bundesrepublik Deutschland.* Bremerhaven: Wirtschaftverlag NW.

Meyer, Th. (2001). *Mediokratie. Die Kolonialisierung der Politik durch das Mediensystem.* Frankfurt a.M.: Suhrkamp Verlag.

Mitscherlich, A. (1963). *Auf dem Weg zur vaterlosen Gesellschaft.* Frankfurt a.M.: Piper.

Müller-Amenitsch, R. (2009). *AGG und Mobbing. Neue rechtliche Möglichkeiten von Mobbingbetroffenen im Anwendungsbereich des Allgemeinen Gleichbehandlungsgesetzes AGG.* Unpublished Manuscript.

Niethammer, L. (2003). Sind Generationen identisch? In J. Reulecke (Hrsg.), *Generationalität und Lebensgeschichte im 20. Jahrhundert* (pp. 1–16). München: Oldenbourg.

Parin, P. (1978). Warum die Psychoanalytiker so ungern zu brennenden Zeitproblemen Stellung nehmen. *Psyche, 32*(5/6), pp. 385–399.

Parin, P., Morgenthaler, F. & Parin-Matthèy, G. (1971). *Fürchte deinen Nächsten wie dich selbst. Psychoanalyse und Gesellschaft am Modell der Agni in Westafrika.* Frankfurt a.M.: Suhrkamp Verlag.

Parsons, T. (1968). *The structure of social action.* New York: Free Press.

Presch, G. (1985). Verdeckte Beurteilungen in qualifizierten Arbeitszeugnissen. Beschreibung, Erklärung, Änderungsvorschläge. In F. Januschek (edt.), *Politische Sprachwissenschaft. Zur Analyse von Sprache als kultureller Praxis* (pp. 307–360). Opladen: Westdeutscher Verlag.

Prosch, A. (1995). *Mobbing am Arbeitsplatz. Literaturanalyse mit Fallstudie.* Konstanz: Hartung Gorre.

Puig, M.A. (2012). Emotional. The Inner Journal. In Global Agenda Coucil on New Models of Leadership. Available online: http://reports.weforum.org/global-agenda-council-on-new-models-of-leadership

Racker, H. (1978). *Übertragung und Gegenübertragung. Studien zur psychoanalytischen Technik.* München: Reinhardt.

Radebold, H., Heuft, G. & Fooken, I. (Edts.). (2006). *Kindheiten im Zweiten Weltkrieg. Kriegserfahrungen und deren Folgen aus psychohistorischer Perspektive.* Weinheim/München: Juventa.

Reiche, R. (1988). Sexuelle Revolution – Erinnerung an einen Mythos. In L. Baier et al. (Hrsg.), *Die Früchte der Revolte. Über die Veränderung der politischen Kultur durch die Studentenbewegung* (pp. 45–71). Berlin: Wagenbach.

Reiche, R. (1995). Von innen nach außen? Sackgassen im Diskurs über Psychoanalyse und Gesellschaft. *Psyche, 49*(3), pp. 227–258.

Reulecke, J. (2010). »Vaterlose Söhne« in einer »vaterlosen Gesellschaft«. Die Bundesrepublik nach 1945. In D. Thomä (Hrsg.), *Vaterlosigkeit. Geschichte und Gegenwart einer fixen Idee* (pp. 142–159). Berlin: Suhrkamp Verlag.

Richter, H.-E. (1979). *Der Gotteskomplex. Die Geburt und die Krise des Glaubens an die Allmacht des Menschen.* Reinbek bei Hamburg: Rohwohlt.

Rosenbaum, B. & Sonne, H. (1986). *The Language of Psychosis.* New York/ London: New York University Press.

Roszak, T. (1994). *Ökopsychologie: Der entwurzelte Mensch und der Ruf der Erde.* Stuttgart: Kreuz.

Rutschky, K. (Hrsg.). (1977). *Schwarze Pädagogik. Quellen zur Naturgeschichte bürgerlicher Erziehung.* Frankfurt a.M./Berlin/Wien: Ullstein.

Schäfer, M. & Herpell, G. (2010). *Du Opfer! Wenn Kinder Kinder fertigmachen. Der Mobbing-Report.*Reinbek/H.: Rowohlt.

Scheithauer. H. & Bull, H.D. (2010). Das fairplayer.manual zur unterrichtsbegleitenden Förderung sozialer Kompetenzen und Prävention von Bullying im Jugendalter: Ergebnisse der Pilotevaluation. Prax. Kinderpsycholog. Kinderpsychiat., *59*(4), pp. 266–281.

Scherer, K. (1979). *Der aggressive Mensch – Ursachen der Aggression in unserer Gesellschaft.* Königstein: Athenäum.

Schmidbauer, W. (1981). *Ohnmacht des Helden. Unser alltäglicher Narzißmus.* Reinbek/H.: Rohwohlt.

Schmidt, S. (2012). *Das Gesetz der Krise. Wie die Banken die Politik regieren.* München: Droemer.

Schreyögg, G. & Steinmann, H. (1990). *Management – Grundlagen der Unternehmensführung.* Wiesbaden: Gabler.

Stephan, A. (1989). *Sinn als Bedeutung. Bedeutungstheoretische Untersuchungen zur Psychoanalyse Sigmund Freuds.* Berlin/New York: de Gruyter.

Schülein, J.A. (1999). *Die Logik der Psychoanalyse. Eine erkenntnistheoretische Studie.* Gießen: Psychosozial-Verlag.

Schülein, J.A. & Wirth, H.-J. (2011). *Analytische Sozialpsychologie. Klassische und neuere Perspektiven.* Gießen: Psychosozial-Verlag.

Schumpeter, J.A. (1950). *Kapitalismus, Sozialismus und Demokratie.* Bern: Francke.

Schütz, A. (1964). The Stranger. In ders., *Collected Papers II. Studies in Social Theory* (pp. 91–105). Den Haag: Martinus Nijhoff.

Sennett, R. (1998). *Der flexible Mensch. Die Kultur des neuen Kapitalismus.* Berlin: Berlin-Verlag.

Sohm, H. (1995). *Mobbing. Ein Fall für den Vorgesetzten?* Unpublished diploma thesis.

Spitz, R. (o.J.). *Nein und Ja. Die Ursprünge der menschlichen Kommunikation. Beiheft zur Psyche.* Stuttgart: Klett.

Stephan, A. (1989). *Sinn als Bedeutung.* Berlin/New York: de Gruyter.

Strauss, A. (1974). *Spiegel und Masken. Die Suche nach Identität.* Frankfurt a.M: Suhrkamp Verlag.

Strenger, C. (1991). Between Hermeneutics and Science. An Essay on the Epistemology of Psychoanalysis, Madison: *Psychological Issues Monograph, 59.*

Taylor, Ch. (1995). *Das Unbehagen an der Moderne.* Frankfurt/M: Suhrkamp Verlag.

Thomä, D. (2010). Statt einer Einleitung: Stationen einer Geschichte der Vaterlosigkeit von 1700 bis heute. In ders. (Hrsg.), *Vaterlosigkeit. Geschichte und Gegenwart einer fixen Idee* (pp. 11–64). Berlin: Suhrkamp Verlag.

Timpanaro, S. (1976). *The Freudian Slip.* Thetford: Lowe & Brydon.

Treher, W. (1966). *Hitler, Steiner, Schreber. Ein Beitrag zur Phänomenologie des kranken Geistes.* Emmendingen im Breisgau: Selbstverlag.

Twenge, J.M. & Campbell, W.K. (2010). *The Narcissism Epidemic.* New York: Simon & Schuster.

Volkan, V. & Ast, G. (1994). *Spektrum des Narzissmus.* Göttingen: Vandenhoeck & Ruprecht.

Volkan, V. (2005). *Blindes Vertrauen.* Gießen: Psychosozial-Verlag.

Von Wright, G. H. (2008). Erklären und Verstehen. Hamburg: EVA.

Weber, M. (1987 [1919]). *Politik als Beruf.* Berlin: Duncker & Humblot.

Weintrobe, S. (2013) *Introduction.* In S. Weintrobe (Editor), *Engaging with Climate Change* (pp. 1–15). Sussex: Routledge.

Weintrobe, S. (2013) *The difficult problem of anxiety in thinking about climate change.* In S. Weintrobe (Editor), *Engaging with Climate Change* (pp. 33–47). Sussex: Routledge.

Wieland, J. (2004). *Handbuch Wertemanagement. Erfolgsstrategien einer modernen Corporate Governance.* Hamburg: Murmann.

Willi, J. (1975). *Die Zweierbeziehung.* Reinbek/H.: Rowohlt.

Winnicott, D.W. (1973). *Vom Spiel zur Kreativität.* Stuttgart: Klett.

Wirth, H.-J. (2011 [2002]). *Narzissmus und Macht. Zur Psychoanalyse seelischer Störungen in der Politik* (4. edition). Gießen: Psychosozial-Verlag.

Wittgenstein, L. (2001). *Philosophische Untersuchungen. Kritisch-genetische Edition.* Frankfurt a.M.: Suhrkamp Verlag.

Wygotski, L.S. (1969). *Denken und Sprechen.* Frankfurt a.M.: S. Fischer Verlag.

Zeul, M. (2007). *Das Höhlenhaus der Träume. Filme, Kino & Psychoanalyse.* Frankfurt a.M.: Brandes & Apsel.

Žižek, S. (1997). *Looking Awry. An Introduction to Jacques Lacan through Popular Culture* (7. Aufl.). Cambridge, Mass: MIT Press.

Žižek, S. (2001). *Die gnadenlose Liebe.* Frankfurt a.M.: Suhrkamp Verlag.

Films

Eyre, R. (Regie). (1988). *Tumbledown.*

Hitchcock, A. (Regie). (1954). *Rear Window.*

Hitchcock, A. (Regie). (1963). *The Birds.*

King, S. (Regie). (1995). *The Langoliers* [Produktionsstudio/s].

Polański, R. (Regie). (1974). *Chinatown* [Paramount Pictures, Penthouse & Long Road Productions].

»Unser täglich Tier« (21.10.2014). Folge der ZDF-Dokumentationsreihe *37 Grad.*

Index

For Product Safety Concerns and Information please contact our EU
representative GPSR@taylorandfrancis.com
Taylor & Francis Verlag GmbH, Kaufingerstraße 24, 80331 München, Germany